Drupal 8 Theming with Twig

Master Drupal 8's new Twig templating engine to create fun and fast websites with simple steps to help you move from concept to completion

Chaz Chumley

[PACKT] open source *
PUBLISHING   community experience distilled

BIRMINGHAM - MUMBAI

Drupal 8 Theming with Twig

First published: March 2016

Production reference: 1170316

Published by Packt Publishing Ltd.
Livery Place
35 Livery Street
Birmingham B3 2PB, UK.

ISBN 978-1-78216-873-7

www.packtpub.com

Credits

Author
Chaz Chumley

Reviewer
Vincent Lark

Acquisition Editor
Larissa Pinto

Content Development Editor
Onkar Wani

Technical Editor
Pramod Kumavat

Copy Editor
Dipti Mankame

Project Coordinator
Bijal Patel

Proofreader
Safis Editing

Indexer
Rekha Nair

Graphics
Jason Monteiro

Production Coordinator
Aparna Bhagat

Cover Work
Aparna Bhagat

About the Author

Ever since Chaz can remember, he has been picking up a crayon, a pencil, a pen, or a computer, whether to draw a picture, write a poem, share an article, or develop the next great website. Looking back at these qualities, it's the reason why he chose to use those passions to give back to the open source community. His journey has opened doors to great experiences as a consultant, instructor, trainer, author, web developer, technical architect, Drupalist, and most importantly, a father. However, he could be none of these without first being a student and learning from life, love, and a passion for education, community development, and of course, science and technology.

The sum of these things has allowed Chaz to share his experiences as an active member of the Drupal community, having participated in developing Lynda.com Drupal training videos, authoring multiple Drupal books for Packt Publishing, and giving back his knowledge by contributing numerous articles and presentations at NYCCamp, BadCamp, and DrupalCon, and bringing top-notch Drupal expertise to his clients' work.

However, his greatest journey is still in front of him as he continues to learn new creative ways to architect open source websites, write about the next best things, and laugh with his colleagues along the way.

Acknowledgments

When I first started this journey of writing a Drupal 8 book, I thought to myself, "what could be so hard about that. Well, let me tell you?" Trying to catch up with every Alpha, Beta, and Release candidate was like chasing that third grade crush around the schoolyard. You were always able to catch her but then she would run again.

Speaking of crushes, I still have one on my beautiful wife. Without her even harder work, dedication, and support, this book would have not been possible. The long hours and lost time cannot be made up, but her smile always fills my heart. She is my friend, colleague in life, love, and spirit. Rebecca has allowed me to grow as an author and pursue the dream of putting my knowledge to pen and paper, even though she will tell you that I have been doing this for a while now ever since I wrote her the first poem. Well honey, I hope you enjoy this latest poem because it's finally published.

I also want to thank my two beautiful children, who while writing this book, have grown up a little bit more. My son Brendan makes me proud every day to be his father and friend. He is a young man in his own mind but always my little buddy, quickly on his way to becoming an Eagle Scout. The other one is my daughter Kayla who is getting ready to go off to college to pursue Graphic Design and just may write a book of her own some day. I definitely look forward to seeing you grow into the beautiful woman you will be.

I would like to thank Colin Panetta and Last Call Media for letting me use the great Drupal 8 chalkboard for the book cover.

I thank the Drupal community without whose support, I wouldn't be working with such an awesome content management framework.

I have to thank my colleagues. There are too many to name but without the absolutely great friends at Forum One I would have lost my mind writing this book: rock star developers, awe-inspiring designers, breathtaking UX, and amazing marketing. Not only is it the best place I have ever worked, we are always hiring!

About the Reviewer

Vincent Lark is a French Full Stack developer with a strong web development background. After working on frontend and backend software in multiple companies, he's still very interested in every technical part of a product, especially on emergent technologies.

When not coding for work, he also likes developing games as hobby in local game jams.

Vincent previously reviewed other books for Packt Publishing, including *Learning JavaScript Data Structures and Algorithms* and *WebGL Hotshot*.

www.PacktPub.com

eBooks, discount offers, and more

Did you know that Packt offers eBook versions of every book published, with PDF and ePub files available? You can upgrade to the eBook version at www.PacktPub.com and as a print book customer, you are entitled to a discount on the eBook copy. Get in touch with us at customercare@packtpub.com for more details.

At www.PacktPub.com, you can also read a collection of free technical articles, sign up for a range of free newsletters and receive exclusive discounts and offers on Packt books and eBooks.

https://www2.packtpub.com/books/subscription/packtlib

Do you need instant solutions to your IT questions? PacktLib is Packt's online digital book library. Here, you can search, access, and read Packt's entire library of books.

Why subscribe?

- Fully searchable across every book published by Packt
- Copy and paste, print, and bookmark content
- On demand and accessible via a web browser

Table of Contents

Preface

Starting from the bottom, *Drupal 8 Theming with Twig* will walk you through setting up and configuring a new Drupal 8 website. Navigate across the admin interface, learn how to work with core themes, and create new custom block layouts. Take a real-world project and create a Twig theme that adopts best practices to implement CSS frameworks and JavaScript libraries. See just how quick and easy it is to create beautiful and responsive Drupal 8 websites along with avoiding some of the common mistakes many frontend developers run into.

If you consider yourself a frontend developer, you will be right at home. However, since no PHP knowledge will be necessary, anyone who can create HTML websites with basic HTML5 and CSS3 skills will learn how to create a great Drupal 8 theme.

What this book covers

Chapter 1, Setting up Our Development Environment, will begin with walking you through setting up a development workflow. You will learn how to use an AMP (Apache, MySQL, PHP) stack to configure a local web server. We will introduce the process of installing Drupal 8 and walk through the admin interface in preparation for working with the new Twig templating engine.

Chapter 2, Theme Administration, provides a glance at the Appearance page, where you will learn how to install, uninstall, and configure various themes and settings. We will take a look at the new Block layout system as we explore how to add fields to blocks, reuse blocks, and assign chunks of content to various regions. Learn how Drupal 8 has reconfigured files and folders, where themes are now placed, and how to find core themes.

Chapter 3, Dissecting a Theme, begins with discussing the importance of a proper development environment and the steps involved to ensure that you're ready for Drupal 8. This will help you learn the differences and similarities between core and custom themes and how configuration has changed. Break down the metadata that makes up a theme, libraries, and regions. You will learn the role of templates and how the theme layer interacts with the Twig templating engine.

Chapter 4, Getting Started – Creating Themes, starts with creating a starter theme that allows us to work with assets while learning common techniques to integrate various CSS frameworks. You can learn how to rethink layout strategies as we dive into the theme layer and work with Twig. Then, we will wrap up with creating a subtheme that extends the new Classy base theme.

Chapter 5, Prepping Our Project, covers reviewing a real-world project that we will be building and how to break down how design and functionality should come together in Drupal 8. We will create the new theme structure, define metadata, add regions, and implement several CSS and JavaScript libraries.

Chapter 6, Theming Our Homepage, begins with working with the site branding block to add a logo. We will create a basic HTML wrapper and homepage template using Twig as we convert our homepage mockup into a fully functioning Drupal 8 front page. You will learn how to convert static markup into Twig variables as we theme global components, such as the Search block, menus, and custom blocks. Use the new libraries.yml file to work with assets, such as Twitter Bootstrap and Flex Slider and then attach them to specific templates using the new {{ attach_library() }} function.

Chapter 7, Theming Our Interior Page, will show you how to review mockups and identify what regions, blocks, content types, and views will need to be developed to recreate functionality. You will learn how to reuse Drupal 8 regions, work with the new Page title block, and how Twig plays an important part in rewriting Views output.

Chapter 8, Theming Our Blog Listing Page, starts with the best practice approaches to managing content types. From adding new display modes to enabling and formatting fields, learn how to use content display modes with Views to display data in lieu of using fields directly. You can work with Node templates to add CSS classes directly to our markup, work with content variables, and learn how to suppress fields. You will use Twig filters to format dates and manage individual field templates while creating a listing page.

Chapter 9, Theming Our Blog Detail Page, teaches us how to reuse Twig templates and display different content simply by using file name suggestions to target-specific display modes. You will work with the new comment types to add commenting functionality to pages as fields, learn how to alter comment display using field templates to theme comment threads, and add social sharing functionality to pages using custom blocks and JavaScript libraries that we can attach directly to a block.

Chapter 10, Theming Our Contact Page, introduces contact forms in Drupal 8 that we can use to create fieldable forms that users can interact with. You will learn how to integrate Google Maps into custom blocks that take advantage of library assets and vendor JavaScript.

Chapter 11, Theming Our Search Results, covers core search functionality, how to index database content, and work with search results templates. Core search can sometimes be limited, so we will take a more advanced look at the Search API module to create a better search experience. You will learn how to add individual fields to search and use display modes to output content while creating a Search view that allows us to expose filters to the users to find exactly what they are looking for.

Chapter 12, Tips, Tricks, and Where to Go from Here, introduces how to theme common admin sections of Drupal 8. You will learn how to modify the markup for local tasks and status messages. Reuse Twig templates using extends to share layouts while working with pages and blocks. Finally, we will leave you with some great contributed modules to take a look at and introduce you to the Drupal community.

What you need for this book

To follow along with this book, you need an installation of Drupal 8, preferably in a local development environment located on a Windows, Mac, or Linux-based computer. Documentation regarding setting up a local development environment can be found at https://www.drupal.org/setting-up-development-environment. Specific system requirements are listed at https://www.drupal.org/requirements. An introduction to MAMP for Windows and Mac is also covered in *Chapter 1, Setting Up Our Development Environment*.

To follow along with each lesson, you will need a text editor or IDE. To see a list of software to consider when developing in Drupal 8 you can refer to https://www.drupal.org/node/147789.

Who this book is for

Drupal 8 Theming with Twig is intended for frontend developers, designers, and anyone who is generally interested in learning all the new features of Drupal 8 theming. Discover what has changed from Drupal 7 to Drupal 8 and immerse yourself in the new Twig PHP templating engine. Familiarity with HTML5, CSS3, JavaScript, and the Drupal Admin interface would be helpful. Prior experience of setting up and configuring a standalone development environment is required as we will be working with PHP and MySQL.

Conventions

In this book, you will find a number of text styles that distinguish between different kinds of information. Here are some examples of these styles and an explanation of their meaning.

Code words in text, database table names, folder names, filenames, file extensions, pathnames, dummy URLs, user input, and Twitter handles are shown as follows "Rename `page.html.twig` as `page--front.html.twig`.":

A block of code is set as follows:

```
name: Tweet
type: theme
description: 'A Twitter Bootstrap starter theme'
core: 8.x
base theme: false
```

New terms and **important words** are shown in bold. Words that you see on the screen, for example, in menus or dialog boxes, appear in the text like this: "Click on the **Continue** button, which will take us to the license information."

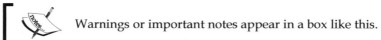

Warnings or important notes appear in a box like this.

Tips and tricks appear like this.

Reader feedback

Feedback from our readers is always welcome. Let us know what you think about this book—what you liked or disliked. Reader feedback is important for us as it helps us develop titles that you will really get the most out of.

To send us general feedback, simply e-mail feedback@packtpub.com, and mention the book's title in the subject of your message.

If there is a topic that you have expertise in and you are interested in either writing or contributing to a book, see our author guide at www.packtpub.com/authors.

Customer support

Now that you are the proud owner of a Packt book, we have a number of things to help you to get the most from your purchase. You can contact the author at http://www.forumone.com/books/drupal-8-theming-with-twig if you are facing a problem with any aspect of this book.

Downloading the example code

You can download the example code files for this book from your account at http://www.packtpub.com. If you purchased this book elsewhere, you can visit http://www.packtpub.com/support and register to have the files e-mailed directly to you.

You can download the code files by following these steps:

1. Log in or register to our website using your e-mail address and password.
2. Hover the mouse pointer on the **SUPPORT** tab at the top.
3. Click on **Code Downloads & Errata**.
4. Enter the name of the book in the **Search** box.
5. Select the book for which you're looking to download the code files.
6. Choose from the drop-down menu where you purchased this book from.
7. Click on **Code Download**.

Once the file is downloaded, please make sure that you unzip or extract the folder using the latest version of:

* WinRAR / 7-Zip for Windows
* Zipeg / iZip / UnRarX for Mac
* 7-Zip / PeaZip for Linux

Errata

Although we have taken every care to ensure the accuracy of our content, mistakes do happen. If you find a mistake in one of our books—maybe a mistake in the text or the code—we would be grateful if you could report this to us. By doing so, you can save other readers from frustration and help us improve subsequent versions of this book. If you find any errata, please report them by visiting http://www.packtpub. com/submit-errata, selecting your book, clicking on the **Errata Submission Form** link, and entering the details of your errata. Once your errata are verified, your submission will be accepted and the errata will be uploaded to our website or added to any list of existing errata under the Errata section of that title.

To view the previously submitted errata, go to https://www.packtpub.com/books/content/support and enter the name of the book in the search field. The required information will appear under the **Errata** section.

Piracy

Piracy of copyrighted material on the Internet is an ongoing problem across all media. At Packt, we take the protection of our copyright and licenses very seriously. If you come across any illegal copies of our works in any form on the Internet, please provide us with the location address or website name immediately so that we can pursue a remedy.

Please contact us at copyright@packtpub.com with a link to the suspected pirated material.

We appreciate your help in protecting our authors and our ability to bring you valuable content.

Questions

If you have a problem with any aspect of this book, you can contact us at questions@packtpub.com, and we will do our best to address the problem.

1
Setting Up Our Development Environment

Regardless of you being a seasoned web developer or someone who is just about to start learning Drupal, there are few things that everybody needs to have in place before we can get started:

- First, is to make sure that we have an Application stack that will meet Drupal 8's system requirements. MAMP provides us with a standalone web server that is generally referred to as an AMP (Apache, MySQL, PHP) stack and is available for both OS X and Windows. We will look at installing and configuring this local web server in preparation to install Drupal 8.

- Second, is to set up a Drupal 8 instance and learn the process of installing Drupal instances into our AMP stack. There are a few changes on how the configuration and installation processes work in Drupal 8, so we will take a closer look to ensure that we all begin development from the same starting point.

- Third, we will be reviewing the Admin interface, including the new responsive Admin menu and any configuration changes that have been made as we navigate to familiar sections of our site. We will also look at how to extend our website using contributed modules, review changes to the files and folder structure that make up Drupal 8, and discuss best practices to manage your files.

- Finally, we will review the exercise files that we will be using throughout the series, including how to download and extract files, how to use phpMyAdmin—a database administration tool to back up and restore database snapshots—and how to inspect elements within our HTML structure using Google Chrome.

Let's get started by installing our web environment that we will be using as we take an exciting look at Drupal 8 theming with Twig.

Installing an AMP (Apache, MySQL, PHP) stack

To install and run Drupal 8, our server environment must meet and pass certain requirements. These requirements include a web server (Apache, NGINX, or Microsoft IIS) that can process server-side languages such as PHP, which Drupal 8 is built on.

Our server should also contain a database that can manage the data and content that Drupal 8's content management system will store and process. The preferred database is MySQL. However, Drupal 8 can also support PostgreSQL along with Microsoft SQL Server and Oracle with an additional module support.

Finally, Drupal 8 requires PHP 5.5.9 or later, with the CURL extension.

However, because this book is not meant to be a "How-to" on installing and configuring Apache, MySQL, or PHP, we will take all the guesswork and trial by fire out of the equation and instead turn to MAMP.

Introducing MAMP

MAMP can be found at `https://www.mamp.info/en` and is a tool that allows us to create Drupal sites locally without the need or knowledge of installing and configuring Apache, MySQL, or PHP on a specific platform.

The application stack will consist of the following:

- Apache: The world's most popular web server
- MySQL: The world's most popular database server
- PHP: Various versions of PHP
- phpMyAdmin: A tool to manage MySQL databases via your browser

Downloading MAMP

Let's begin with the steps involved in quickly downloading, installing, and configuring our very own AMP stack along with an initial instance of Drupal that we will be using throughout the rest of this book. Begin by opening up our web browser and navigating to `https://www.mamp.info/en/downloads` and selecting either Mac OS X or Windows and then clicking on the **Download** button, as shown in the following image:

MAMP will allow us to install a local web server on either Mac or Windows and provides us with all the tools we will need to develop most open source websites and applications including Drupal 8.

Installing MAMP

Once the download has completed, we will need to locate the .dmg (Mac users) or .exe (Windows users) installation file and double-click on it to begin the installation process. Once the executable is opened, we will be presented with a splash screen that will guide us through the process of installing and configuring MAMP.

Clicking on the **Continue** button located on the **Introduction** pane, will take us to the **Read Me** information. MAMP will notify us that two folders will be created: one for MAMP and the other for MAMP PRO. It is important to not move or rename these two folders.

Click on the **Continue** button, which will take us to the license information. Simply accept the terms of the license agreement by clicking on **Continue** and then on **Agree** when prompted.

We can finally click on the **Install** button to complete the installation process. Depending on the operating system, we may need to enter our credentials for MAMP to be able to continue and configure our local web server. Once the install has completed, we can click on the **Close** button.

A quick tour of MAMP PRO

Let's begin by opening up MAMP and taking a quick tour of the various settings and how we can go about using our local web server to install and configure a new Drupal 8 instance.

When we first open up MAMP, we will be prompted to launch either MAMP or MAMP PRO, as shown in the following image:

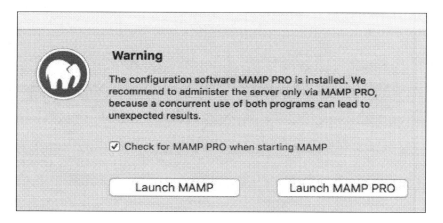

While MAMP is the free version of the local web server, it is strongly recommended that we use MAMP PRO for configuration and easy setup of a website. We can continue by clicking on **Launch MAMP PRO**, which will prompt us one more time to accept the **Initialization** of the remaining components that MAMP PRO needs before we can begin using it. Now, click on **OK** to continue.

We can use MAMP PRO free for 14 days and at the end of that period, we can decide whether to purchase a license or continue using the free version. Click on **OK** to continue.

General settings for MAMP PRO

If this is the first time you're using MAMP PRO, then there is some quick housekeeping we will want to take care of, beginning with the general settings. MAMP PRO tries to make sure that it does not interfere with any other possible web servers we may be running by setting the default ports of Apache to 8888 and MySQL to 8889. Although this is nice, the recommendation is to click on the **Set ports to 80, 443 & 3306** button that will make sure that MAMP PRO is running on more standardized ports for web development.

If we want to make sure that Apache or MySQL are active at all time, we will also check **Start Apache and MySQL on system startup** and uncheck **Stop Apache and MySQL when quitting MAMP PRO**. Once we have made these changes, we can click on the **Save** button. Our changes should now be applied as shown in the following image and MAMP PRO will now prompt us to **Start servers now**.

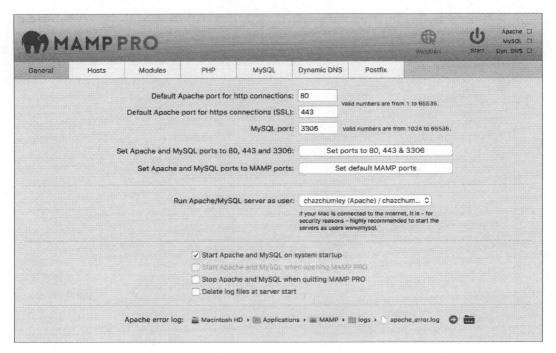

Host settings

The next tab we will look at is the **Hosts** tab, which is where we will create and configure basic websites. By default, MAMP PRO creates a localhost entry for us, which is common when developing a web application.

We will be using the **Hosts** tab to create an additional website when we install Drupal 8, so let's take a moment to locate some of the common settings we will need to know. Take a look at the following image; we can see that **localhost** is the **Server name** of our default website, uses the default **PHP version** of **5.6.10**, and has a **Document root** pointing to the **htdocs** folder of our MAMP installation.

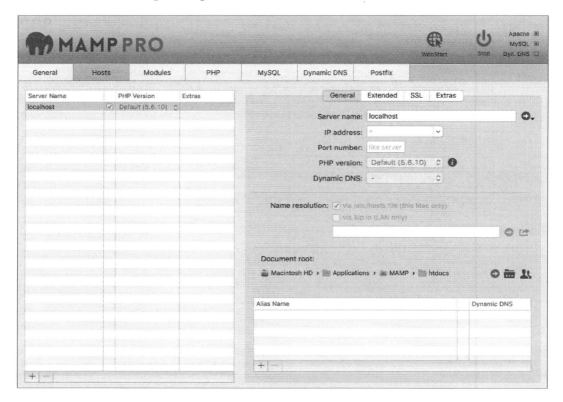

Another nice ability of MAMP PRO is to be able to click on the arrow icon located to the right of the **Server name** and have our default web browser open up to the localhost page, as shown in the following image:

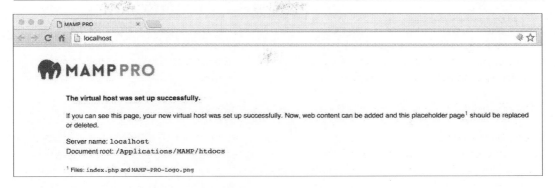

It is important to point out that the **Server name** always equates to the name of the URL in our browser that displays our website.

MAMP PRO is quite a robust and powerful local web server and while there are many more configuration options and settings that we could spend time looking through, most of our time will be spent on working from the **Hosts** tab creating new websites or configure existing sites.

So far, MAMP PRO has configured everything for us, but how to create a new website and, in more general, install a Drupal 8 instance? Let's look at it in the following section.

Installing Drupal 8

In order to install Drupal 8 within our local MAMP PRO server, we will need to perform a series of steps:

1. We will need to grab a copy of the latest Drupal 8 release and extract the files to a location on our computer that will be the document root of our website.

2. We will have to create a new host entry with the server name that we will want to use for our URL and point our host entry to the proper document root containing our Drupal 8 instance.

3. We will have to create a MySQL database that we can point Drupal to during the installation process.

We will walk through each of these steps in detail to ensure that we all have a copy of Drupal 8 installed properly that we will build upon as we work through each lesson.

Downloading Drupal 8

Drupal.org is the authority on everything about Drupal. We will often find ourselves navigating to Drupal.org to learn more about the community, look for documentation, post questions within the support forum, or review contributed modules or themes that can help us extend Drupal's functionality. Drupal.org is also the place where we can locate and download the latest release of Drupal 8.

We can begin by navigating to `https://www.drupal.org/node/2627402` and locate the latest release of Drupal 8. Click on the compressed version of Drupal 8 that we prefer, which will begin downloading the files to our computer. Once we have a copy of Drupal 8 on our computer, we will want to extract the contents to a location where we can easily work with Drupal and its folders and files.

Creating our document root

A document root is the main folder that our host entry will point to. In the case of Drupal, this will be the extracted root folder of Drupal itself. Generally, it is a best practice to maintain some sort of folder structure that is easy to manage and that can contain multiple websites.

For the sake of demonstration, we will create a `Sites` folder and then copy the compressed Drupal files to our new folder and extract the contents, as shown in the following image:

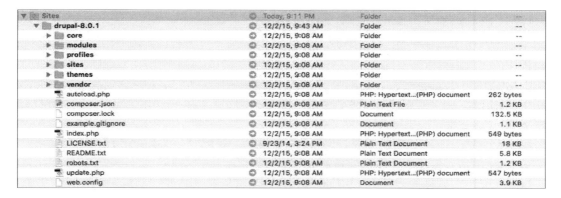

Creating our host entry

A host entry represents our website, which, in this case, is our Drupal 8 instance. Hosts always contain a server name that equates to the URL we will use to navigate to Drupal within our browser.

Begin by opening MAMP PRO and clicking on the **Hosts** tab. To add a new host entry, we can click on the plus icon at the bottom of the **Server Name** column, as shown in the following image:

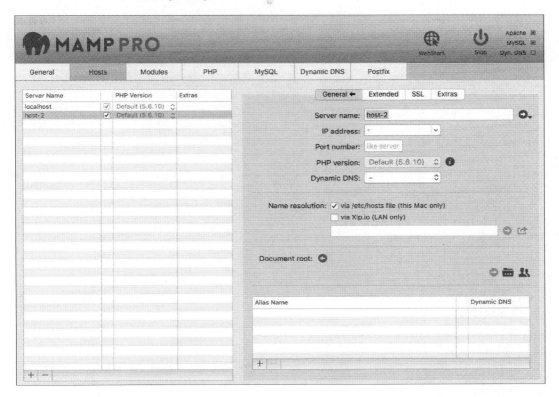

By default, this will add a new host entry that will require us to configure with three very important pieces of information:

- We will have to change the **Server name** from the default to drupal8.

- Then, we will want to verify that the required version of PHP is being used; in our case, the default of **5.6.10** will work just fine.

- Finally, we will need to click on the folder icon within the **Document root** section and choose our Drupal 8 folder that we placed within our sites folder earlier from the **Please select a Document Root folder** dialog.

The **General** settings for our new host entry should look as shown in the following image:

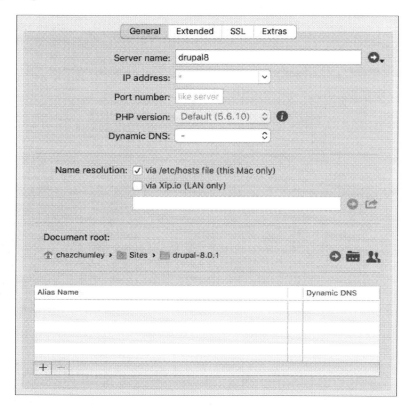

We can now apply our changes by clicking on the **Save** button and then clicking on the **Yes** button when prompted to have MAMP PRO restart the servers.

Creating a new database for Drupal

Drupal 8 requires a database available to install any tables that make up the content management system. These tables will hold configuration data, users and permissions, content, and any extendable functionality that makes Drupal 8 so powerful.

Lucky for us, MAMP PRO installs a MySQL database server that we can take advantage of to create a new database that Drupal 8 can point to. This same database server we will also be working with to back up and restore our database content as we progress through each lesson.

Using phpMyAdmin

MAMP PRO also installs a free software tool written in PHP for the sole purpose of managing MySQL databases. phpMyAdmin allows us to perform a multitude of tasks from browsing tables, views, fields, and indexes to exporting and importing database backups and much more.

If we switch back over to MAMP PRO, we can locate the **MySQL** tab and click on the **phpMyAdmin** link located in the **Administer MySQL with** region, as shown in the following image:

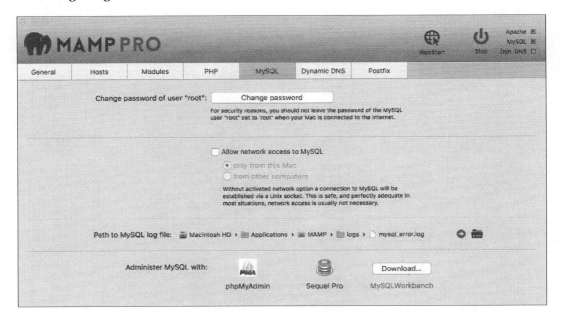

We should now be presented with **phpMyAdmin** within our browser. Currently, we are interested in creating a new database. We will revisit phpMyAdmin a little later to learn how to back up and restore our database. The following are the steps to create a database:

1. Begin by clicking on the **New** link in the left sidebar, as shown in the following image:

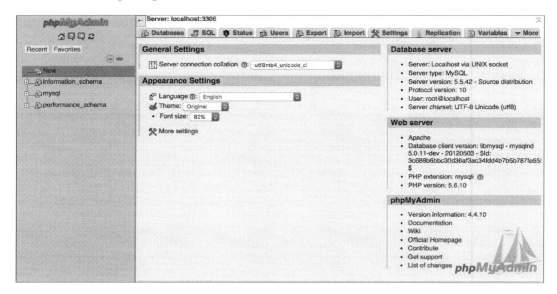

2. Next, we will want to enter a name of **drupal8** within the **Create database** field, as shown in the following image, and then click on the **Create** button.

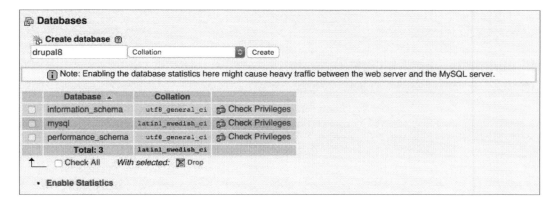

We have now created our first MySQL database, which we will use when configuring Drupal 8 in the next step.

Completing Drupal 8 installation

Now that we have all of our basic requirements completed, we can open up our favorite web browser and navigate to `http://drupal8/core/install.php` to begin the installation process.

Since this may be the first time installing Drupal 8, one thing we will notice is that the install screen looks a little different. The install screen has been given a makeover, but the steps are similar to that of Drupal 7, starting with choosing a language.

Choosing a language

The installation process will prompt us to choose a language that we want Drupal 8 to be installed in. This language will control how the Admin area appears, and in many cases, the default of English is acceptable. We will need to click on the **Save and continue** button to proceed to the next step, as shown in the following image:

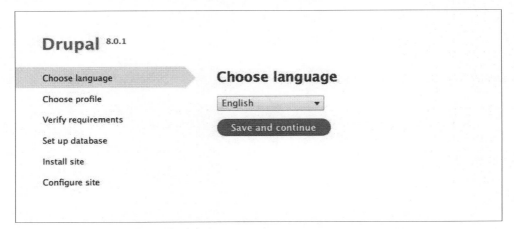

Choosing a profile

Our next step is to choose an installation profile. We can think of this as Drupal's way of preconfiguring items for us that will make our job easier when developing. By default, we can leave the **Standard** profile selected, but if we choose to configure Drupal ourselves, we can always choose **Minimal**. Click on the **Save and continue** button to proceed to the next step, as shown in the following image:

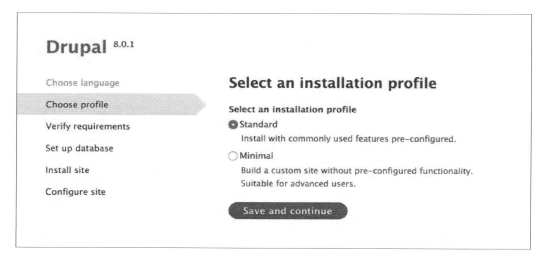

Verifying requirements

The next screen allows us to review any requirements that Drupal needs or recommends for optimal performance. From here, we can see web server information, PHP version, memory limits, and more:

The requirements review can also alert us to any configuration settings that will allow Drupal to perform better. In our example, we forgot to enable OPcode caching, which allows PHP to compile down to bytecode. Without going into the details of caching, we can easily enable this feature in MAMP PRO.

Begin by opening up the MAMP PRO console and clicking on the **PHP** tab. Next, we will want to select **OPcache** from the **Cache module to speed up PHP execution** dropdown, as shown in the following image:

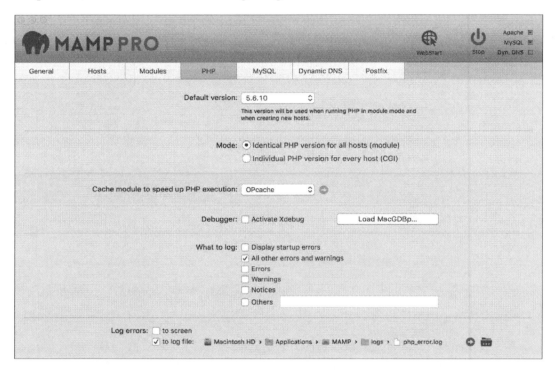

Click on the **Save** button and then allow MAMP PRO to restart servers if prompted. Now, we can refresh our Drupal install in the browser, and we will be taken to the next step in the installation process.

Database configuration

Database configuration can sometimes be a tricky part of installing Drupal for the first time. This is generally due to selecting the incorrect database type, wrong database name, or password, or by not specifying the correct host or port number.

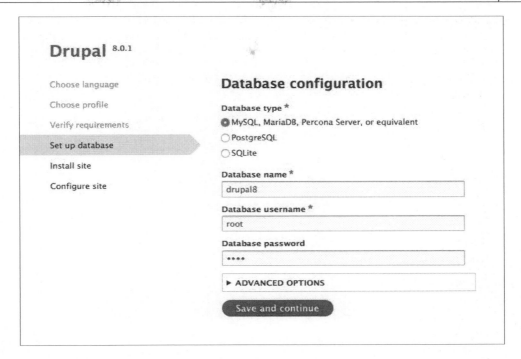

The settings we will want to use are as follows:

- **Database type**: Leave the default of MySQL selected.
- **Database name**: This is the name of the database that was created upon import. In our case, it should be drupal8.
- **Database username**: root.
- **Database password**: root.

With these settings, we can click on the **Save and continue** button to proceed.

If this is successful, we can see the **Installing Drupal** screen and watch as Drupal installs the various modules and configurations. This process may take a few minutes. If this process fails in any way, please go back and review the previous steps to make sure that they match what we have used.

Configuring the site

Before we can wrap up our Drupal 8 installation, we need to configure our site by inputting various settings for site information, site maintenance account, regional settings, and update notifications. Let's proceed now by entering our **Site Information**.

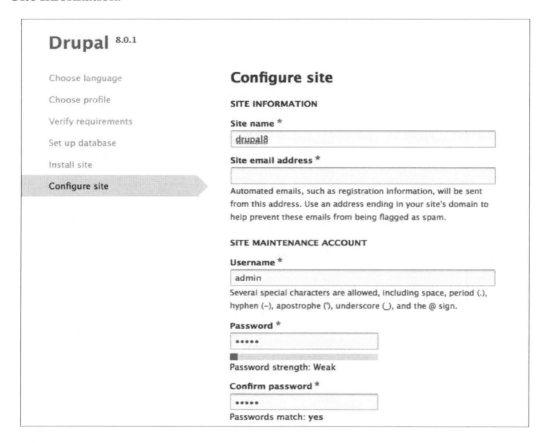

The site information consists of the following:

- **Site name**: To be consistent, let's call our site drupal8. We may give our new site any name that we like. As usual, we can change the site name later from the Drupal admin.

- **Site e-mail address**: Enter an e-mail address that we will want to use for automated e-mails such as registration information. It is the best practice to use an e-mail that ends in our site's domain to prevent e-mails from being flagged as spam.

Next, we will want to set up the site maintenance account. This is the primary account used to manage Drupal to perform such tasks as updating the core instance, module updates, and any development that needs user 1 permissions.

Site maintenance account

The site maintenance account information consists of the following:

- **Username**: Because we are developing a demo site, it makes sense to generally use admin for the username. Feel free to choose whatever is easy to remember, but don't forget it.

- **Password**: Security sticklers will ask to create something strong and unique, and Drupal displays a visual interface to let us know how strong our password is. For the sake of demonstration, we will use admin as our password so that your username and password match and are easy to remember.

- **E-mail address**: Generally, using the same e-mail that is used for the site e-mail address makes for consistency but is not required as we can choose any e-mail that we don't mind receiving security and module update notices.

Regional settings

Regional settings consist of default country and default time zone. These are often neglected and left with their defaults. The defaults are not recommended, as they are important in the development and design of Drupal 8 websites, specifically, when it comes to dates and how they are used to capture data and display dates back to the end user.

For our specific installation, choose the country and time zone for our region.

Update notifications

At last, we have come to our final set of configurations. Update notifications should always be left-checked unless we have no reason to receive security updates to Drupal core or module updates. By default, they should be checked. Click on **Save and continue** to finalize the configuration and installation of Drupal 8.

Drupal installation is now complete, and we should see the home page of our new website. Say "hello" to Drupal 8.

Reviewing the new admin interface

Our local instance of Drupal 8 is similar to Drupal 7 when first viewing the site. You will note the default Bartik theme with the friendly Drupal drop logo and a tabbed main menu. It is here though where the similarities stop. Drupal 8 has been reworked from the ground up, including a brand new responsive layout and admin menu.

Exploring the admin menu

One of the nice new features of Drupal 8 is the rebuilt admin menu. Everything has been moved under the **Manage** menu item. The admin menu itself is responsive and will change from text and icon to icon only, as soon as the browser is resized to tablet screen size.

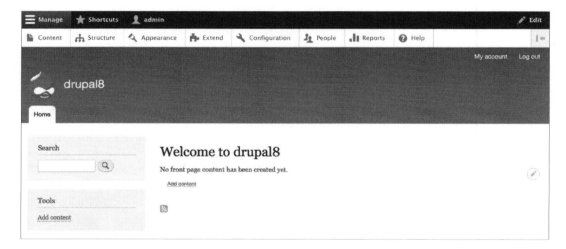

The admin menu can also be pinned to the left side of the window by clicking on the **arrow** icon to the right of the **Help** menu item.

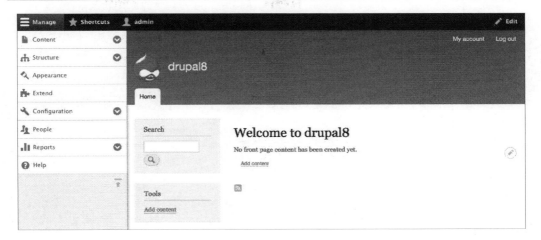

The flexibility of the new admin menu enables the admin user to manage Drupal 8 websites from the browser or a tablet or a smartphone very easily.

Previewing the interface

Taking a closer look at the menu items contained in our admin menu, we begin to see some differences in how things are named and may wonder where to find once familiar settings and configurations. Let's quickly walk through these menu items now so that it is easier to find things as we progress later on in future chapters:

- **Content**: This section displays any user-generated content, comments, and files with the ability to filter by **Published status**, **Type**, **Title**, and **Language**. The display for content is also now a view and can be customized with additional fields and filters as needed.

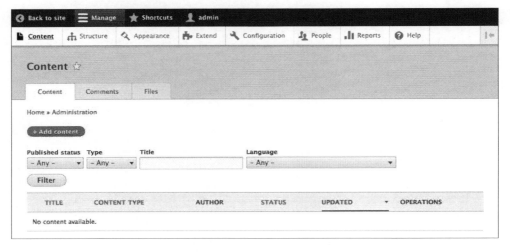

- **Structure**: This section is to manage **Block layout**, **Comment types**, **Contact forms**, **Content types**, **Display modes**, **Menus**, **Taxonomy**, and **Views**. We will explore some of the changes and new functionality contained within this section later on in the book.

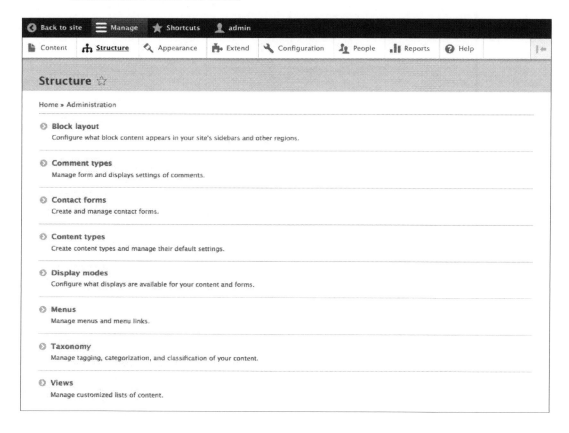

- **Appearance**: This section is to enable, disable, and configure default themes as well as administrative themes.

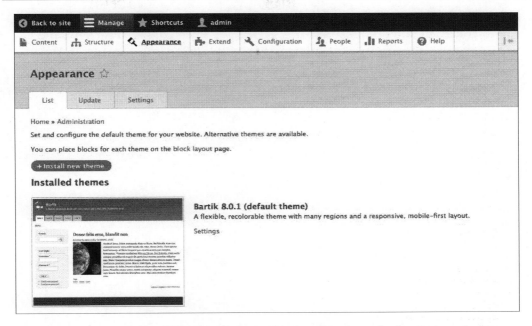

- **Extend**: Formerly known as Modules, this section is for listing, updating, and uninstalling core, custom, and contributed modules. New is the ability to search for modules using a filter. Various contributed modules have been moved into core, including Views and CKEditor.

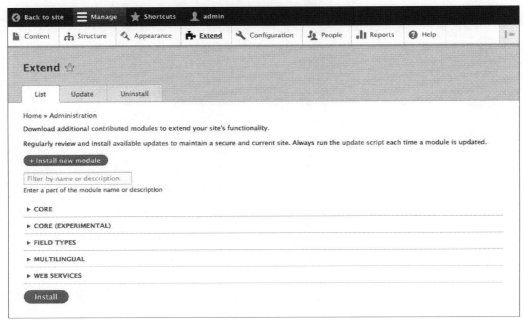

- **Configuration**: This section is designed to configure both core and contributed modules. Each area is grouped into functional sections and allows us to manage site information to file system to performance tuning.

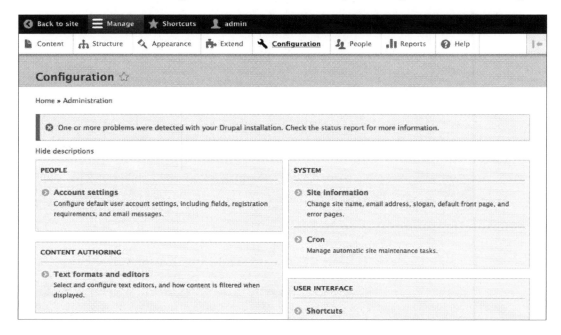

- **People**: This section allows us to manage users, permissions, and roles. The display for users is now a View as well and can be customized to add additional fields and filters as needed.

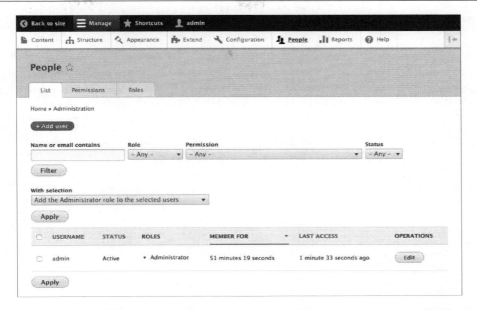

- **Reports**: This section is designed to view available updates, recent log messages, field lists, status reports, top "access denied" errors, top "page not found" errors, top search phrases, and View plugins.

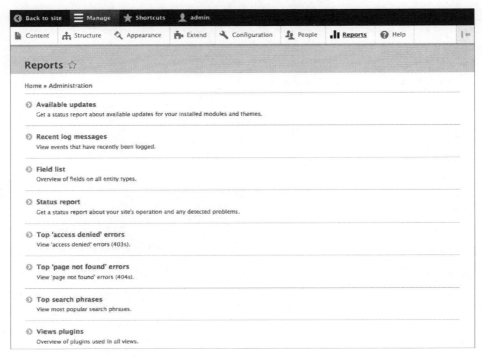

- **Help**: This section is designed to obtain helpful information on functionality necessary to know in administering a Drupal 8 website. This includes a **Getting Started** section and help topics on items, such as **Block**, **Views**, **User**, and more.

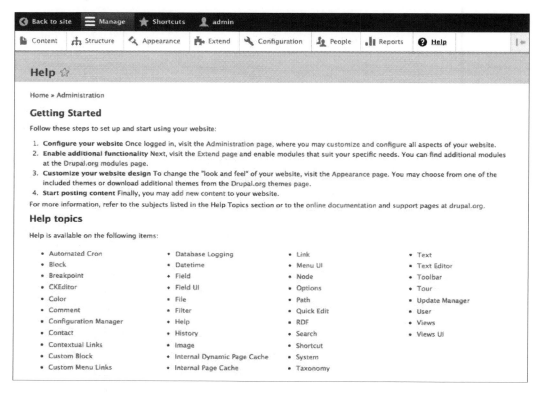

Exploring Drupal 8 folder structure

There are several changes to Drupal 8 with regard to how files and folders are structured. Let's walk through the `core`, `modules`, `sites`, and `themes` folders and discuss some best practices for how each of these folders should be managed when creating a Drupal 8 website.

The core folder

One of the first things to point out is that the files and folder structure of Drupal 8 have changed from its predecessor Drupal 7. The first change is that everything that Drupal 8 needs to run is contained within the new `core` folder. No longer is there any confusion of having the `modules` and `themes` folders contained within a `sites` folder and having to ask "did I place my files in the correct location?".

Name	^	Date Modified	Size	Kind
▼ 📁 core		12/2/15, 9:08 AM	--	Folder
▶ 📁 assets		12/2/15, 9:08 AM	--	Folder
📄 authorize.php		12/2/15, 9:08 AM	7 KB	PHP
📄 CHANGELOG.txt		12/2/15, 9:08 AM	64 KB	Plain Text Document
📄 composer.json		12/2/15, 9:08 AM	6 KB	JSON
📄 composer.txt		12/2/15, 9:08 AM	886 bytes	Plain Text Document
▶ 📁 config		12/2/15, 9:08 AM	--	Folder
📄 COPYRIGHT.txt		12/2/15, 9:08 AM	2 KB	Plain Text Document
📄 core.api.php		12/2/15, 9:08 AM	118 KB	PHP
📄 core.libraries.yml		12/2/15, 9:08 AM	21 KB	YAML
📄 core.services.yml		12/2/15, 9:08 AM	62 KB	YAML
📄 globals.api.php		12/2/15, 9:08 AM	2 KB	PHP
▶ 📁 includes		12/2/15, 9:08 AM	--	Folder
📄 INSTALL.mysql.txt		12/2/15, 9:08 AM	2 KB	Plain Text Document
📄 INSTALL.pgsql.txt		12/2/15, 9:08 AM	2 KB	Plain Text Document
📄 install.php		12/2/15, 9:08 AM	1 KB	PHP
📄 INSTALL.sqlite.txt		12/2/15, 9:08 AM	1 KB	Plain Text Document
📄 INSTALL.txt		12/2/15, 9:08 AM	18 KB	Plain Text Document
▶ 📁 lib		12/2/15, 9:08 AM	--	Folder
📄 LICENSE.txt		12/2/15, 9:08 AM	18 KB	Plain Text Document
📄 MAINTAINERS.txt		12/2/15, 9:08 AM	17 KB	Plain Text Document
▶ 📁 misc		12/2/15, 9:08 AM	--	Folder
▶ 📁 modules		12/2/15, 9:08 AM	--	Folder
📄 phpcs.xml.dist		12/2/15, 9:08 AM	4 KB	Document
📄 phpunit.xml.dist		12/2/15, 9:08 AM	3 KB	Document
▶ 📁 profiles		Today, 1:12 PM	--	Folder
📄 rebuild.php		12/2/15, 9:08 AM	2 KB	PHP
▶ 📁 scripts		12/2/15, 9:08 AM	--	Folder
▶ 📁 tests		12/2/15, 9:08 AM	--	Folder
▶ 📁 themes		12/2/15, 9:08 AM	--	Folder
📄 UPGRADE.txt		12/2/15, 9:08 AM	6 KB	Plain Text Document
📄 example.gitignore		12/2/15, 9:08 AM	1 KB	Document
📄 index.php		12/2/15, 9:08 AM	549 bytes	PHP
📄 LICENSE.txt		9/23/14, 3:24 PM	18 KB	Plain Text Document

The core folder consists of miscellaneous files needed by Drupal to bootstrap the content management system as well as the following folders:

- assets: Various external libraries used by core (jquery, modernizr, backbone, and others)
- config: It contains misc configuration for installation and database schema
- includes: It contains files and folders related to the functionality of Drupal

- `lib`: Drupal core classes
- `misc`: Various JavaScript files and images used by core
- `modules`: Drupal core modules and Twig templates
- `profiles`: Installation profiles
- `scripts`: Various CLI scripts
- `tests`: Drupal core tests
- `themes`: Drupal core themes

The modules folder

While a lot of functionality, which was generally contained in a contributed module, has been moved into the core instance of Drupal 8, you will still find yourself needing to extend Drupal. Previously, you would locate a contributed module, download it, and then extract its contents into your `sites/all/modules` folder so that Drupal could then use it.

Contributed and custom modules are now placed into the `modules` folder, which is no longer contained inside your `sites` folder.

Name	Date Modified	Size	Kind
autoload.php	12/2/15, 9:08 AM	262 bytes	PHP
composer.json	12/2/15, 9:08 AM	1 KB	JSON
composer.lock	12/2/15, 9:08 AM	133 KB	Document
▶ core	Today, 11:35 PM	--	Folder
example.gitignore	12/2/15, 9:08 AM	1 KB	Document
index.php	12/2/15, 9:08 AM	549 bytes	PHP
LICENSE.txt	9/23/14, 3:24 PM	18 KB	Plain Text Document
▼ modules	12/2/15, 9:08 AM	--	Folder
README.txt	12/2/15, 9:08 AM	2 KB	Plain Text Document
▶ profiles	12/2/15, 9:08 AM	--	Folder
README.txt	12/2/15, 9:08 AM	6 KB	Plain Text Document
robots.txt	12/2/15, 9:08 AM	1 KB	Plain Text Document
▶ sites	Today, 9:31 PM	--	Folder
▶ themes	12/2/15, 9:08 AM	--	Folder
update.php	12/2/15, 9:08 AM	547 bytes	PHP
▶ vendor	12/2/15, 9:08 AM	--	Folder
web.config	12/2/15, 9:08 AM	4 KB	Document

Best practices are to create a few subdirectories inside the `modules` folder for contributed modules—the modules built by third parties that we will use to extend your project, such as `contrib`, and `custom`, for the modules that we create on a per project basis. We will also occasionally find ourselves with a `features` folder if we plan to use the Features module to break out functionality that needs to be managed in code for purposes of migrating it easily to development, staging, and production instances of our website.

The sites folder

We are all familiar with the `sites` folder in Drupal 7. However, in Drupal 8, the `sites` folder only contains our Drupal instance configuration and files.

Name	^	Date Modified	Size	Kind
autoload.php		12/2/15, 9:08 AM	262 bytes	PHP
composer.json		12/2/15, 9:08 AM	1 KB	JSON
composer.lock		12/2/15, 9:08 AM	133 KB	Document
▶ core		Today, 11:35 PM	--	Folder
example.gitignore		12/2/15, 9:08 AM	1 KB	Document
index.php		12/2/15, 9:08 AM	549 bytes	PHP
LICENSE.txt		9/23/14, 3:24 PM	18 KB	Plain Text Document
▶ modules		12/2/15, 9:08 AM	--	Folder
▶ profiles		12/2/15, 9:08 AM	--	Folder
README.txt		12/2/15, 9:08 AM	6 KB	Plain Text Document
robots.txt		12/2/15, 9:08 AM	1 KB	Plain Text Document
▼ sites		Today, 11:47 PM	--	Folder
▼ default		Today, 9:31 PM	--	Folder
default.services.yml		12/2/15, 9:08 AM	6 KB	YAML
default.settings.php		12/2/15, 9:08 AM	28 KB	PHP
▼ files		Today, 10:44 PM	--	Folder
▶ config_ac....38-1802		Today, 9:31 PM	--	Folder
▶ config_c...17wlglaDQ		Today, 10:20 PM	--	Folder
▶ css		Today, 11:11 PM	--	Folder
▶ js		Today, 11:11 PM	--	Folder
▶ php		Today, 10:20 PM	--	Folder
▶ styles		Today, 10:20 PM	--	Folder
settings.php		Today, 10:20 PM	29 KB	PHP
development.services.yml		12/2/15, 9:08 AM	249 bytes	YAML
drupal8.dd		Today, 9:31 PM	7 bytes	Alias
example.settings.local.php		12/2/15, 9:08 AM	3 KB	PHP
example.sites.php		12/2/15, 9:08 AM	2 KB	PHP
README.txt		12/2/15, 9:08 AM	515 bytes	Plain Text Document
sites.php		Today, 9:31 PM	2 KB	PHP
▶ themes		12/2/15, 9:08 AM	--	Folder
update.php		12/2/15, 9:08 AM	547 bytes	PHP
▶ vendor		12/2/15, 9:08 AM	--	Folder
web.config		12/2/15, 9:08 AM	4 KB	Document

The themes folder

Finally, we have the `themes` folder. So, why don't we see the default themes that Drupal generally ships with inside this folder? That is because Drupal's default themes now are contained within the `core` folder. Finally, we will actually use the `themes` folder to place our custom or contributed themes inside it for use by Drupal.

We will be exploring the `themes` folder in more detail in later chapters as we begin creating custom themes.

Name	⌃	Date Modified	Size	Kind
autoload.php		12/2/15, 9:08 AM	262 bytes	PHP
composer.json		12/2/15, 9:08 AM	1 KB	JSON
composer.lock		12/2/15, 9:08 AM	133 KB	Document
▶ core		Today, 11:35 PM	--	Folder
example.gitignore		12/2/15, 9:08 AM	1 KB	Document
index.php		12/2/15, 9:08 AM	549 bytes	PHP
LICENSE.txt		9/23/14, 3:24 PM	18 KB	Plain Text Document
▶ modules		12/2/15, 9:08 AM	--	Folder
▶ profiles		12/2/15, 9:08 AM	--	Folder
README.txt		12/2/15, 9:08 AM	6 KB	Plain Text Document
robots.txt		12/2/15, 9:08 AM	1 KB	Plain Text Document
▶ sites		Today, 11:47 PM	--	Folder
▼ themes		12/2/15, 9:08 AM	--	Folder
README.txt		12/2/15, 9:08 AM	1 KB	Plain Text Document
update.php		12/2/15, 9:08 AM	547 bytes	PHP
▶ vendor		12/2/15, 9:08 AM	--	Folder
web.config		12/2/15, 9:08 AM	4 KB	Document

Using the project files

As we work through each chapter of the book, we will be using exercise files that contain examples of how each page will be themed is laid out. This will include database snapshots, HTML, CSS, and images for our Home, About, Portfolio, Blog, and Contact pages. Before we begin using these files, we need to know where to download them from and the best location to extract them to for future use.

Downloading and extracting the exercise files

We can find the exercise files at `https://www.packtpub.com/support`. Click on the download link and save the compressed file to the desktop. Once the download is finished, we will need to extract the contents. Let's take a quick look at what we have:

- Several chapter folders containing files that we will use for whatever task we are working on in that chapter
- A `Mockup` folder that contains the finished HTML version of our theme
- A database snapshot contained within various chapter folders that we will use to restore on top of our current Drupal instance to ensure that we always have the same configuration at specific points along the way

Since we will be working with database snapshots at various points, we will want to look at how we can manage these files using the MySQL database tool named phpMyAdmin.

Database backup

It is important to know how to backup our database when working in Drupal 8 as most of our content and configurations are contained within a database. Make sure that phpMyAdmin is open in the browser.

Next, we will want to make sure that any database exports are saved as a file versus just plain SQL script. Because this is a global setting, we will need to make sure that we have not selected any specific database. We can make sure that we are affecting global settings by clicking on the house icon in the left-hand sidebar underneath the phpMyAdmin logo. Next, we can navigate to **Settings** and then **Export**, as shown in the following image:

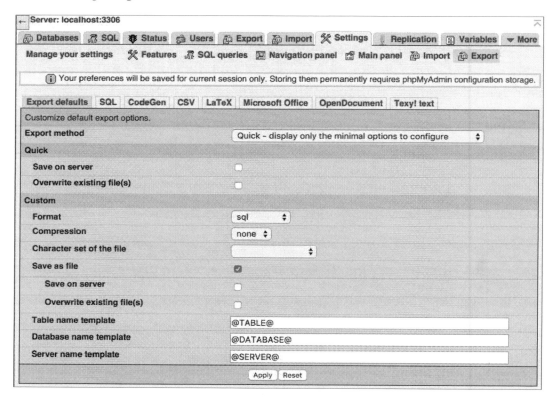

Next, click on the **Save as file** option and the **Apply** button.

Export settings

One little gotcha when using phpMyAdmin is making sure that when we create our database export, we ensure that the SQL also drops any tables before trying to recreate them when we do the import later.

We can create our database export by following these steps:

1. Select the `drupal8` database from the left sidebar.
2. Click on the **Export** tab.

3. Select **Custom - display all possible options** as our export method.

4. Select **SQL** as our format.

5. Choose **Add DROP TABLE / VIEW / PROCEDURE / FUNCTION / EVENT / TRIGGER statement** from **Object creation options**.

6. Click on the **Go** button.

At this point, we have a new file named `drupal8.sql`, which contains a backup of our database. Next, we will use this file we just created to restore our database.

Database restore

Restoring a database is simpler than backing our database up. Except this time, we will be using an existing database snapshot that either we have taken or that we were provided to overwrite our current database files with. Let's begin by following these steps:

1. Click on the **Import** tab.

2. Click on the **Choose File** button and locate the `drupal8.sql` file we created earlier.

3. Click on the **Go** button to begin the restoration process.

The process of restoring the file can sometimes take a minute to complete, so please be patient while the file is being restored.

While phpMyAdmin allows us to manage database operations, we can choose to use other database tools or even the command line, which is a lot faster to export and import databases.

Now that we have a good understanding of how to back up and restore our database, it's time to take a quick look at how we will be using Google Chrome to review our HTML and CSS structure within Drupal 8 and our theme Mockup.

Using Google Chrome to inspect elements

While there are many different browsers to view web content on, Google Chrome is definitely a favorite browser when theming in Drupal. It is not only standards compliant ensuring that most HTML and CSS work properly but Chrome also allows us to inspect the HTML and CSS and preview changes "live" within the browser using the **Developer Tools** option.

Begin by browsing to our local Drupal 8 instance in Google Chrome and then selecting **Developer Tools** from the **View | Developer | Developer Tools** menu. The **Developer Tools** will open up in the bottom of your browser, as shown in the following image:

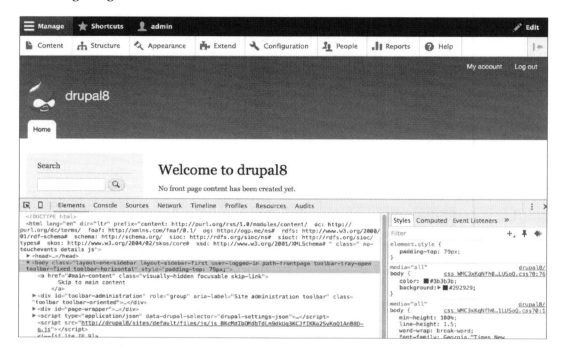

There are several tools available for our use, but the one we will use the most is inspecting **Elements** on the page, which allows us to view the HTML structure and any CSS being applied to that element from the **Elements** and **Styles** panels. We can navigate through the HTML structure, or if we prefer to isolate an element on the page, we can place our cursor on that element and right-click to open up a context menu where we can select **Inspect**. Doing so will target that element in the **Elements** pane for us.

As we dive deeper into theming, we will use this set of tools to help preview changes as well as isolate any issue we may be experiencing as our HTML structure changes based on what Drupal 8 outputs.

Summary

We collected a lot of information to start our series on Drupal 8 themes. Let's review exactly what we covered so far:

- We successfully configured an AMP (Apache MySQL, PHP) stack by downloading and installing MAMP PRO.

- We set up our first Drupal 8 instance by downloading the latest version from Drupal.org, importing the Drupal instance into our AMP stack, and completing the Drupal 8 install by choosing our language, profile, database settings, and site information.

- We also had our first look at Drupal 8 and some of the new responsive functionality that it provides. We familiarized ourselves with the admin menu and the new admin interface, which included the **Content**, **Structure**, **Appearance**, **Extend**, **Configuration**, **People**, **Reports**, and **Help** sections. Having a better knowledge of Drupal 8 and its folder structure has given us insight into how to apply best practices to manage our theme and its assets.

- By using the project files, we learned how to manage database snapshots through importing and exporting SQL files inside phpMyAdmin.

- Finally, we learned how to use Google Chrome to inspect our HTML and CSS to have a better understanding of our theme and its markup.

In the next chapter, we will take a closer look at "theme administration" and answer the question: what is a theme? We will explore the "appearance interface" and discuss how Drupal's default themes function. Finally, we will follow up with looking closer at how to use prebuilt themes and managing content with blocks and custom block layouts.

2
Theme Administration

Before we can get started with creating or managing themes in Drupal 8, we need to have a better understanding of exactly what a theme is. From there we will have the basis for how we work with themes in Drupal and the various configuration and components that are considered to be part of the theming ecosystem.

Let's get started by exploring what we will be covering along the way:

- First, we will explore the Appearance interface and the core default themes. We will learn how themes are administered, how to install and uninstall themes, how they are configured, and the different settings a theme can have.

- Second, we will take a closer look at a prebuilt theme, where to find themes that we can use, and how we can easily install themes using the Drupal 8 admin.

- Third, we will take a closer look at the `themes` folder structure and how to manually install a theme in preparation to create a custom theme.

- Fourth, we will take a look at the new Block layout and how we can manage chunks of content and assign content to regions. This will include configuring a block and controlling the visibility of blocks based on certain settings.

- Finally, we will take a look at the new Custom Block library and explore how to add fields to blocks, something not previously available to us in Drupal 7.

We have a lot to cover, so let's get started by discussing, what is a theme?

What is a theme?

In simple terms, a theme is the presentational layer to content. Regardless of you working in Drupal or another **content management system (CMS)** without a theme, all you have is content that looks very similar to a Word document.

A theme generally consists of HTML markup, CSS, JavaScript, and media (images, video, and audio). It is this combination of technologies that allow the graphic designer to build something visually rich that can then be applied on top of the logic a web developer is building in Drupal. Sometimes, a web developer may be the person who implements the theme, but in most cases, you will hear the term themer or interface engineer, which describes the person who actually fills that role.

This book helps you learn that role. So, as long as you have a good knowledge of HTML, CSS, and JavaScript, you are well on your way to filling a much-needed role in the Drupal community.

We will begin by exploring the Appearance interface in Drupal 8.

Exploring the Appearance interface

The Appearance interface in Drupal 8 can be located by clicking on the **Manage** menu item from the administrative toolbar and then by choosing the **Appearance** link. We can also directly navigate to the Appearance interface by entering the address of /admin/appearance in our browser.

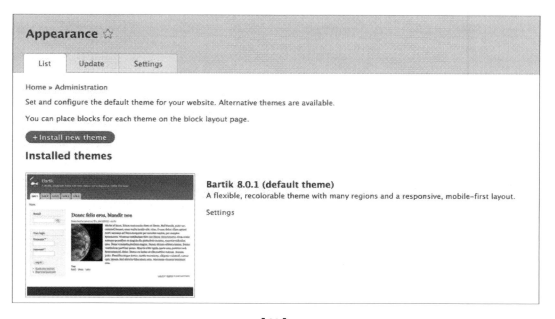

The **Appearance** interface allows us to work with themes in Drupal, that is, anything from installing, uninstalling, and configuring the default theme for our website. We will be exploring the various functions within this section starting with taking a look at the default themes that Drupal 8 ships with.

Drupal's core themes

By default, Drupal 8 ships with three themes. As part of the standard installation profile, Drupal will install and configure Bartik, Seven, and Stark themes. Each of these themes serves a specific function in the workflow. Let's look at them in more detail.

Bartik

Bartik is considered the default theme in Drupal and is familiar to most as it has been part of the Drupal ecosystem for quite a while now. We can think of Bartik as the frontend theme or what we see when we first install Drupal. The Bartik theme is what you will visually see when you are not navigating within the Drupal administrative screens.

Seven

Seven is the default admin theme, and it provides a clean separation between the frontend and backend of Drupal. This is great as it will always allow us to navigate through the administrative areas if our default theme generates any errors that may cause a blank white screen while theming.

Stark

Stark is an intentionally plain theme with no styling at all to help demonstrate the default HTML and CSS that Drupal will output and is great for learning how to build a custom theme.

Classy

Wait, this is the fourth theme! Actually, Classy is a base theme that both Bartik and Seven use that provides both with clean well-documented markup and CSS classes. Classy is hidden from the Appearance admin screen by default, and we will learn more about Classy as a base theme and how to use it within our own themes later in *Chapter 4, Getting Started – Creating Themes*.

Theme states

One of the advantages of Drupal is the ability to have multiple themes available to use at any time, and as we discussed earlier, Drupal provides us with three themes to start with. However, it is important to differentiate between installed, uninstalled, and default. We can consider these as the theme's states.

Installed themes

Installed themes are always located in the **Installed themes** section of the Appearance admin and are available for Drupal to use for either the frontend or backend of the CMS. However, there can only be one theme set as the default at any given time. We can see a list of installed themes, as shown in the following image:

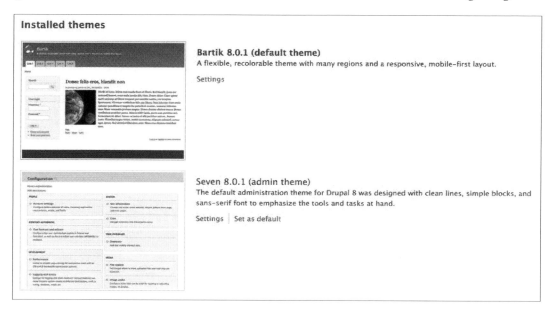

Uninstalled themes

Uninstalled theme(s) are themes that Drupal is aware of within the core themes folder or the custom themes folder but have not been placed into an installed state. One or multiple themes can be present at any time within the **Uninstalled theme** section, as shown in the following image:

Uninstalled theme

Stark 8.0.1
An intentionally plain theme with no styling to demonstrate default Drupal's HTML and CSS. Learn how to build a custom theme from Stark in the Theming Guide.

Install | Install and set as default

Default theme

Finally, we will often hear the term default theme being used, so it's important to remember that the default theme is always the current theme being displayed to users when viewing our website as an anonymous or logged out user or when logged in but not within an Administrative section of Drupal. Anytime a theme is set as default, it will always be considered installed as well.

Installing and uninstalling themes

The act of installing or uninstalling a theme is a common practice when administering a Drupal website. Let's try installing Stark and making it our default theme in place of Bartik.

Step one – installing a theme

Currently, the only uninstalled theme is **Stark**, and we can easily move this into the installed state by following these two steps:

1. Click on the **Install and set as default** link.
2. Scroll back to the top of **Appearance** admin.

3. If we now look at the **Installed themes** section, we should see that we now have three themes installed: Stark, Bartik, and Seven. We can also tell that Stark is now our default theme by looking to the right of the themes name, which will be marked as **(default theme)** as shown in the following image:

We can also see what the Stark theme looks like by clicking on the **Back to site** link in the Admin menu, which will take us back to the frontend of our website. We are now presented with an unstyled page, which is to help demonstrate the clean markup of Drupal.

Step two – uninstalling a theme

It is just as easy to uninstall a theme, and one nice feature of Drupal 8 is that it ensures that we have at least one installed theme set as default. Otherwise, we won't even have the option of uninstalling the theme.

Let's navigate back to the Appearance admin located at /admin/appearance and uninstall the Stark theme by following these two steps:

1. Locate the **Bartik** theme and click on **Set as default**.
2. Locate the **Stark** theme and click on **Uninstall**.

We saw how simple it is to install and uninstall themes within Drupal 8. Another common task we will find ourselves completing within the Appearance admin is adjusting the settings of a theme.

Theme settings

Under the **Settings** tab of the Appearance admin, the options to control the default display settings for your entire site are located, across all themes or individually. These settings range from toggling the display of certain page elements, updating the default logo supplied by the theme, to providing a shortcut icon or favicon that is displayed in the address bar of most browsers.

Let's explore these in more detail by clicking on the **Settings** tab and previewing the interface, as shown in the following image:

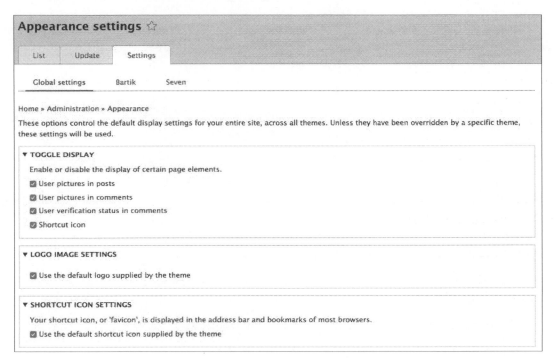

Toggling the display of page elements

Having control over certain page elements of a theme can come in handy when we want to hide or show specific items. Most of the items listed pertain to user settings, such as user pictures in posts or comments, user verification status in comments, and the Shortcut icon from displaying.

Simply checking or unchecking an item will toggle that item on or off. Also, keep in mind that toggling the Shortcut icon will disable the ability to add a shortcut icon as the visibility of that section is also toggled on and off.

Gone are Logo, Site name, Site slogan, Main menu, and Secondary menu from the theme settings. These were present in Drupal 7 but have now been moved into Blocks and block configuration. We will be addressing each of these moved settings in a few moments.

Logo image settings

Another nice option within the Appearance settings admin is the ability to manage the themes logo. By default, Drupal displays the infamous Drop logo, but we have the power to replace that logo with our own.

Let's begin by following these five steps:

1. Locate the **LOGO IMAGE SETTINGS** section.
2. Uncheck **Use the default logo supplied by the theme**.
3. Click on the **Choose file** button under the **Upload logo image** field.
4. Locate the exercise files and select `logo.png` from the `mockup/assets/img` folder. Click on the **Open** button.
5. Click on the **Save configuration** button.
6. Our new logo has now been placed into the `sites/default/files` folder of our Drupal installation, as shown in the following image:

With the path to our custom logo now pointing to our new logo, we can preview it by clicking on the **Back to site** link in the Admin menu, which will take us to the frontend of our website, as shown in the following image:

One thing to note is that there is no simple way to delete logo images we upload using the Logo image settings, so Drupal will append a sequential number to the end of the file versus overriding it if it has the same name. In the case where we ever need to delete a logo image, we would have to navigate to the `sites/default/files` directory and manually delete the file.

Shortcut icon settings

If you are wondering what a shortcut icon is, don't worry. The shortcut icon is also known as a favicon. It is the small image located in the browser window next to the URL address or if you are using Google Chrome, next to the page title of the website you are visiting.

Often this step is overlooked when creating or working with themes in Drupal, but the steps involved in adding a shortcut icon is exactly like adding a logo. Start by navigating to `/admin/appearance/settings` and follow these five steps:

1. Locate the **SHORTCUT ICON SETTINGS** section.
2. Uncheck **Use the default icon supplied by the theme**.
3. Click on the **Choose file** button under the **Upload icon image** field.
4. Locate the exercise files and select `favicon.ico` from the `mockup/assets/img` folder; click on the **Open** button.
5. Click on the **Save configuration** button.

Our new favicon has now been placed into the `sites/default/files` folder of our Drupal installation, as shown in the following image:

We can now preview our shortcut icon by clicking on the **Back to site** link in the Admin menu and navigating to the homepage, as shown in the following image:

So far, we have been working with Global settings. However, individual theme settings can be applied as well. In fact, if we navigate back to the Appearance settings admin located at `/admin/appearance/settings`, we will see that Bartik and Seven can each have their own settings.

Theme-specific settings

Drupal 8 allows for the configuration of theme-specific settings. These can vary based on the theme and the amount of extensibility that a theme provides. For example, if we click on the **Bartik** theme, we will notice that it provides us with an ability to change the **COLOR SCHEME** through a series of presets, as shown in the following image:

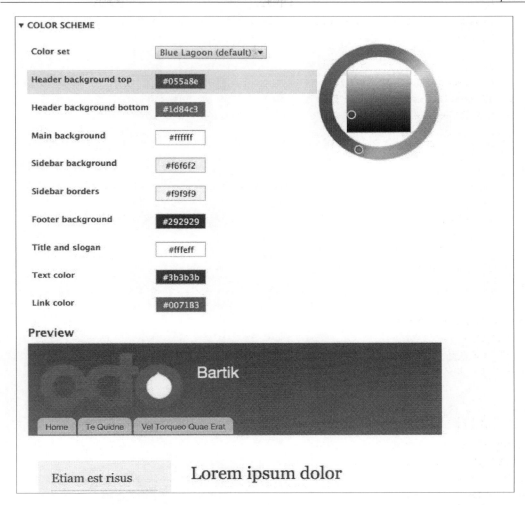

Feel free to experiment by selecting various color sets and then previewing what those selections would look like if applied. Outside the core themes shipped with Drupal 8, we can apply prebuilt themes to provide various features.

Using prebuilt themes

Additional themes for Drupal 8 may be limited at first, but we can find prebuilt themes at several places. Some of these themes have to be purchased, whereas others are free to use. We will take a look at Drupal.org to find some prebuilt themes and how to install them using the Drupal admin, how to manually install a theme, and finally how to uninstall a theme once we're done using it.

Begin by opening up a new tab in our browser and navigating to `https://drupal. org/project/project_theme`.

The **Download & Extend** section of Drupal.org allows us to filter results based on various options. We can find Drupal 8-specific themes by performing the following steps:

1. Select **8.x** from the **Core compatibility** dropdown.

2. Click on the **Search** button.

3. With a selection of themes compatible with Drupal 8 to choose from, one result looks promising and that is the Bootstrap 3 theme, as shown in the following image:

Bootstrap

Posted by markcarver on *May 18, 2008 at 1:15pm*

> Sleek, intuitive, and powerful mobile first front-end framework for faster and easier web development. Bootstrap has become one of the most popular front-end frameworks and open source projects in the world.

This base theme bridges the gap between Drupal and the Bootstrap Framework.

Features

- jsDelivr CDN for "out-of-the-box" styling and faster page load times.
- Bootswatch theme support, if using the CDN.
- Glyphicons support via Icon API.
- Extensive integration and template/preprocessor overrides for most of the Bootstrap Framework CSS, Components and JavaScript
- Theme settings to further enhance the Drupal Bootstrap integration:
  - Breadcrumbs
  - Navbar
  - Popovers
  - Tooltips
  - Wells (per region)

Documentation

Visit the project's official documentation site or the markdown files inside the ./docs folder.

Installing a new theme

At this point, we should have two tabs opened in our browser. One opened to the Bootstrap 3 theme and the other tab opened to the Appearance admin of our Drupal instance.

From the Appearance admin, we can install a new theme by clicking on the **Install new theme** button, which will take us to the **Install new theme** interface, as shown in the following image:

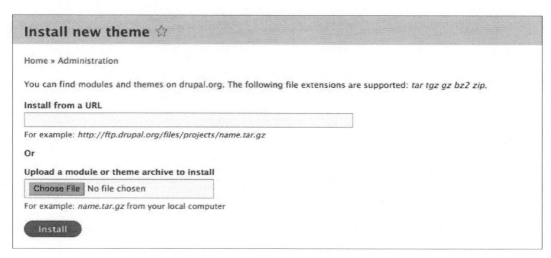

We will first take a look at using the **Install from a URL** option to install the Bootstrap 3 theme.

Installing from a URL

To install a theme from a URL, we only need to know the URL path to the archived theme file. This can be obtained from the Theme project page where the theme was found.

Downloads

Recommended releases

This theme has a pre-release version for Drupal 8. To find out more, follow this issue or download below.

Version	Download	Date
8.x-3.0-beta2	tar.gz (211.08 KB) | zip (572.35 KB)	2015-Dec-19
7.x-3.4	tar.gz (199.55 KB) | zip (828.34 KB)	2015-Dec-19

Follow these four steps:

1. Right-click on the tar.gz link located under the **Download** column of the 8.x version of the theme.

2. Select **Copy Link Address** from the context menu.

3. Paste the link into the **Install from a URL** textbox on the **Install new theme** admin screen.

4. Click on the **Install** button.

5. We should now be presented with the **Update manager** screen notifying us that the **Installation was completed successfully**, as shown in the following image:

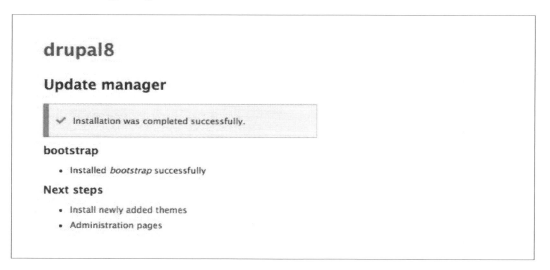

6. Click on the **Install newly added themes** link to take us back to the **Appearance** admin.

7. If we look at the **Uninstalled themes** section, we will see the **Bootstrap 3** theme where we can click on the **Install and set as default** link.

8. To verify that our theme is installed, navigate to the frontend of our site by clicking on the **Back to site** link in the Admin menu. We should now see our new theme being displayed, as shown in the following image:

Congratulations, we have installed our first prebuilt theme. As we can see, the process of installing a theme from a URL is quite simple. In fact, the process of installing a new theme from a file is not that different, as we will see.

Uploading a module or theme archive to install

If we navigate to /admin/theme/install, we will be back on the **Install new theme** screen. The **Upload a module or theme archive to install** option requires that we have a copy of the archived theme downloaded.

If we navigate back to the Drupal.org Theme project page and look a little further down our search results, we will see another popular theme based on the ZURB Foundation framework, as shown in the following image:

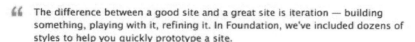

ZURB Foundation

Posted by ishmael-sanchez on *November 4, 2011 at 7:33pm*

Do you like grid systems? How about rapid prototyping? Do you believe in mobile first? Then this theme is for you.

From the Zurb Foundation homepage:

> An easy to use, powerful, and flexible framework for building prototypes and production code on any kind of device.

> **Mockups don't tell a story. Build a prototype in no time.**

> The difference between a good site and a great site is iteration — building something, playing with it, refining it. In Foundation, we've included dozens of styles to help you quickly prototype a site.

See Zurb Foundation in the wild.

Read the Zurb Foundation Docs

In order to use this theme effectively, it may help if you learn how to use Zurb Foundation's built in classes and components:

* **Learn how to use the Foundation framework.**
* See the kitchen sink! See all of Zurb Foundation 4's components on one page

We will be downloading the current Drupal 8 Development release of the theme by clicking on either the tar.gz or zip links. This will initiate a file download to our specified downloads folder. We will use this downloaded file to perform the following steps from the **Install new theme** admin:

1. Click on the **Choose file** button from the **Upload a module or theme archive to install** input.
2. Locate the downloaded file and select it.

3. Click on the **Open** button.

4. Click on the **Install** button.

5. Click on the **Install newly added themes** link from the Drupal 8 **Update manager**.

6. If we look at the **Uninstalled themes** section, we will see the **ZURB Foundation** theme where we can click on the **Install and set as default** link.

7. Navigate back to the frontend by clicking on the **Back to site** link and verify that our new theme is being displayed, as shown in the following image:

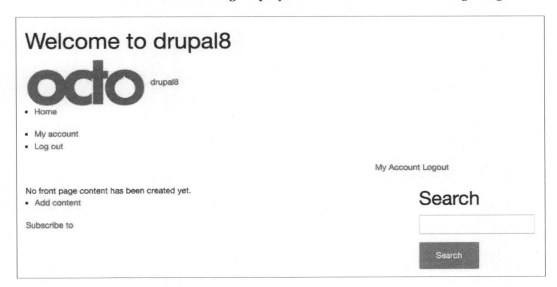

We have now mastered using the Drupal Admin to install themes from both a URL and an archive. However, the preferred method to install a theme is by manually installing it. The benefit to choose this method is that we have full control over the themes folder, and if we are doing any type of custom theming, we will need to be familiar with this process anyway.

Manually installing a theme

In order to manually install a theme, we will need a copy of the archive downloaded to our local machine. Start by navigating to the Drupal Theme project page and locate the Drupal 8 theme named **Neato**. Neato is based on the Neat grid system and is part of the Bourbon Sass framework.

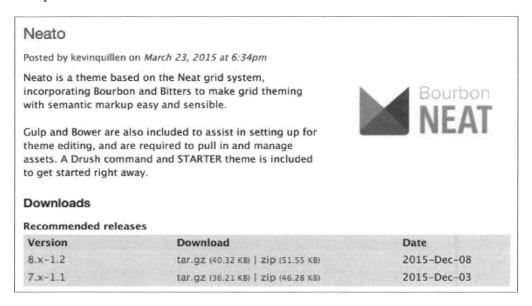

Click on the tar.gz or zip file next to the 8.x version of the theme to initiate the download. Next, we need to locate the tar or zipped file on our machine and extract the contents of the file. We should now have a theme folder named `neato`.

In order for Drupal 8 to recognize a new theme, all we need to do is copy the theme into the `themes` directory inside our Drupal 8 installation, as shown in the following image:

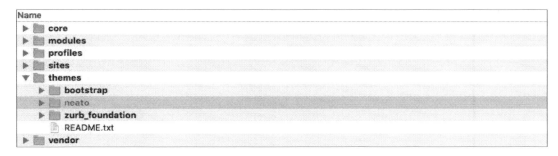

Our `themes` folder should now contain three themes. Two of the themes are installed through the Drupal admin and the third is manually placed. As long as a Drupal 8 theme is configured properly, simply placing it into the `themes` folder will allow it to be found by the Drupal admin. However, some themes may come with an `INSTALL.txt` or `README.txt` file that provides additional installation instructions.

Navigate back to the Appearance admin located at `/admin/appearance`, and we should see our Neato theme within the **Uninstalled themes** section. We can now click on the **Install and set as default** link to activate our new theme.

With our new theme enabled, we can now view it by navigating back to our homepage, as shown in the following image:

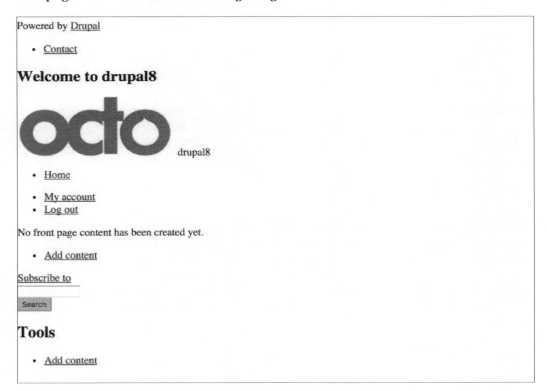

By now, we should be getting used to working with prebuilt themes. However, the more themes we play around with, the more our `themes` folder can become bloated. It is much easier to manage themes if we have a clean directory structure.

Cleaning up our themes folder

To have a much more manageable theme folder, let's take a few moments to do some housecleaning. First, let's set the Bartik theme back as our default. Once that is complete, we can uninstall Bootstrap 3, ZURB Foundation, and Neato themes. Finally, once the three themes are uninstalled, we can remove them from our `themes` folder as we will not be using them anymore.

Managing content with blocks

Themes are much more than just layout with their respective HTML, CSS, and JavaScript. Without content, we would not have much to display. In Drupal 8, a lot of content has been moved into blocks that are then assigned to various regions.

Think of blocks as small sections of content. These blocks can contain a menu, a search form, a listing of content, plain HTML, and more. Drupal 8 uses this content within the Block layout system that makes up a good part of a website.

If you are familiar with blocks in Drupal 7, you will be happily surprised to find that blocks have matured and are now fieldable, similar to content types. This new implementation of blocks also allows the same block to be reused and displayed using different view modes. As we explore the Block layout, we will learn how to place blocks, configure them, and create custom blocks.

Exploring the Block layout

Begin by navigating to `/admin/structure/block` or by clicking on **Structure** and then **Block layout** from the Admin menu. The Block layout page provides an interface in order to manage block content and place them into regions, as shown in the following image:

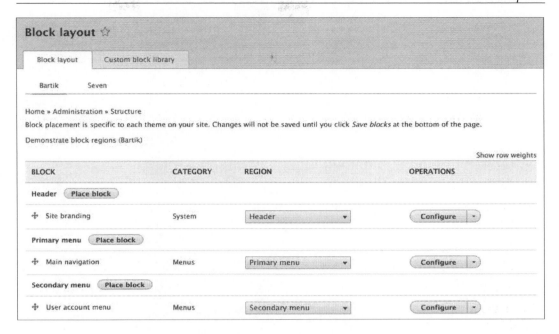

Blocks and regions

A block can be thought of as a chunk of content as small as a single line of HTML markup or as complicated as a listing of content types. Blocks can be categorized based on their functionality with the most common types of blocks categorized:

- **Core**: Blocks contained within the core installation consisting of items such as page title, primary admin actions, and tabs.

- **System**: Blocks that provide system functionality consisting of breadcrumbs, main-page content, messages, site branding, and a few others.

- **Forms**: Blocks that contain embedded forms such as the search form and user login.

- **Menus**: Blocks that contain menus and menu items, such as Administration, Footer, Main navigation, and Tools.

- **Lists (Views)**: Blocks consisting of Views generated for block content. Generally, these types of blocks will be created during configuration or site building.

- **Custom**: Blocks are created from the Custom block library consisting of fieldable blocks with one or more display modes.

If blocks consist of content, regions are the containers that hold blocks and make up a themes layout.

Drupal 8 provides the following regions:

- Header
- Primary menu
- Secondary menu
- Highlighted
- Help
- Content
- Sidebar first
- Sidebar second
- Footer
- Breadcrumb

Also, each theme can define its own regions. An example of this is the Bartik theme, which implements additional regions for the footer. We will look at how to add custom regions later in *Chapter 3, Dissecting a Theme*.

Demonstrating block regions

To view defined regions within a theme, we can click on the **Demonstrate block regions** link located on the **Block layout** page. Clicking on this link will take us to the homepage with the regions highlighted, as shown in the following image:

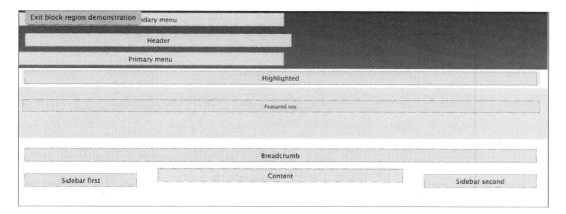

To return to the **Block layout** page, we click on the **Exit block region demonstration** link located at the top of the page.

Placing blocks into regions

If we scroll down the **Block layout** page and locate the **Sidebar second** region, we can see that it is currently empty. Empty regions will not output anything until we have placed a block within it. To place a block, we can follow these steps:

1. Click on the **Place block** button next to the **Sidebar second** region.

2. Locate the **Powered by Drupal** block and click on the **Place block** button.

3. Leave the default settings within the **Configure block** dialog.

4. Click on the **Save block** button.

5. We now have a new **Powered by Drupal** block placed within the **Sidebar second** region, as shown in the following image:

Let's verify that the **Powered by Drupal** block is displaying properly by navigating to our homepage. Since the **Sidebar second** region now contains a block, we will see the content appear in the right-hand column of the page, as shown in the following image:

So far, we have placed a block successfully within a region, but we can also configure a block based on the type of block it is.

Configuring a block

Although we can navigate back and forth between the specific page a block is located on and the Block layout screen, it is much easier to use the context menu provided by the block. If we hover over a block, we will see a **Configure block** link as, shown in the following image:

Clicking on this link takes us directly to the **Configure block** screen for the block, as shown in the following image:

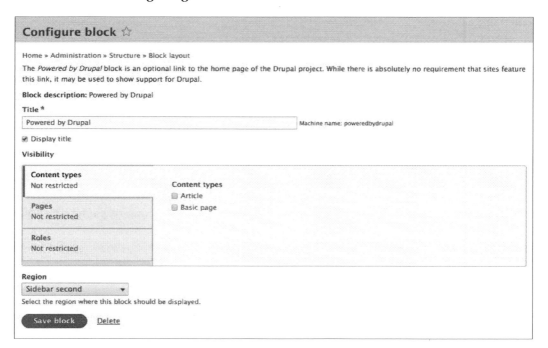

All blocks contain three common areas of configuration: **Title**, **Visibility**, and **Region**. Keep in mind that additional configuration options may be available based on the type of block. We will only be covering the basic configuration options.

Managing the title

Block content, whether system generated or custom, can have its display title changed or even suppressed. In the case of our **Powered by Drupal** block, we can change the title by simply inputting a different value in the **Title** field:

1. Locate the **Title** field.
2. Change the value to Powered by Drupal 8.
3. Click on the **Save block** button.
4. We return to the homepage, and we can see that our block title has changed, as shown in the following image:

Let's try suppressing the block title all together by clicking on the **Configure block** context link and following these steps:

1. Uncheck the **Display title** checkbox.
2. Click on the **Save block** button.

We should now only see the content of our block being displayed as the title is gone.

Managing visibility settings

Sometimes, we may want to control the visibility of a particular block of content based on various contexts. If we navigate back to the **Configure block** screen and scroll down to the **Visibility** section, we will see three different contexts to restrict visibility based on **Content types**, **Pages**, and **Roles**.

Content types restriction

Content types' visibility allows us to determine whether a block is displayed based on the content type of the node or page that the block is placed on. For example, if we have a block listing of recent articles that we only want to display in the sidebar on an Article Detail node, we could specify **Article** for the **Content types** restriction. This restriction would ensure that the same block did not accidentally show on a Basic page node.

Page restriction

Page restriction allows us to whitelist or blacklist blocks of content based on the path to a specific page or set of pages. The path to the page needs to be entered one line at a time and can utilize a wildcard "*" character to specify all children pages. Once we have entered the path, we can choose to *negate the condition* by either selecting **Show for the listed pages** or **Hide for the listed pages**.

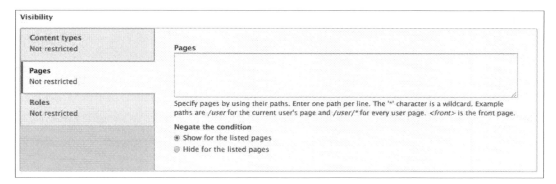

Page restriction visibility is probably the most common visibility setting used for blocks. Especially with Drupal 8 introducing the ability to reuse blocks, being able to control what page a block displays on is important to make sure that a block is not duplicated.

Role restriction

The last way to restrict block content is by role. A role is defined by the site administrator and generally consists of an administrator, editor, contributor, an authenticated user, and an anonymous user. Visibility to block content can be restricted by selecting the specific role, as shown in the following image:

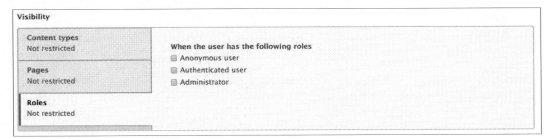

Role-specific visibility can be useful to display admin-only content or membership content to authenticated users without the anonymous user seeing it.

Creating a custom block

So far, we have worked with system-generated blocks. However, with the introduction of fieldable blocks in Drupal 8, we now have the ability to create custom blocks. Custom blocks are quite powerful and will be used to display content in ways not possible previously without a contributed module.

We can create a custom block by navigating back to the **Block layout** admin located at /admin/structure/block and following these steps:

1. Locate the **Sidebar second** region.
2. Click on the **Place block** button.
3. Click on the **Add custom block** button.

We are now presented with the **Add custom block** screen that will allow us to create a default custom block that includes a **Block description** and a **Body** field, as shown in the following image:

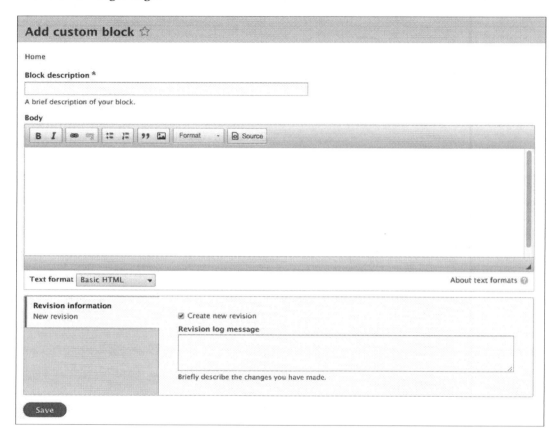

We can continue filling out our custom block by entering the following values:

- **Block description**: Our custom block
- **Body**: This is some basic content

Click on the **Save** button to proceed to the **Configure block** screen as follows:

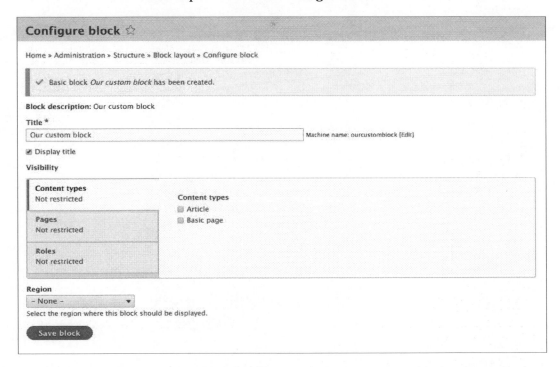

We can complete the creation of our custom block by leaving the defaults and clicking on the **Save block** button.

We have now created our first custom block, and if we scroll to the bottom of the Block layout admin, we will see our block displayed in the **Disabled** section, as shown in the following image:

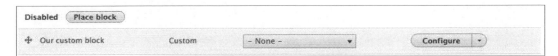

At this point, we can place our custom block within any region by using another method of placing blocks, the **Region** dropdown. The **Region** dropdown is visible within each region and allows a block to quickly move another region by selecting the specified region from the dropdown.

Let's move our custom block into the **Sidebar second** region by following these steps:

1. Select **Sidebar second** from the **Region** dropdown.
2. Click on the **Save blocks** button to save our changes.

If we navigate to the homepage, we will see our new custom block displayed in the right sidebar directly under our other block.

Managing custom blocks

If we want to edit the block content of a custom block, we will not find it by selecting the **Configure block** button in its context menu or by clicking on the **Configure** button next to the block from the **Block layout** page. Custom blocks can only be configured from the custom block library located at /admin/structure/block/ block-content or by clicking on the **Custom block library** tab from the **Block layout** admin.

Exploring the custom block library

The **Custom block library** tab displays any custom blocks that have been created. It is from here that we can **Edit** any custom block:

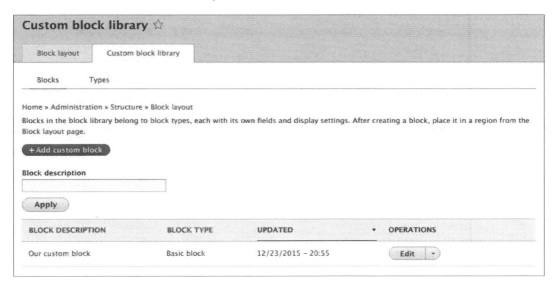

Clicking on the **Edit** button will bring up the **Edit custom block** page where any content, including the **Block description**, **Body**, or additional fields, can be changed.

The **Custom block library** consists of both the **Blocks** tab, which displays all custom blocks, and the **Types** tab, which displays the various block types that have been created. A block type is similar to a content type and contains a lot of the same traits as a content type. Let's take a closer look at the custom block type.

Exploring block types

Selecting the **Types** tab from the **Custom block library** exposes that we currently have a single block type named **Basic block**.

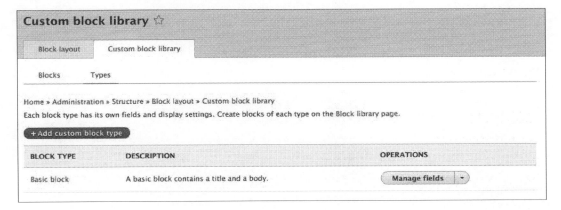

A Basic block contains a title and a body field, similar to that of the Page content type. However, we now have the ability to manage both the View mode of a block as well as to manage the fields a block can have. This new functionality allows us to extend the normal block way further than before. Let's take a look at how we can manage the fields of a basic block by adding a new field.

Managing fields

The minute we click on the **Manage fields** button, we are seeing something quite familiar to us, the Fields UI. The Fields UI allows us to manage existing fields as well as add new fields, as shown in the following image:

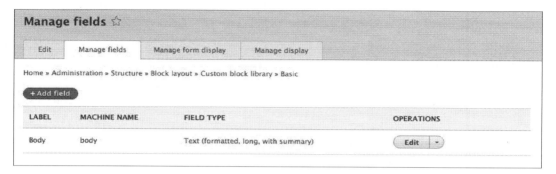

The Fields UI consists of the following:

- **LABEL**: This is a descriptive name of our field that will be used as a label when inputting content into this field.
- **MACHINE NAME**: The machine name is a lower case field name used by Drupal to distinguish this field from others.
- **FIELD TYPE**: This allows us to choose from various field types, such as date, file, text, and more.

We can add an additional field to our basic block type now by following these steps:

1. Click on the **Add field** button.
2. Select **Image** from the **Add a new field** dropdown.
3. Enter a **Label** of Featured Image.
4. Click on the **Save and continue** button.

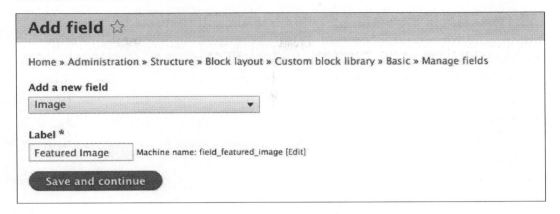

5. Leave the default settings on the field settings page.

6. Click on the **Save field settings** button.

7. Leave the default settings on the Edit page.

8. Click on the **Save settings** button.

9. We have successfully added a new field to the Basic block type that all future custom blocks can use to add a Featured Image to, as shown in the following image:

We could continue to add additional fields as needed, but we will stop at this point and focus on how to manage the display of custom blocks and their respective **View modes**.

Managing display

The **Custom block library** not only allows us to manage fields using the Fields UI, but we can also manage the display of the fields. Continuing with **Our custom block**, we will click on the **Manage display** tab. Managing the display of a block is exactly like managing the display of a content type.

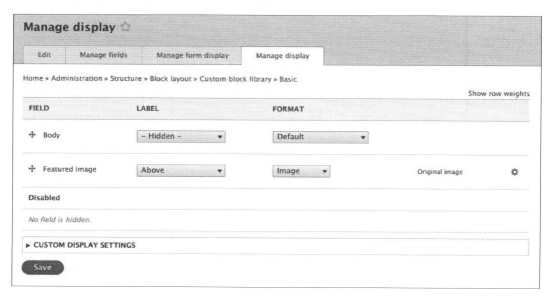

From the **Manage display** page, we can manage several display options ranging from showing or hiding the label to configuring the format of a field. The format options will vary based on the field type it is referring to. Feel free to play around with the various settings and preview the changes.

The final thing to point out is the custom display settings or view modes that a block can have. If we expand the **CUSTOM DISPLAY SETTINGS** field, we will only see one **View mode** which is called **Full**. Drupal 8 allows us to create additional View modes for use with custom blocks the same way we create content types.

If we navigate to /admin/structure/display-modes/view or using the Admin menu, click on **Structure, Display Modes**, and finally **View modes**. We will see all the options available to create additional **View modes** for **Content** as well as **Custom blocks**.

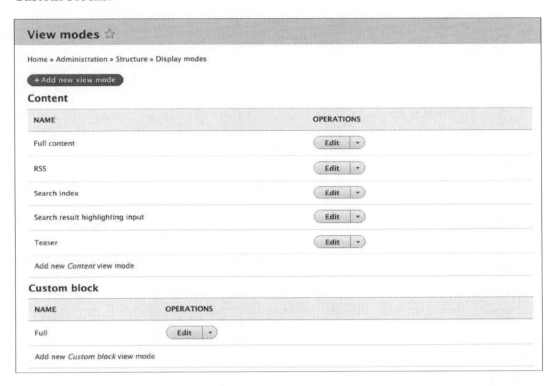

The **View modes** page contains several prebuilt displays based on **Content, User, Taxonomy term, Comment**, and **Custom Block**. If we scroll down to the **Custom block** section, we will see **Full** display. We can **Edit** or **Delete** this display or add additional displays by clicking on the **Add new Custom Block view mode** link. New view modes are simply containers to hold the display of our fields when we specify one to be used back on the **Manage display** page.

Summary

We have covered a lot of information surrounding the administration of themes in Drupal 8. So, let's recap exactly what we have covered so far:

- We answered the question, "What is a theme?"

- We took an in-depth look at the Appearance interface and how we can use it to install, uninstall, and configure settings, including toggling the display of certain page elements.

- We learned how to work with the logo image settings and shortcut icon settings that can be configured for themes.

- We worked with prebuilt themes and learned where to find them, how to install them using the Drupal admin, and manually using a theme archive.

- Finally, we took a detailed look at blocks and regions, including how to configure blocks and control their appearance using the new custom blocks layout to add additional fields and view modes.

In the next chapter, we will begin dissecting a theme. This includes taking a look at the file and folder structure of a theme, configuration management, and what makes up a core theme versus a custom theme. We will also explore the new `info.yml` configuration, the role of assets in Drupal, and how templates function with an introduction to Twig. Finally, we will follow up with looking closer at the theme file and how it can control variables within our templates.

3
Dissecting a Theme

Drupal 8 provides us, as developers and designers, with a unique opportunity to change the appearance of the output content. We have the ability to manage the configuration from the admin user interface as well as work with the actual templates and variables that output the HTML, CSS, and JavaScript. To get a better understanding, we will take a look at dissecting a theme, as we cover the following:

- Having a proper development environment is important when working with themes, so we will take a look at the steps involved in configuring our local environment.

- Next, we will compare the similarities and differences between core default themes and custom themes while looking at how configuration has changed in Drupal 8 with the introduction of the info.yml file.

- Being able to breakdown how the metadata of the info.yml works in conjunction with general information, libraries, and regions will ensure that we have a better understanding of Drupal's theme configuration.

- The role of templates, where to find core templates, and the process of overriding templates plays a major role in theming, so we will introduce ourselves to the Twig templating system.

- Finally, we will look at the role the theme file plays in manipulating template variables and how we can use it to our advantage when working with the content.

Setting up a local development environment

Everything we will be creating with Drupal revolves around having a proper local development environment, and with the move from Drupal 7 to Drupal 8, there has been a more aligned workflow between local development, staging, and production environments. This is evident with the introduction of the additional files and services that are now included within our sites folder, all aimed at allowing us to have more control during development.

For example, while creating a theme, we will often find ourselves having to clear Drupal's cache to see any changes that we applied. This includes render cache, page cache, and Twig cache. Having to go constantly through the process of clearing cache not only takes up time but also becomes an unnecessary step.

Let's discuss the setup and configuration of our local environment to use a local settings file that will allow us to disable CSS/JS aggregation, disable render and page cache, and enable Twig debugging.

Managing sites/default folder permissions

The first step in configuring our local development environment requires making changes to various files that will live within our sites/default folder or need to be placed within it. By default, Drupal protects the sites/default folder and any files within it from being written to. We will need to modify the permissions to make sure that the owner of the folder has read, write, and execute permissions while everyone else has only read and execute.

These steps assume that we are familiar with managing permissions, but for further reference, we can take a look at http://www.wikihow.com/Change-File-Properties.

Once we have made the required permission changes, we can proceed to creating and configuring our local settings file.

Configuring settings.local.php

We are all familiar with Drupal's settings.php file. However, in Drupal 8, we can now have different configurations per environment by creating a settings.local.php file that the default settings.php file can reference.

We can follow these simple steps to create and enable the new file:

1. First, we will need to copy and rename `example.settings.local.php` located in the `sites` folder to `settings.local.php` within the `sites/default` folder.

2. Next, we need to open `settings.php` located in our `sites/default` folder and uncomment the following lines:

```
if (file_exists(__DIR__ . '/settings.local.php')) {
  include __DIR__ . '/settings.local.php';
}
```

3. Save the changes to our `settings.php` file.

Uncommenting the lines allows `settings.php` to include our new `settings.local.php` file within our default settings while allowing us to manage different environment configurations.

Disabling CSS and JS aggregation

As part of the performance settings, Drupal will aggregate both CSS and JS to optimize bandwidth. During development, we are not concerned with bandwidth as we are developing locally. Using a `settings.local.php` file, CSS and JS aggregation are disabled for us. However, if for some reason we want to re-enable aggregation, we would simply change the TRUE values to FALSE as follows:

```
/**
 * Disable CSS and JS aggregation.
 */
$config['system.performance']['css']['preprocess'] = TRUE;
$config['system.performance']['js']['preprocess'] = TRUE;
```

Disabling render and page cache

Another configuration option we can address while having the `settings.local.php` file open is render and page cache. This setting allows us to avoid having to clear Drupal's cache constantly when we make a file change.

Locate and uncomment the following lines:

```
$settings['cache']['bins']['render'] = 'cache.backend.null';
$settings['cache']['bins']['dynamic_page_cache'] = 'cache.backend.null';
```

Disabling test modules and themes

One last configuration we will want to make to our `settings.local.php` file has to do with test modules and themes. By default, our local settings file enables the display of various modules and themes meant for testing purposes only. We can disable them by changing the following TRUE value to FALSE:

```
$settings['extension_discovery_scan_tests'] = FALSE;
```

With all of these changes made, we will want to make sure that we save our `settings.local.php` file. Now, each time we refresh our browser, we will get a new copy of all files without the need to clear Drupal's cache to see any changes.

In some instances, we may need to rebuild Drupal's cache before the above settings will work. If that is the case, we can navigate to `/core/rebuild.php`, which will fix any issues.

Now that we have our local development environment configured its time we took a closer look at default versus custom themes.

Default themes versus custom themes

We have a couple of options when it comes to what themes we want to use in Drupal 8; that is default themes, such as Bartik and Seven that ship with Drupal, or custom themes that a designer creates and which then get converted into themes. Both of these are similar in structure and configuration, which we will look closer at in a minute, but the main separation begins with the folder structure.

Folder structure and naming conventions

In Drupal 8, the folder structure is changed to make it more logical. Everything that ships with Drupal now resides in a `core` folder including the default themes, which are now contained within the `core/themes` folder. However, any themes that we download or develop ourselves now reside within the `themes` folder.

The folder structure comprises the following:

- **Default themes**: These themes reside in the `core/themes` directory and include Bartik, classy, seven, stable, and stark.
- **Custom themes**: These themes reside in the `themes` directory at the root level of our Drupal installation and will contain any contributed themes or custom themes.

Before we can begin creating our own custom themes, we need to have a better understanding of how themes are configured and exactly how they let Drupal know where to display content and how the content should look.

Managing configuration in Drupal 8

Theme configuration in Drupal 8 has now adopted YAML. YAML is a human-friendly data serialization standard used by many programming languages, including Symfony, which Drupal 8 is now built on. With this adoption, the syntax to create an info file has now changed as well. One important concept when creating or editing any *.yml file is that proper indentation is required. Failure to properly indent configuration can lead to errors or to the configuration not loading at all. We can dive deeper into the specifics of YAML and find out more detailed information at the Symfony website (http://symfony.com/doc/current/components/yaml/yaml_format.html).

Reviewing the new info.yml file

The Info.yml file is required when creating any theme. It helps notify Drupal that a theme exists and provides information to the Appearance interface that a theme is available to install. We will be working with *.info.yml files when creating our first theme, so let's take a look at the makeup of a basic example.info.yml file:

```
name: Example
description: 'An Example theme.'
type: theme
package: Custom
base theme: classy
core: 8.x

libraries:
  - example/global-styling

regions:
  header: Header
  primary_menu: 'Primary menu'
  secondary_menu: 'Secondary menu'
  page_top: 'Page top'
  page_bottom: 'Page bottom'
  highlighted: Highlighted
  breadcrumb: Breadcrumb
  content: Content
  sidebar_first: 'Sidebar first'
  sidebar_second: 'Sidebar second'
  footer: 'Footer'
```

At first glance, the example.info.yml file is logical in structure and syntax. Starting from the top and moving our way down, the file is broken down by different sections of metadata containing general information, libraries, and regions. This information is described using a key: value format. We should begin with understanding how basic metadata works.

Metadata

The metadata contained within any themes *.info.yml file helps to describe what type of document it is. In our case, it begins to describe a theme, including the name, description, and the version of Drupal the theme works with. Some metadata is required for the theme to function properly, so let's explore the keys in more detail as follows:

- **name** (*required*): This is the name of our theme.
- **type** (*required*): This is the type of extension (theme, module, or profile).
- **base theme** (*required*): This is the theme that the current theme is inheriting. In most cases, it is recommended we reference either classy or stable as our base theme. If we choose not to reference a based theme, then we will need to set the value to false (base theme: false).
- **description** (*required*): This is the description of our theme.
- **package** (optional): This is used to group similar files when creating modules.
- **version** (optional): This is created by packaging script.
- **core** (*required*): This specifies the version of Drupal that a theme is compatible with.

One of the most common mistakes when first creating a *.info.yml file is forgetting to change the core value to 8.x. Failure to set this value will result in the theme not being displayed within the Appearance interface in the admin.

The next section of a *.info.yml file allows us to manage assets (CSS or JS) using the new concept of libraries.

Libraries

Drupal 8 introduced a new, high-level principle of managing assets using a libraries configuration file that can be loaded globally or on a per page basis. This concept helps to improve frontend performance as well as ensure that any dependencies that a particular asset needs is loaded properly. One advantage of this is that jQuery no longer loads on every page as it did in the previous versions of Drupal.

The concept of a `*.libraries.yml` configuration file also means that the style sheets and scripts properties that we may have been familiar with in Drupal 7 no longer exist. Instead, the process to manage assets includes saving any CSS or JS files to our theme's `css` or `js` folder and then defining a library file that references the files we want to use in our theme.

Defining a library

When defining a `*.libraries.yml` file for a theme, each library will reference the location of individual CSS or JS files and be organized using the SMACSS (`https://smacss.com/`) style categorization.

- **Base**: This defines CSS reset/normalize plus HTML element styling
- **Layout**: This defines the macro arrangement of a web page, including any grid system
- **Component**: This defines the discrete, reusable UI elements
- **State**: This defines the styles that deal with client-side changes to components
- **Theme**: This is purely visual styling for a component

In most cases, a simple library reference will follow the theme categorization. For example, if we wanted to create an `example.libraries.yml` file that included assets for CSS and JS, we would create a library that pointed to our assets, as shown here:

```
libraryname:
  css:
    theme:
      css/style.css: {}
      css/print.css: { media: print }
  js:
    js/scripts.js
```

We would then reference the library within our `example.info.yml` configuration simply by adding the following:

```
libraries:
  - example/libraryname
```

This would result in Drupal adding to every page both CSS and JS files contained in our library. Where this becomes powerful is in the management of assets, as we would only ever need to make modifications to our `example.libraries.yml` file if we ever needed to add or remove assets.

Overriding libraries

Libraries can also be overridden to modify assets declared by other libraries, possibly added by a base theme, by a module, or even the Drupal core. The ability to override libraries includes removing as well as replacing assets altogether. The same way we reference a library from our `*.info.yml` file, we can override libraries by adding the following:

```
libraries-override:

  # Replace an entire library.
  core/drupal.vertical-tabs: example/vertical-tabs

  # Replace an asset with another.
  core/drupal.vertical-tabs:
    css:
      component:
      misc/vertical-tabs.css: css/vertical-tabs.css

  # Remove an asset.
  core/drupal.vertical-tabs:
    css:
      component:
      misc/vertical-tabs.css: false

  # Remove an entire library.
  core/modernizr: false
```

In this case, the `libraries-override` configuration achieves something different for each line. Whether it is replacing an entire library or removing an asset, we now have the flexibility to control assets like never before.

Extending libraries

Libraries can also be extended to allow overriding CSS added by another library without modifying the original files. This can be done by adding the following to our `*.info.yml` configuration as follows:

```
libraries-extend:
  core/drupal.vertical-tabs:
    - example/tabs
```

In this case, the `libraries-extend` configuration is extending Drupal's own `core.libraries.yml` file and extending the `drupal.vertical-tabs` library with additional styling.

While we now have a general understanding of how libraries are defined, overridden, and extended, we have only dealt with libraries globally loaded into our Drupal instance using our configuration file. However, there are two more methods to include assets within a page directly, without the need to add it to every page.

Attaching a library

In many cases, we may be developing some CSS or JS functionality that is specific to an individual page. When we are presented with this requirement, we have the ability to attach a library to a page using two different methods.

Using Twig to attach a library

While we will be learning all about Twig a little later in the chapter, we need to pause for a moment to reference a Twig function named `{{ attach_library() }}`. This function allows us to add to any Twig template a library that may include CSS or JS that will load on that page only.

For example, if we wanted to add the Slick Carousel (`http://kenwheeler.github.io/slick/`) to our page, we may define the library within our `example.libraries.yml` file as follows:

```
# Slick
slick:
  version: VERSION
  css:
    theme:
      vendor/slick/slick.css: {}
  js:
    vendor/slick/slick.min.js: {}
  dependencies:
    - core/jquery
```

We could then turn around and add the following to our Twig template:

```
{{ attach_library('example/slick') }}
```

This provides us with some nice functionality to define individual libraries for various user functions and also to have those assets used wherever we choose to attach them.

Using the preprocess functions to attach a library

Another method to attach a library to an individual page depends on creating a *.theme file, which allows us to use preprocess functions to manipulate page variables. We will learn a lot more about creating a *.theme file a little later in the chapter, but it's important to note that we could attach the same Slick Carousel to our homepage without globally calling it by using a preprocess function, as shown in the following example:

```
function example_preprocess_page(&$variables) {
  if ($variables['is_front']) {
    $variables['#attached']['library'][] = 'example/slick';
  }
}
```

Here, we are checking to see whether we are on the homepage of our website and attaching our Slick library using the #attached library array. Again, this may seem a little bit advanced at this point but does merit mentioning.

The last section we will want to cover when working with any *.info.yml file is about regions that can be defined for the layout of our theme.

Regions

Regions play a critical part in theming, as Drupal needs to know exactly where content can be displayed. This has an impact on what regions are visible to the Block layout for both system blocks and custom blocks that we may want to use. If we do not specify any regions within our *.info.yml file, then Drupal will provide us with regions by default.

If we decide to add additional regions to our theme, we must also add the defaults or else we will not have access to them. Let's take a look at how this is implemented:

```
regions:
  header: Header
  primary_menu: 'Primary menu'
  secondary_menu: 'Secondary menu'
  page_top: 'Page top'
  page_bottom: 'Page bottom'
  highlighted: Highlighted
  breadcrumb: Breadcrumb
  content: Content
  sidebar_first: 'Sidebar first'
  sidebar_second: 'Sidebar second'
  footer: 'Footer'
```

The value for each key is what is displayed in the Block layout within the Drupal UI and can be named whatever we want to name it. We can add additional regions based on our theme as needed. We will look at this in more detail in *Chapter 4, Getting Started – Creating Themes.*

Now that we have covered the basics of theme configuration, it's time for us to set up a local development environment that will enable us to work with files and templates without worrying about having to clear the Drupal cache or guess what Twig templates are being used.

The role of templates in Drupal

We may have heard the term "template" before when talking to someone about theming and Drupal. But what exactly is a template? We can think of a template as a text file no different from any HTML document that provides a method for separating the presentation layer from the business logic. In traditional PHP websites, we have the ability to mix PHP with HTML and CSS, which makes managing web pages both difficult and dangerous. Drupal provides us with the ability to use templating engines to enforce the separation of the two, so we can begin to focus more on the HTML and CSS and worry less about the PHP.

How templates work

In general, templates can contain HTML markup and PHP variables that output content contained within a Drupal database. Templates can be as small as a few lines of HTML that hold the presentational layer for a block that is displayed in a region on the page, or the actual page itself, with containers defined for header, content, and so on.

To get a better idea of what this looks like, let's take a look at the following image:

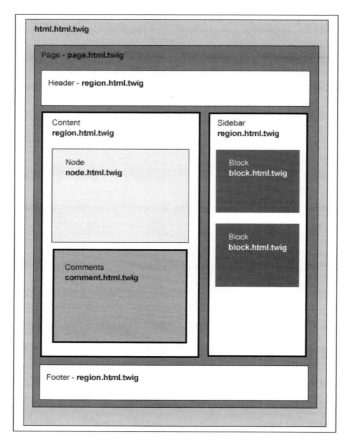

If we break down the image into logical sections of a website, we can begin to get an idea of what constitutes a template. A template can be any of the following:

- **HTML wrapper**: This contains the top-level HTML markup, including title, metadata, style sheets, and scripts, and it is commonly referred to as `html.html.twig`.

- **Page wrapper**: This contains the content generally found between the body tags of an HTML document, and it is commonly referred to as `page.html.twig`.

- **Header**: This is also known as a region, generally containing the header content of our web page. This can be part of the `page.html.twig` template or may reside in a region specified within our configuration file. This is commonly referred to as `region.html.twig`.

- **Content**: This is also considered a region, generally containing our main content. This can consist of multiple subcontent regions, such as nodes and comments. Nodes and comments each have their own respective templates referred to as `node.html.twig` and `comment.html.twig`.

- **Sidebar**: This is also considered a region. This can contain blocks of content. Blocks are either created by the end user or by Drupal itself. The content within these blocks generally resides within `block.html.twig`.

- **Footer**: This is another region containing HTML content as well as blocks of content.

Drupal and the theme engine it uses to convert the markup and variables into HTML interpret each individual template or series of templates. We have full control over what is output using the new Twig templating engine.

Once we begin theming, we will start to see a pattern of how templates are used, and as we gain more experience, we will find ourselves using less and less templates. However, to begin with, we will build examples of each to help clarify their functionality within Drupal.

Where to find templates

The nice thing about Drupal is that, by default, the core system provides us with all the templates we need to use. So, knowing where to find the core templates is important because it will allow us to copy them into our own theme folder to override with our own markup.

Let's begin by opening up our Drupal instance in MAC Finder or Windows Explorer and browsing to the `core/modules` folder. Contained within this folder are the core modules that make up Drupal, along with their respective templates. Most of the core templates will be located in the `core/modules/system/templates` folder, as shown in the following image:

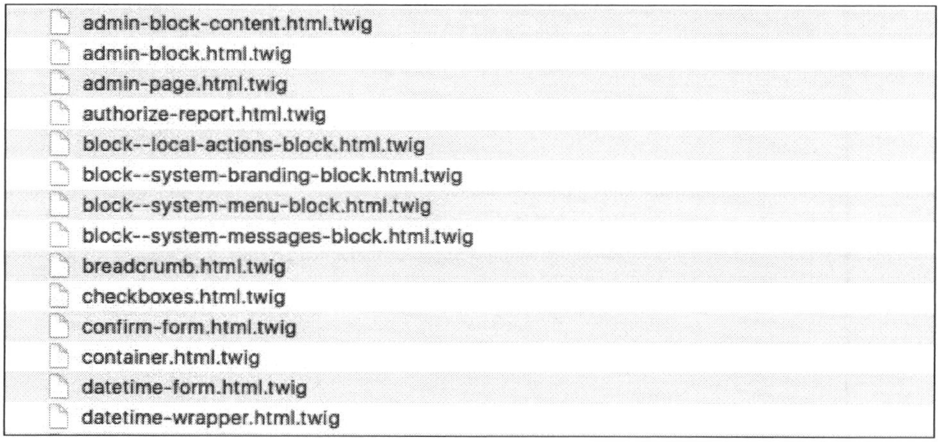

If we browse the contents of the `templates` folder, we will see some of the most common templates we will be using including the following:

- `html.html.twig`: HTML wrapper
- `page.html.twig`: Page wrapper
- `region.html.twig`: Region wrapper

Three more template folders that we need to be aware of are:

- `core/modules/node/templates`: This contains the templates for nodes
- `core/modules/comment/templates`: This contains the comment templates
- `core/modules/block/templates`: This contains the templates for blocks

We will find ourselves frequently overriding templates, so we need to make sure that we know where to find any Twig template that we will be theming.

Most of us have done some PHP development or are at least familiar enough with it to work with the variables that Drupal outputs. So, as we look at the templates, we should be noticing that the files don't end with a file extension of `.php` but instead end with a file extension of `.twig`. In fact, if we were to look at the `html.html.twig` template located in the `core/modules/system/templates` folder, we won't even find PHP syntax inside it:

```
<!DOCTYPE html>
<html{{ html_attributes }}>
  <head>
    <head-placeholder token="{{ placeholder_token|raw }}">
    <title>{{ head_title|safe_join(' | ') }}</title>
    <css-placeholder token="{{ placeholder_token|raw }}">
    <js-placeholder token="{{ placeholder_token|raw }}">
  </head>
  <body{{ attributes }}>
    <a href="#main-content" class="visually-hidden focusable">
      {{ 'Skip to main content'|t }}
    </a>
    {{ page_top }}
    {{ page }}
    {{ page_bottom }}
    <js-bottom-placeholder token="{{ placeholder_token|raw }}">
  </body>
</html>
```

Instead, we will see general HTML markup along with the Twig syntax that will output content within its place. We will take a closer look at Twig in a moment. First, we will try our hand at creating a basic theme.

Creating our first basic theme

Now that we have reviewed the basics of how a theme is constructed, there is no better time than the present to create our first basic theme. We will begin by creating a theme named `twig` that we will use to work with exploring how Twig and the Theme system works in Drupal 8.

In order to make sure that we all are working from the same baseline, let's open up the `Chapter03/start` folder located in the exercise files and select the `drupal8.sql` database file. We will use this database snapshot to restore our current database instance. Refer to *Chapter 1, Setting Up Our Development Environment* for instructions on how to perform a database restore.

Now that we all have the same baseline Drupal instance, we can navigate to our Drupal 8 folder using MAC Finder or Windows Explorer and follow these next six steps to create a theme.

Step One – creating a new folder

Create a new folder under our `themes` folder and call it `twig`, as shown in the following image:

Step two – create an info file

Create a new `*.info.yml` file named `twig.info.yml` and add the following configuration information to the file:

```
name: Twig
type: theme
description: 'A Twig theme for demonstrating TWIG syntax'
core: 8.x
base theme: false
```

Step three – copy core templates

Copy the `html.html.twig` and `page.html.twig` templates from the `core/modules/system/templates` folder and paste it into our `themes/twig` folder. Open up `page.html.twig` in our editor and replace the HTML structure below the comments with the following code:

```
<h1>Welcome to Twig</h1>
{{ page.content }}
```

Step four – include a screenshot

Not always a required step but one that will definitely help is including a screenshot that displays or represents our theme within the Appearance admin. In general, we would generate a screenshot based on the finished theme, but because we are just starting out, we can copy an existing one from our exercise files.

Begin by navigating to the `Chapter03/end` folder and copy the `screenshot.png` file to our newly created `themes/twig` folder.

Step five – installing our theme

Next, we will need to install our new theme by navigating to /admin/appearance and locating our new theme named **Twig** under the **Uninstalled themes** section. Click on the **Install and set as default** link to install our new theme, as shown in the following image:

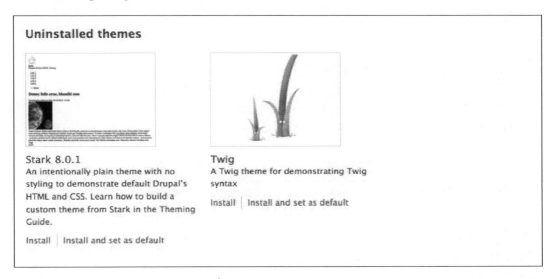

Step six – Welcome to Twig

We have successfully created our first theme. Although there is not much to it, we can preview what our website looks like by browsing back to the home page of our Drupal instance. We should see our new theme displaying a message of **Welcome to Twig**, as shown in the following image:

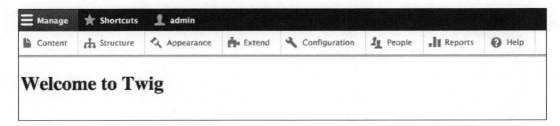

With our new theme in place, we can begin taking a deeper look into Twig and all of the great features that Drupal 8 introduces to us with this new templating engine.

Introducing Twig

Twig (`http://twig.sensiolabs.org`) is the new template engine introduced to Drupal 8 and is a companion to Symfony, the new PHP framework that Drupal 8 is built on. Twig provides us with a fast and secure way to separate content from PHP logic in a manner that makes it easier for non-developers to work with templates. To help us get a better feel in order to work with Twig, let's first dive into the steps involved in enabling Twig debugging.

Enabling Twig debug

When Twig debugging is turned on within Drupal, we are able to trace which template is being used, where a template is located, and a list of suggested file names to override a template. This functionality is very advantageous and actually quite simple to set up by following these steps:

1. Open the `development.services.yml` file located in the `sites` folder.

2. Add the following lines to the bottom of the file:

```
parameters:
  twig.config:
    debug : true
    auto_reload: true
    cache: false
```

3. Save the file.

4. Clear Drupal's cache.

If we navigate back to the homepage and inspect the markup using Google Chrome's Developer Tools, we can now see Twig debug outputting information, as shown in the following image:

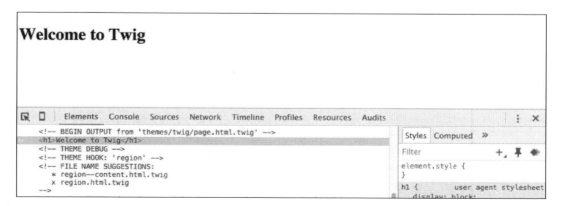

There are a couple of items we should make note of when Twig debugging is enabled:

- **FILE NAME SUGGESTIONS**: This displays suggestions to name Twig HTML templates and displays in the order of precedence in which Drupal folders would look for templates.

- **OUTPUT**: This displays the location of the template currently being displayed, which, in our case, is `themes/twig/page.html.twig`.

Remember that we will only see the debug output when we have the Twig debugging enabled as part of our local development environment. It is best to remember to disable debugging before moving a Drupal site to production. So now that we have an understanding of what Twig debug provides us with, let's begin writing some of our own Twig syntax, beginning with comments.

Twig fundamentals

A Twig template outputs PHP with a template-oriented syntax using opening and closing curly brackets {{ ... }}. This syntax interprets the variable between the brackets and outputs HTML in its place. The following are three kinds of delimiters in Twig that trigger an evaluation to take place:

- The first is Twig commenting, which uses the comment tag {# ... #} to provide comments inline or around a section of HTML.

- Next is the print tag {{ ... }}, which is used to print the result of an expression or variable. The print tag can be used by itself or within a section of HTML.

- The third tag is to execute a statement such as conditional logic, looping structures, or the assignment of values to variables and is expressed by using {% ... %}.

Each of the three delimiters will be used when we do any type of theming projects within Drupal 8. We will find that they are just as simple as using any regular HTML element, and we will quickly be writing these tags.

Commenting variables

We are familiar with HTML commenting such as `<!-- This is a comment -->`, which allows us to add descriptive text to our markup. We saw an example of this in the Twig debug output once we enabled it. Twig provides us with the ability to add comments as well using the {# comment #} syntax.

If we open `page.html.twig` within our editor, we can add a Twig comment by adding the following:

```
{# This is a comment in Twig #}
<h1>Welcome to Twig!</h1>
```

Once we save our template, refresh the browser and inspect the heading. We will note that we don't actually see the comment being displayed. Unlike HTML comments, Twig comments are meant to be hidden from browser output and are meant only for the developer.

Setting variables

Twig can also assign values to variables using a technique named Assignment. Assignment uses the `set` tag to place a value into a variable, which can then be used later within a template to output the value.

Open `page.html.twig` and add the following above our heading:

```
{# Setting a variable #}
{% set name = 'Drupal' %}

{# This is a comment in Twig #}
<h1>Welcome to Twig!</h1>
```

If we save our template and refresh the browser, we will not see any changes to our HTML as we are only setting a variable but not using it anywhere in our document. So how do we then use a variable?

Printing variables

Twig allows us to print variables by simply referencing them within our document using the `{{ variable }}` syntax to trigger the interpreter to replace the variable name with the value stored in it. We can try this by replacing the word `Twig` in our heading with the `name` variable.

Open `page.html.twig` and add the following:

```
{# Setting a variable #}
{% set name = 'Drupal' %}

{# This is a comment in Twig #}
<h1>Welcome to {{ name }}</h1>
```

If we save our template and refresh the browser, we will see that our heading now says **Welcome to Drupal**. The name variable we set has output the word **Drupal** in its place. This is the same technique that we will be using to output variables in our Twig templates to display content from Drupal. In fact, if we sneak a peek at our `html.html.twig` template, we will see a variety of twig variables being used to output content.

Dumping variables

While theming in Drupal, we will be working with both simple and complex variables consisting of PHP arrays that contain multiple values. Knowing that there can be multiple values, it is sometimes useful to dump the contents of the variable to know exactly what we are working with. The `{{ dump() }}` function allows us to view information about a template variable and is only available to us when Twig debugging is turned on. Let's take our name variable for instance and dump the contents to see what it contains.

Open `page.html.twig` and add the following to the bottom of the template:

```
{# Dumping variables #}
{{ dump(name) }}
```

If we save our template and refresh the browser, we will now see the name variable being dumped to the page displaying some additional info about our variable.

Using the `dump()` function, we can introspect more than one variable at a time by passing multiple arguments. Let's try this by adding an additional Drupal variable named is_front, as shown in the following code sample:

```
{# Dumping variables #}
<pre>{{ dump(name, is_front) }}</pre>
```

If we save our template and refresh the browser, we will now see the is_front variable being dumped to the page as well as displaying some more information, as shown in the following image:

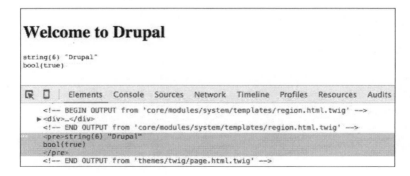

By now, we should be comfortable working with a Twig template and variables. However, we can do much more with Twig than just print variables though. We can also apply filters to variables to achieve different functionality.

Filters

Filters provide us with a way to modify variables. The filters are generally separated by a pipe character (|) and may accept arguments depending on the filter's purpose. Twig provides us with currently 30+ filters that we can apply to variables. Let's try out filters now by applying an uppercase filter on our name variable.

Open `page.html.twig` and add the following:

```
{# Apply filter to name variable #}
<p>{{ name|upper }} Rocks.</p>
```

If we save our template and refresh the browser, we will now see that the name variable is converted to uppercase inside our paragraph tag, as shown in the following image:

Welcome to Drupal

```
string(6) "Drupal"
bool(true)
```

DRUPAL Rocks.

| R | ☐ | Elements | Console | Sources | Network | Timeline | Profiles | Resources | Audits |

```
-->
<!-- BEGIN OUTPUT from 'themes/twig/page.html.twig' -->
<h1>Welcome to Drupal</h1>
<pre>string(6) "Drupal"
bool(true)
</pre>
<p>DRUPAL Rocks.</p>
<!-- THEME DEBUG -->
<!-- THEME HOOK: 'region' -->
<!-- FILE NAME SUGGESTIONS:
   * region--content.html.twig
   x region.html.twig
-->
<!-- BEGIN OUTPUT from 'core/modules/system/templates/region.html.twig' -->
► <div>...</div>
<!-- END OUTPUT from 'core/modules/system/templates/region.html.twig' -->
<!-- END OUTPUT from 'themes/twig/page.html.twig' -->
```

We can also use filters to wrap sections of HTML and variables, which apply the filter to more than one item at a time. An example of this would be if we wanted to uppercase a whole paragraph versus just the `name` variable.

Open `page.html.twig` and add the following:

```
{% filter upper %}
<p>{{ name }} is the best cms around.</p>
{% endfilter %}
```

If we save our template and refresh the browser, we will now see that the entire paragraph including the `name` variable is converted to uppercase, as shown in the following image:

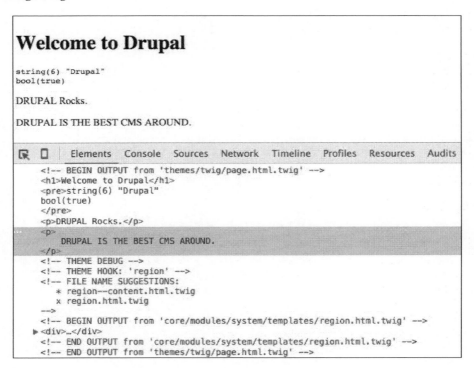

This is just an example of one of the many filters that can be applied to variables within Twig. For a detailed list of filters, we can refer to `http://twig.sensiolabs.org/doc/filters/index.html`.

Control structures

There will be situations while theming with Twig where we will need to check whether a variable is True or False or need to loop through a variable to output multiple values contained in an array.

Control structures in Twig allow us to account for these types of functions using {% ... %} blocks to test for expressions and traverse through variables that contain arrays. Each control structure contains an opening and closing tag similar to PHP logic. Let's take a look at a couple of the most commonly used control structures starting with the if tag used to test an expression.

Open page.html.twig and add the following:

```
{# Conditional logic #}
{% set offline = false %}

{% if offline == true %}
  <p>Website is in maintenance mode.</p>
{% endif %}
```

If we save our template and refresh the browser, we will not see anything actually displaying yet. The reason is that the offline variable is currently set to false and we are checking to see whether it is true.

Open page.html.twig and edit the offline variable changing its value to true:

```
{# Conditional logic #}
{% set offline = true %}

{% if offline == true %}
  <p>Website is in maintenance mode.</p>
{% endif %}
```

Now resave our template and view the page in the browser. This time, we will see our paragraph displayed, as shown in the following image:

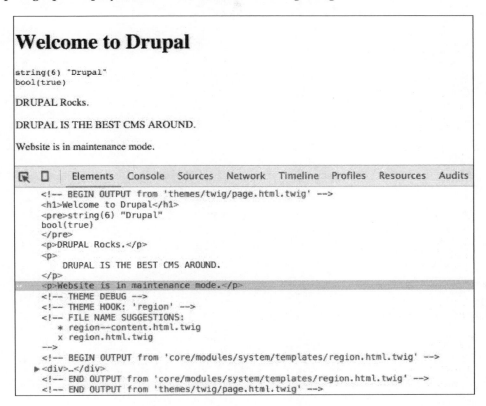

By now, we are starting to see how control structures within Twig can come in handy to hide or show certain markup within our template based on the value of a variable. This will come in handy when we have certain Drupal regions that we want to display when a block is placed into a region.

The other commonly used control structure in Twig is looping. The `for` tag is used to loop over each item in a sequence. For our example, let's try looping based on a number of items and outputting the count.

Open `page.html.twig` and add the following:

```
{# Looping #}
{% for i in 0 ..10 %}
  {{ i }}
{% endfor %}
```

If we save our template and view the page in the browser, we will be presented with the count within our loop displaying on the page starting at 0 and going to 10, as shown in the following image:

Welcome to Drupal

string(6) "Drupal"
bool(true)

DRUPAL Rocks.

DRUPAL IS THE BEST CMS AROUND.

Website is in maintenance mode.

0 1 2 3 4 5 6 7 8 9 10

This is a simple loop, and it only really demonstrates the use of the `for` tag. Once we start creating additional Twig templates, we can loop through more complex Drupal variables. More extensive documentation regarding the `for` tag can be found at `http://twig.sensiolabs.org/doc/tags/for.html`.

Template variables

Drupal 8 uses variables to output data within Twig templates. We know that variables generally consist of anything from a simple string to a complex object containing an array of values. If we look at the `html.html.twig` template, we will see documentation that outlines the variables available to us along with the name of the variable and a description of what the variable contains:

```
Variables:
 logged_in: A flag indicating if user is logged in.
 root_path: The root path of the current page (e.g., node, admin,
user).
 node_type: The content type for the current node, if the page is a
node.
 head_title: List of text elements that make up the head_title
variable.
    May contain or more of the following:
    - title: The title of the page.
    - name: The name of the site.
    - slogan: The slogan of the site.
    - page_top: Initial rendered markup. This should be printed before
'page'.
    - page: The rendered page markup.
```

```
        - page_bottom: Closing rendered markup. This variable should be
printed after 'page'.
        - db_offline: A flag indicating if the database is offline.
        - placeholder_token: The token for generating head, css, js and js-
bottom placeholders.
```

Each of the variables that our template has access to can be output using Twig syntax. For example, the `head_title` variable outputs the title of our page within the `<title>` element. Drupal also uses `{{ attributes }}` to print out additional information to our page, for example, the `<body>` element to output CSS classes needed by modules or themes.

Each template we will work with uses variables to output database content. What if we want to add additional variables to Drupal? This is where the role of the theme file comes into use.

The role of the theme file in Drupal

Themes can be simple to compose, sometimes containing a single configuration file, a couple of Twig templates, and a few assets. However, there will be times when we need to intercept and override variables and data that Drupal outputs before them reaching our Twig templates. Drupal's API (https://api.drupal.org/api/drupal/8) allows us to create a `*.theme` file where we can add theme functions that can hook into the API using different types of function calls.

- **Preprocess**: This is a set of function calls specific to different templates that allow us to manipulate variables before they are output to the page.
- **Hooks**: This is a set of function calls to hook into the Drupal API that allows us to alter variables and override default implementations.

Preprocessors and hooks

The main role of preprocessor functions is to prepare variables to be used within our Twig templates using `template_preprocess` functions. These functions reference the theme and template we want to intercept. We would write an example of intercepting the `html.html.twig` template variables used within our Twig theme as follows:

```
twig_preprocess_html(&$variables) {

}
```

With this simple function call, we can hook into the theme preprocessing to intercept the `$variables` argument and manipulate it as needed before our template receives the variables. In order for us to use this function, we need to do the following steps:

1. Create a `twig.theme` file within the `themes/twig` folder. The `twig.theme` file will contain all the PHP functions we will write to work with Drupal's API.

2. Add the following within our `twig.theme` file and then save the file as:

```php
<?php

/**
 * Implements hook_preprocess_html().
 */
function twig_preprocess_html(&$variables) {
    // add to classes
    $variables['attributes']['class'][] = 'twig';
}
```

Whenever we add a file or template for the first time, we will need to clear the Drupal cache.

Overriding variables

Now that we have created our `twig.theme` file and have the outline of our first preprocess hook, let's take a look at how to override a variable. Previously, we saw that Drupal was adding classes to our body tag using the `$attributes` variable. But what if we want to add additional classes specific to our theme?

Open `twig.theme` and edit the preprocess function to include the following:

```php
/**
 * Implements hook_preprocess_html().
 */
function twig_preprocess_html(&$variables) {
    // add to classes
    $variables['attributes']['class'][] = 'twig';
}
```

Now if we save our `twig.theme` file and refresh the browser, we will see that our class is added, as shown in the following image.

```
<!-- BEGIN OUTPUT from 'themes/twig/html.html.twig' -->
<!DOCTYPE html>
<html lang="en" dir="ltr" prefix="content: http://purl.org/rss/1.0/modules/content/  dc: http://purl.org/d
 ▶ <head>…</head>
 ▼ <body class="twig toolbar-tray-open toolbar-fixed toolbar-horizontal" style="padding-top: 78.9861px;">
```

While we have only touched the surface of the functionality that we can use when theming, we are purposely not going into depth regarding all the API calls that we have access to with Drupal 8. If you are interested in taking a deeper look, you can find the reference at `https://api.drupal.org/api/drupal/8`.

One last thing to note is that we can reference the completed exercise files for *Chapter 3*, *Dissecting a Theme*, if we need to compare any of the work we just completed or perform a database restore.

Summary

From core themes to custom themes, we covered a lot of information. Remember that it's ok to go back and review any section to ensure that everything is understood. As we continue working through creating themes, our skills will only increase, and hopefully, we will all become theming experts when we're all done.

- We reviewed the new `info.yml` file and how Drupal recognizes metadata, stylesheets, scripts, regions, and settings.

- We looked at the role of assets in Drupal and what has changed since Drupal 7 with the addition of new JavaScript libraries and CSS best practices.

- Templates play a large part in theming, and we covered the basics of how they function including setting up our first theme and local development environment.

- We answered what Twig is and how much it empowers themers to build templates without having to worry about the laborious knowledge of PHP.

- Finally, we took a brief look at the `*.theme` file and how simple it is to override Drupal variables for use within our templates.

In the next chapter, we will dive even deeper into theming by creating a subtheme using Classy. We will also look at how easy it is to create a responsive starter theme following best practice methods to add CSS and JavaScript frameworks, such as Twitter Bootstrap. This will be followed up with a more detailed look at the `*.theme` file while using the Devel module to output variables within our Twig templates.

4
Getting Started – Creating Themes

Drupal developers and interface engineers do not always create custom themes from scratch. Sometimes, we are asked to create starter themes that we begin any project from or subthemes that extend the functionality of a base theme. Having the knowledge of how to handle each of these situations is important, and in this chapter, we will be learning it as we cover the following:

- First, we will create a starter theme that will walk us through managing folder and file structures, configuring a `*.info.yml` file, and allow us to work with a `*.libraries.yml` file to manage both CSS and JS assets. Our starter theme will involve multiple techniques that are common to any theme, including integrating a CSS framework such as Twitter Bootstrap.

- Next, we will rethink over layout strategies when creating a starter theme and discuss best practices to separate layout from presentation. This will include diving deeper into the Theme layer and how we can use contributed modules such as Devel to work with variables.

- Finally, we will create a subtheme that extends the base theme Classy. Having the ability to take advantage of a base theme's Twig templates and assets will allow us to focus on techniques to override CSS without changing the actual base themes files.

While we work through each section, we have the ability to refer back to the `Chapter04` exercise files folder. Each folder contains a `start` folder and an `end` folder with files that we can use to compare our work when needed. This also includes database snapshots that allow us to start from the same point when working through various lessons. Information on how to restore database snapshots is covered in *Chapter 1, Setting Up Our Development Environment.*

Starter themes

Whenever we begin developing in Drupal, it is preferable to have a collection of commonly used functions and libraries that we can reuse. Being able to have a consistent starting point when creating multiple themes means that we don't have to rethink much from design to design. This concept of a starter theme makes this possible, and we will walk through the steps involved in creating one.

Before we begin, take a moment to browse the `Chapter04/start` folder and use the `drupal8.sql` file to restore our current Drupal instance. This file will add additional content and configuration needed while creating a starter theme. Once the restore is complete, our homepage should look like the following image:

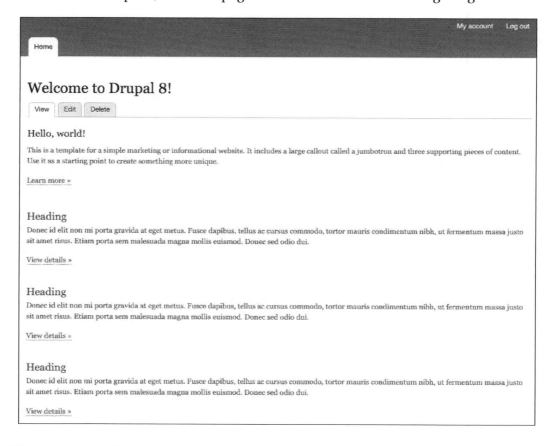

This is a pretty bland-looking homepage with no real styling or layout. So, one thing to keep in mind when first creating a starter theme is how do we want our content to look? Do we want our starter theme to include another CSS framework or do we want to create our own from scratch?

Since this is our first starter theme, we should not be worried about recreating the wheel but instead should leverage an existing CSS framework such as Twitter Bootstrap.

Creating a Bootstrap starter

Having an example or mockup that we can refer to when creating a starter theme is always helpful. So, to get the most out of our Twitter Bootstrap starter, let's browse `http://getbootstrap.com/examples/jumbotron/` where we will see an example of a homepage layout:

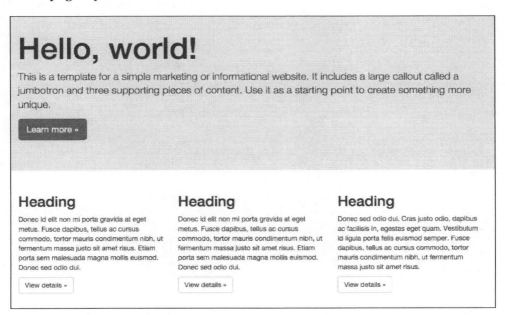

As we take a look at the mockup, we can see that the layout consists of two rows of content with the first row containing a large callout known as a Jumbotron. The second row contains three featured blocks of content. The remaining typography and components are taking advantage of the Twitter Bootstrap CSS framework to display the content.

One advantage of integrating the Twitter Bootstrap framework into our starter theme is that our markup will be responsive in nature. It means that as the browser window is resized, the content will scale down accordingly. At smaller resolutions, the three columns will stack on top of one another enabling the user to view the content easier on smaller devices.

We will be recreating this homepage for our starter theme, so let's take a moment and familiarize ourselves with some basic Bootstrap layout terminology before creating our theme.

Understanding grids and columns

Bootstrap uses a 12-column grid system to structure content using rows and columns. Page layout begins with a parent container that wraps all children elements and allows us to maintain a specific page width. Each row and column then have CSS classes identifying how the content should appear. So, for example, if we wanted to have a row with two equal width columns, we would build our page using the following markup:

```
<div class="container">
    <div class="row">
        <div class="col-md-6"></div>
        <div class="col-md-6"></div>
    </div>
</div>
```

The two columns within a row must combine to a value of 12 because Bootstrap uses a 12-column grid system. Using this simple math, we can have various size columns and multiple columns as long as their total is 12. We should also make a note of the column classes, as we have great flexibility in targeting different breakpoints:

- Extra small (col-xs-x)
- Small (col-sm-x)
- Medium (col-md-x)
- Large (col-lg-x)

Each breakpoint references the various devices from smartphones all the way up to television-sized monitors. We can use multiple classes `class="col-sm-6 col-md-4"` to manipulate our layout, which gives us a 2-column row on small devices and a 3-column row on medium devices when certain breakpoints are reached.

To get a more detailed comprehension of the remaining Twitter Bootstrap documentation, we can browse `http://getbootstrap.com/getting-started/` any time. For now, it's time we begin creating our starter theme.

Setting up a theme folder

The initial step in our process of creating a starter theme is simple. We need to open up MAC finder or Windows Explorer and navigate to the `themes` folder and create a folder for our theme. We will name our theme `tweet`, as shown in the following image:

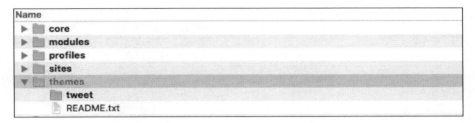

Adding a screenshot

Every theme deserves a screenshot, and in Drupal 8, all we need to do is simply have a file named `screenshot.png`, and the Appearance screen will use it to display an image above our theme.

Go ahead, copy `screenshot.png` from the `Chapter04/start/themes/tweet` folder, and place it within the `themes/tweet` folder.

Configuring our theme

Next, we will need to create our themes configuration file, which will allow our theme to be discoverable. We will only worry about general configuration information to start and then add library and region information in the next couple of steps.

Begin by creating a new file in our `themes/tweet` folder named `tweet.info.yml` and add the following metadata to our file:

```
name: Tweet
type: theme
description: 'A Twitter Bootstrap starter theme'
core: 8.x
base theme: false
```

Note that we are setting the `base theme` configuration to `false`. Setting this value to `false` lets Drupal know that our theme will not rely on any other theme files. This allows us to have full control over our theme's assets and Twig templates.

We will save our changes here and clear the Drupal cache. Now we can take a look to check whether our theme is available to be installed.

Installing our theme

Navigate to `/admin/appearance` within our browser, and we should see our new theme located in the **Uninstalled themes** section. Go ahead and install the theme by clicking on the **Install and set as default** link.

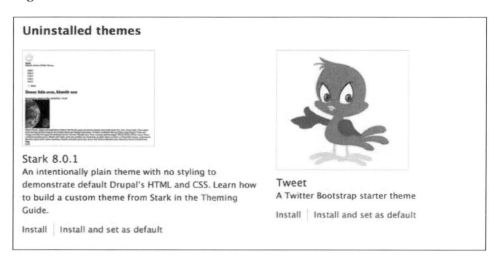

If we navigate to the homepage, we should see an unstyled homepage:

This clean palette is perfect when we are creating a starter theme as it allows us to begin theming without worrying about overriding any existing markup that a base theme may include.

Working with libraries

While Drupal 8 ships with some improvements to its default CSS and JavaScript libraries, we will generally find ourselves wishing to add additional third-party libraries that can enhance the function and feel of our website. In our case, we have decided to add Twitter Bootstrap (`http://getbootstrap.com`), which provides us with a responsive CSS framework and JavaScript library that utilizes a component-based approach to theming.

The process really involves three steps. First is downloading or installing the assets that make up the framework or library. Second is creating a `*.libraries.yml` file and adding library entries that point to our assets. Finally, we will need to add a library reference to our `*.info.yml` file.

Adding assets

We can easily add the Twitter Bootstrap framework assets by following these steps:

1. Navigate to `http://getbootstrap.com/getting-started/#download`.
2. Click on the **Download Bootstrap** button.
3. Extract the `zip` file.
4. Copy the contents of the bootstrap folder to our `themes/tweet` folder.

5. Once we are done, our `themes/tweet` folder content should look like the following image:

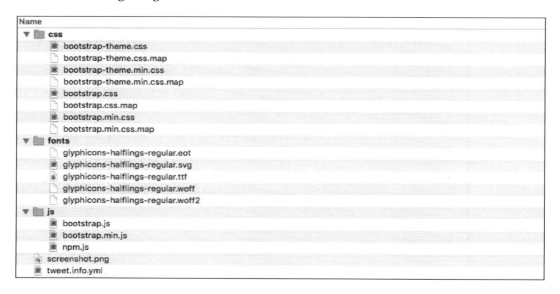

Now that we have the Twitter Bootstrap assets added to our theme, we need to create a `*.libraries.yml` file that we can use to reference our assets.

Creating a library reference

Anytime we want to add CSS or JS files to our theme, we will need to either create or modify an existing `*.libraries.yml` file that allows us to organize our assets. Each library entry can include one to multiple pointers to the file and location within our theme structure. Remember that the filename of our `*.libraries.yml` file should follow the same naming convention as our theme.

We can begin by following these steps:

1. Create a new file named `tweet.libraries.yml`.
2. Add a library entry named `bootstrap`.
3. Add a version that reflects the current version of Bootstrap that we are using.
4. Add the CSS entry for `bootstrap.min.css` and `bootstrap-theme.min.css`.
5. Add the JS entry for `bootstrap.min.js`.

6. Add a dependency to jQuery located in Drupal's core:

```
bootstrap:
  version: 3.3.6
  css:
    theme:
      css/bootstrap.min.css: {}
      css/bootstrap-theme.min.css: {}
  js:
    js/bootstrap.min.js
  dependencies:
    - core/jquery
```

7. Save `tweet.libraries.yml`.

We have added a more complex library entry than we did in *Chapter 3*, *Dissecting a Theme*. However, in the previous library entry, we have added both CSS and JS files as well as introduced `dependencies`.

Dependencies allow any JS file that relies on a specific JS library to make sure that the file can include the library as a dependency, which makes sure that the library is loaded before our JS file. In the case of Twitter Bootstrap, it relies on jQuery and since Drupal 8 has it as part of its `core.libraries.yml` file, we can reference it by pointing to that library and its entry.

Including our library

Just because we have added a library to our theme, it does not mean that it will automatically be added to our website. In order for us to add Bootstrap to our theme, we need to include it in our `tweet.info.yml` configuration file.

We can add Bootstrap by following these steps:

1. Open `tweet.info.yml`.
2. Add a `libraries` reference to `bootstrap` to the bottom of our configuration as follows:

```
libraries:
  - tweet/bootstrap
```

3. Save `tweet.info.yml`.

Make sure to clear Drupal's cache to allow our changes to be added to the Theme registry. Finally, navigate to our home page and refresh the browser so that we can preview our changes.

If we inspect HTML using Chrome's developer tools, we should see that the Twitter Bootstrap library is being included along with the rest of our files. Both the CSS and JS files are loaded into the proper flow of our document.

```
        Elements   Console   Sources   Network   Timeline   Profiles   Resources   Audits
   ▶ <style media="all">...</style>
   ▼ <style media="all">
       @import url("http://drupal8/themes/tweet/css/bootstrap.min.css?o08cbj");
       @import url("http://drupal8/themes/tweet/css/bootstrap-theme.min.css?o08cbj");
   </style>
```

Creating a Jumbotron

Many times, a designer will create a section of content that they want to call the users' attention to. This is sometimes known as a Call to Action or a Hero. Bootstrap calls this visual treatment a Jumbotron and makes up the first part of our homepage mockup that we will be creating.

In order for us to implement the Jumbotron, we need to think about how our current homepage is laid out. We have a custom block called Jumbotron placed within the Content region. This means that potentially every page will have this block. Also, every page contains a page title block as well, and based on the mockup, we don't want that to display on our homepage. So, we need to address these two tasks while modifying our page to accommodate the Jumbotron.

First, we will take advantage of Drupal's new default WYSIWYG to directly edit the source HTML. This will allow us to add HTML markup directly into our custom block without worrying about creating a Twig template for it.

Second, we will need to hide the title block on the homepage using page restrictions on the Block layout admin.

Step one – managing block content

We can manage a block content in multiple ways, but the easiest is by using the contextual links that Drupal provides. If we navigate to the homepage and locate the first block that displays "Hello, world!," we can hover over it to see the contextual links icon:

The contextual links menu will allow us to quickly get to the markup of the block by following these steps:

1. Click on the **Edit** link.
2. Locate the **Body** field.
3. Click on the **Source** button within the WYSIWYG bar.
4. Add the following markup including the jumbotron and container elements around the current markup:

```
<div class="jumbotron">
    <div class="container">
        existing markup...
    </div>
</div>
```

5. Click on the **Save** button.

This will accomplish part one of our steps. We should now see that our markup and content have been replaced and are now being styled according to the mockup:

Step two – hiding the page title

The page title in Drupal 8 is now contained within a block. This allows us to easily place the page title wherever needed based on our design. It also allows us to manage it using the same visibility rules available in any block.

In our mockup, we need to suppress the page title from displaying on the homepage. We can accomplish this by using the contextual menu on the page title block to configure it, as follows:

1. Click on the **Configure block** contextual link.
2. Click on the **Pages** vertical tab on the **Configure block** screen.
3. Select the **Hide for the listed pages**.
4. Enter into the **Pages** text field the path /home.
5. Click on the **Save block** button.

The page title block is no longer displayed, and our Jumbotron looks pretty close to the mockup. While this was a pretty simple technique of adding HTML and Bootstrap classes directly to our content, this actually promotes some bad practices. Stop and think for a minute about what we just did.

We mixed layout and presentation markup together within a single field and stored that in the database. First, this is not very flexible. Second, we have no way to reuse the markup without continuing to add it to fields directly on a per need basis. The reason we approached the Jumbotron markup this way was to prove a point. There are always multiple ways to theme something, but often, we will need to rethink our layout.

Rethinking our layout

Often, we will find ourselves having to rethink over the layout we are trying to accomplish while first creating a starter theme. In fact, creating a starter theme can actually be challenging at first with a lot of trial and error. Implementing our Jumbotron is quite a perfect example of trying to fit a square peg in a round hole. While Drupal will allow us to accomplish layouts in half a dozen different ways, we always want to follow the best practices.

After taking a look at the Jumbotron example again, we can actually break it down into more manageable and reusable components. To begin with, the Jumbotron example is to represent a homepage layout with one row for the Jumbotron and another row containing three blocks of content that float next to each other equally. When we started similarly with our Jumbotron block, we actually had all our blocks placed into our content region.

Adding regions

Regions are key to any layout in Drupal, and the common rule is that anytime we look at a design or mockup, if we see multiple rows of content, we should equate each row to a Drupal region. In our case, we have identified a couple of different regions, but currently our starter theme has no defined regions at all. Therefore, it is using the default regions provided by Drupal.

What we really need is to add a Jumbotron region and the featured content region. These two regions will allow us to assign blocks of content to them apart from the main content region where we currently have them assigned.

One thing to note when adding regions to a theme is that we can't simply add regions to our configuration without also adding the default regions that Drupal provides. Failure to add the default regions will result in us only having the defined regions available to add content to, which is not ideal for a starter theme.

Let's begin by opening `tweet.info.yml` and adding the following regions to the bottom of our file:

```
regions:
  header: Header
  primary_menu: 'Primary menu'
  secondary_menu: 'Secondary menu'
  page_top: 'Page top'
  page_bottom: 'Page bottom'
  highlighted: Highlighted
  breadcrumb: Breadcrumb
```

```
content: Content
sidebar_first: 'Left sidebar'
sidebar_second: 'Right second'
footer: Footer
jumbotron: Jumbotron
featured: Featured
```

Make sure to save the configuration file, clear the Drupal cache, and visit the Block layout page to view our changes, as follows:

Managing the block content

When we are on the Block layout screen, we will want to move our blocks into their respective regions. We can then take advantage of the different regions to address applying styling that will globally benefit our starter theme.

Begin by following these steps to move our four blocks into place:

1. Locate the **Hero** block within the **Content** region.
2. Select **Jumbotron** from the **Region** dropdown.
3. Locate the **Custom Block One** block within the **Content** region.
4. Select **Featured** from the **Region** dropdown.
5. Locate the **Custom Block Two** block within the **Content** region.
6. Select **Featured** from the **Region** dropdown.
7. Locate the **Custom Block Three** block within the **Content** region.
8. Select **Featured** from the **Region** dropdown.
9. Click on **Save blocks** button.
10. Our four blocks should now be placed within the regions, as shown in the following image:

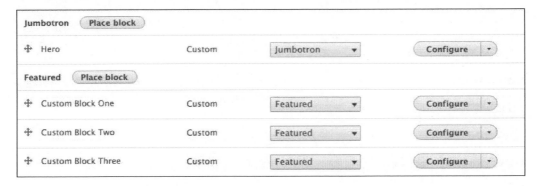

If we were to navigate back to our homepage, we will no longer see any content being displayed. Once we have added two new regions and placed our blocks within those regions, the core Twig templates that Drupal is using to output our content have no idea that these regions exist.

Using Twig templates

The easiest way to work with Twig templates is to allow Drupal and the Twig debug settings we enabled earlier to do the entire work for us. So what do I mean? Begin by navigating to the homepage and inspecting the markup using Chrome's developer tools. Locate the section of markup where we see the `div` element with a class of `layout-container`, as shown in the following image:

```
<!-- THEME DEBUG -->
<!-- THEME HOOK: 'page' -->
<!-- FILE NAME SUGGESTIONS:
   * page--front.html.twig
   * page--.html.twig
   x page.html.twig
-->
<!-- BEGIN OUTPUT from 'core/modules/system/templates/page.html.twig' -->
<div class="layout-container">...</div>
<!-- END OUTPUT from 'core/modules/system/templates/page.html.twig' -->
```

Twig debugging allows us to view all the information we need to identify which Twig template we can use for our homepage. If we look at the information provided, we can identify the following:

- Drupal is currently using `page.html.twig`
- The template is located at `core/modules/system/templates/page.html.twig`
- Drupal suggests that we can use `page--front.html.twig` to display the same content

With these three pieces of information, we can locate, copy, and modify any Twig template we may need in order to modify the layout and markup of the content coming from Drupal.

Creating a homepage template

One rule that comes in handy while creating any Twig template is to be as specific as possible. There is generally multiple **FILE NAME SUGGESTIONS** that Drupal recommends and the more granular we are in choosing to name that template the less we will have to worry about overriding the content we didn't mean to overwrite.

Let's create our homepage template by following these steps:

1. Navigate to the `core/modules/system/templates` folder.
2. Copy `page.html.twig`.

3. Place the copy of `page.html.twig` into `themes/tweet` folder.

4. Rename `page.html.twig` to `page--front.html.twig`.

Clear Drupal's cache, browse the homepage, and use Chrome's developer tools to verify that we are using the `page--front.html.twig` template in the `themes/tweet` folder:

```
<!-- THEME DEBUG -->
<!-- THEME HOOK: 'page' -->
<!-- FILE NAME SUGGESTIONS:
   x page--front.html.twig
   * page--.html.twig
   * page.html.twig
-->
<!-- BEGIN OUTPUT from 'themes/tweet/page--front.html.twig' -->
<div class="layout-container">...</div>
<!-- END OUTPUT from 'themes/tweet/page--front.html.twig' -->
```

Since we have now created a `page--front-html.twig` template, any markup we add or modify within this template will only affect the homepage. Any interior pages that are added to our website will default to using `page.html.twig`.

The Jumbotron mockup only needs to display the header, primary menu, footer, Jumbotron, and featured regions. We can modify our `page--front.html.twig` template by replacing the current markup with the following code:

```
<div class="layout-container">
  <header role="banner">
    {{ page.header }}
  </header>

  {{ page.primary_menu }}
  {{ page.highlighted }}
  {{ page.jumbotron }}
  {{ page.featured }}

  <footer role="contentinfo">
    {{ page.footer }}
  </footer>
</div>
```

Now save the template and refresh the homepage in the browser. We should now see the regions we have defined being displayed along with any blocks that are assigned to them. Speaking of blocks, our Jumbotron block contains markup within the body field when it should really be moved to a region template.

Creating region templates

Just like we were able to create a page-specific Twig template, we can also create region-specific Twig templates. If we inspect the Jumbotron region using Chrome's developer tools, we will see from the **FILE NAME SUGGESTIONS** that we can create a new Twig template named `region--jumbotron.html.twig`.

Create the region template by following these steps:

1. Navigate to the `core/modules/system/templates` folder.
2. Copy `region.html.twig`.
3. Place the copy of `region.html.twig` into `themes/tweet` folder.
4. Rename `region.html.twig` to `region--jumbotron.html.twig`.

Clear Drupal's cache, browse the homepage, and use Chrome's developer tools to verify that we are using the `region--jumbotron.html.twig` template.

Next, we will want to replace the markup within `region--jumbotron.html.twig` with the following markup:

```
{% if content %}
  <div class="jumbotron">
    <div class="container">
      {{ content }}
    </div>
  </div>
{% endif %}
```

Now save the template and refresh the homepage in the browser. If we inspect the Jumbotron region, we will see that our new markup has been added. All we have left to do is to edit the block and remove the layout markup that we added to the content previously.

Locate the Jumbotron block on the homepage, hover over it to reveal the context menu, and follow these steps:

1. Click on the **Edit** link.
2. Locate the **Body** field.
3. Click on the **Source** button within the WYSIWYG bar.

4. Replace the current markup with the following markup:

```
<h1>Hello, world!</h1>
<p>This is a template for a simple marketing or informational
website. It includes a large callout called a jumbotron and three
supporting pieces of content. Use it as a starting point to create
something more unique.</p>
<p><a class="btn btn-primary btn-lg" href="#" role="button">Learn
more »</a></p>
```

5. Click on the **Save** button.

We have now completed our Jumbotron region of the homepage by separating layout markup from presentational markup. This approach is now reusable and makes a great location in our starter theme to add Hero content. Let's replicate this process by adding a Twig template for our featured region as well, as follows:

1. Begin by creating a new file Twig template named `region--featured.html.twig` within our `themes/tweet` folder.

2. Replace the current markup with the following code:

```
{% if content %}
  <div class="container">
    {{ content }}
  </div>
{% endif %}
```

3. Now save the template and refresh the homepage in the browser. Our featured region now has the `container` class. In addition, the featured region is constraining the content to the same width as our Jumbotron region.

In order for us to complete the featured region, we need to know which blocks are within it and add CSS classes to them. Time to look toward the Drupal 8 Theme layer for help.

Working with the Theme layer

Drupal 8 has an extensive API that includes the Theme layer, which gives us the ability to alter and preprocess variables before they are output by Drupal. The API is so extensive that we won't even scratch the surface of the functionality we can use. More detailed information can be found at `https://api.drupal.org/api/drupal/8`.

One such function we will be working with is `template_preprocess_block`, which prepares values passed to each block before them being output by `block.html.twig`. Before we can begin using preprocess functions, we will need to create a `*.theme` file.

Begin by creating a new file named `tweet.theme` within our `themes/tweet` folder. Once our theme file has been created, we can add the following preprocess function:

```php
<?php

function tweet_preprocess_block(&$variables){

}
```

Within our function, we will look for specific blocks based on their IDs and then apply a CSS class to them that allows the blocks to be displayed in three columns. One thing to note is that this is by no means the only way to accomplish this requirement, but to avoid getting too far into the Drupal API we will opt for a simple solution.

While working with the Theme layer, we need some way to print out the `$variables` array that is passed by reference to most functions. Although PHP provides us with the `var_dump()` function, this can be a tedious task of reading through all the information that is printed to the screen, especially since it is not formatted.

Using Devel to print variables

The Drupal community has provided us with a better mechanism of working with variables using a third-party contributed module named Devel. The Devel module can be found at `https://drupal.org/project/devel` and is a set of helper functions to work with variables as well as a list of other functionality that we will not be using at this time.

Because this is our first time installing a contributed module for use with Drupal 8, we can follow these steps to download and install the module:

1. Navigate to the Devel project page `https://drupal.org/project/devel`.
2. Click on the TAR or ZIP download link for the latest Drupal 8.x version.
3. Create a folder named `contrib` within the `modules` folder of our Drupal 8 instance.

4. Extract the contents of the `devel` module to the `contrib` folder, as follows:

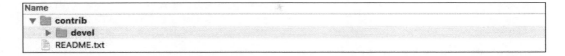

The `contrib` folder will hold any contributed modules that we install, including the Devel module. Now we need to install and configure the Devel module by following these steps:

1. Navigate to `/admin/modules` within the browser.
2. Locate the **Devel** module under the **DEVELOPMENT** section.
3. Click on **checkbox** next to **Devel** to install it.
4. Locate the **Devel Kint** module.
5. Click on **checkbox** next to **Devel Kint** to install it.
6. Click on the **Install** button at the bottom of the **Extend** page.

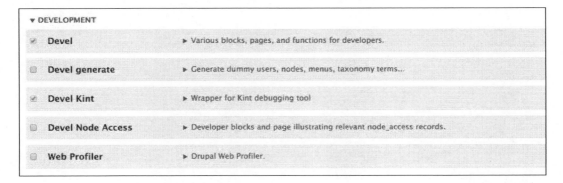

Now that we have Devel and Devel Kint installed, we can move on to using it to display `$variables` within our preprocess function to help identify information we will need to complete our function.

Printing variables from a function

If we open back up our `tweet.theme` file, we currently have an empty preprocess function. This function accepts a parameter that is passed by reference that holds any `$variables` available to be used by blocks. We can use the Devel module to now output `$variables` to our page by adding the following line of code to our function:

```php
<?php

function tweet_preprocess_block(&$variables){
  dpm($variables);
}
```

The `dpm()` function will take whatever values that are passed to it and output the contents in a print friendly format. To see this in action, let's save our file, clear Drupal's cache, and browse to our homepage. If Devel is working properly, we should see six different sections of our site displaying a collapsed information box that contains the contents of the `$variables` array. Each instance represents the values for each block currently assigned to regions. This is due to the fact that our preprocess function runs once for each block, as follows:

We are interested in the three custom blocks that appear in our featured region. Assuming the blocks load in the order that the regions are printed, we should be able to expand the fourth information box to see more information. In particular, we are interested in the block attributes that contain the ID of each block, as follows:

```
$input array (18)
  'elements' => array (17)
  'theme_hook_original' => string (5) "block"
  'attributes' => array (3)
    'data-quickedit-entity-id' => string (15) "block_content/1"
    'id' => string (26) "block-tweet-customblockone"
    'class' => array (1)
      string (17) "contextual-region"
```

The longer we look at the information being output, the more it makes sense how to traverse through the array to access information we can use. For instance, to grab the ID of each block, we could access it by writing `$variables['attributes']['id']` within our preprocess function. Now all we need to do is add some logic to our function that looks for the ID within a list of block IDs and add a CSS class to the block if found. We can accomplish this by adding the following to our preprocess function:

```
function tweet_preprocess_block(&$variables){

  // Add layout class to Featured Blocks
  $featured = array('block-tweet-customblockone','block-tweet-
customblocktwo','block-tweet-customblockthree');

  $id = $variables['attributes']['id'];

  // If block id matches list - add class
  if(in_array($id, $featured)){
    $variables['attributes']['class'][] = 'col-md-4';
  }
}
```

Remember to remove the `dpm()` function we added previously. Next, we can clear Drupal's cache and then browse our homepage where we will see our three custom blocks aligned to our grid:

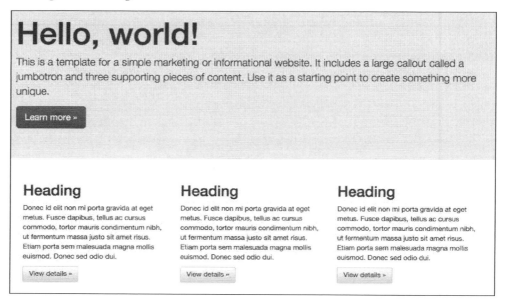

We have definitely mastered using the Twitter Bootstrap framework with our starter theme to recreate the mockup Jumbotron example. By modifying Twig templates, using theme suggestions, working with new regions, and diving deeper into the Theme layer, we were able to have Drupal output HTML markup exactly how we needed it.

While starter themes are very flexible, they do require a little more work than simply using an existing base theme. We can take a quick look at what this means by creating a subtheme next.

Subthemes

One point of interest in Drupal 8 is that there is a new base theme named **Classy**, which both Bartik and Seven reference. This means that Bartik and Seven in reality are subthemes. So why not learn from the best, in this case, Morten Birch Heide-Jørgensen, otherwise known as "Div Killer." Morten has come through, as his nickname suggests, and created one hell of a base theme.

To become a little more intimate with this new base theme, we will create a subtheme of our own called **Sassy**. Since the steps involved to create and install a subtheme are similar to a starter theme, we will progress a little faster through this first part.

Adding the theme folder

Begin by navigating to our `themes` folder and create a new folder inside named `sassy`.

Including a screenshot

Go ahead and copy `screenshot.png` from the `Chapter04/start/themes/sassy` folder and place it within the `themes/sassy` folder.

Configuring our theme

Begin by creating a new file in our `themes/sassy` folder named `sassy.info.yml` and add the following metadata to our file:

```
name: Sassy
type: theme
description: 'A Classy sub theme but a little more Sassy'
core: 8.x
base theme: classy
```

Note that we are setting the `base theme` configuration to `classy` this time. Setting this value to `classy` lets Drupal know that our subtheme will inherit all the configuration and files from the base theme.

We will save our changes at this time and clear the Drupal cache. Now we can take a look to see if our theme is available to install.

Installing our theme

Navigate to `/admin/appearance` within our browser and we should see our new theme located in the **Uninstalled themes** section. Go ahead and install the theme by clicking on the **Install and set as default** link:

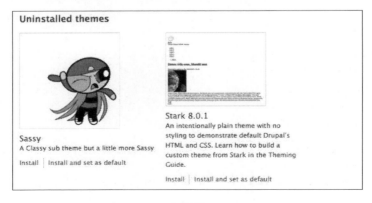

This time when we navigate to our homepage, we will see that our markup has changed, we are now inheriting the markup and libraries from Classy. We can verify this by using Chrome's developer tools to inspect the page. Looking at the **FILE NAME SUGGESTIONS** of any region, we will note that the Twig templates are coming from `core/themes/classy/templates/*`, as follows:

```
<!-- BEGIN OUTPUT from 'core/themes/classy/templates/layout/region.html.twig' -->
▼<div class="region region-sidebar-first">
    <!-- THEME DEBUG -->
    <!-- THEME HOOK: 'block' -->
    <!-- FILE NAME SUGGESTIONS:
       * block--sassy-customblockone.html.twig
       * block--block-content--8e1cf09a-2f14-40de-9100-a1cbae3ab6d4.html.twig
       * block--block-content.html.twig
       * block--block-content.html.twig
       x block.html.twig
    -->
    <!-- BEGIN OUTPUT from 'core/themes/classy/templates/block/block.html.twig' -->
```

Touring Classy

We can take a closer look at Classy by navigating to the `core/themes/classy` folder of our Drupal instance. At first glance, the theme structure of Classy is quite organized. It is well-structured with folders for CSS, images, and a multitude of Twig templates. Each template has been organized based on its functionality as follows:

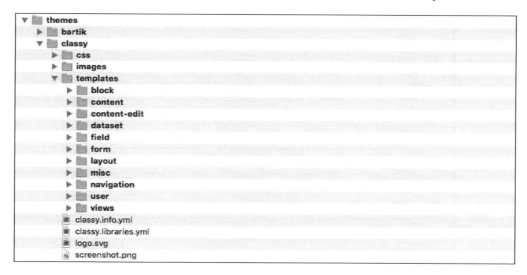

Everything so far screams best practices and is one of the major benefits of creating a subtheme that uses Classy as a base theme. However, we can still add our own regions, libraries, and Twig templates as we would for any other theme. However, in some cases, we may find ourselves also needing to override libraries with our own CSS or JS without modifying any assets directly located in the base theme.

Overriding a library

So when we talk about overriding a library, we have options to replace the entire library, replace an asset with another asset, or remove an asset or entire library simply by using `libraries-override` within our theme's `*.info.yml` file.

Take the status message block as an example. Anytime we edit a block, a node, or anything in Drupal that has an edit form, once we click the save button, we will see a status message letting us know the outcome of our action.

✓ Basic page *Welcome to Drupal 8!* has been updated.

In this case, the default styling for the status message is coming from the base theme Classy. In fact, if we look at the `classy.libraries.yml` file located in the `core/themes/classy` folder, we can see an entry pointing to `css/components/messages.css`:

```
messages:
  version: VERSION
  css:
    component:
      css/components/messages.css: { weight: -10 }
```

What if our subtheme calls for different styling? If we want to override `messages.css` with our own version of the file, we can do so using `libraries-override`.

All we need to override this file is a `*.libraries.yml` file for our subtheme, a library entry pointing to our own `messages.css` file, and a reference within our `*.info.yml` file telling Drupal what we want to override.

Let's override Classy's messages styling by following these steps:

1. Copy the `css` folder from the `Chapter04/start/themes/sassy` folder and place it within the `themes/sassy` folder.
2. Create a new `sassy.libraries.yml` file within the `themes/sassy` folder.

3. Add the following library entry to `sassy.libraries.yml`:

    ```
    messages:
      version: VERSION
        css:
          theme:
            css/messages.css: {}
    ```

4. Save `sassy.libraries.yml`.

5. Open `sassy.info.yml` and add the following configuration:

    ```
    libraries-override:
      classy/messages: sassy/messages
    ```

6. Save `sassy.info.yml`.

Now we can clear Drupal's cache and then browse our homepage where we can edit the homepage by following these steps:

7. Click on the **Edit** tab to open the Welcome to Drupal 8 Edit form.

8. Click on the **Save and keep published** button.

Once back on the homepage, we should see that the status message is now picking up our `messages.css` rules and is now overriding the `messages.css` that was originally coming from the Classy base theme.

Basic page *Welcome to Drupal 8!* has been updated.

It is hoped that by now, we can see how `libraries-override` will come in handy whenever we want to replace assets injected from base themes, modules, or even Drupal core. For more information and examples, such as `libraries-override`, feel free to review the documentation at `https://www.drupal.org/theme-guide/8/assets`.

As we progress to creating custom themes, we will find we often need to add the JS functionality. Although we will not be covering it in this chapter, we will take a look at working with JS libraries in great detail in *Chapter 6, Theming Our Homepage*.

Summary

The starter theme or subthemes are all just different variations on the same techniques. The level of effort to create each type of theme may vary, but as we saw there was a lot of repetition, and by now, we have already created a couple different themes. So, let's look back to what we covered in this chapter:

- We began with a discussion around starter themes and learned what steps were involved in integrating a CSS framework such as Twitter Bootstrap.

- We worked extensively with libraries and best practices for creating a homepage from a mockup. This included how to rethink layouts and how to avoid the pitfalls that we may come across when theming blocks and regions.

- Working with the Theme layer came in handy when needing to understand what was available to us when working with preprocess functions. From using contributed modules such as Devel to print variables to creating Twig templates, we learned how to separate layout from presentation.

- Finally, we took a quick look at subthemes and discussed the benefits of using them while still being able to override any assets they include without modifying the original assets.

In the next chapter, we will prepare ourselves for a large web-based project that will involve setting up our themes structure, using essential modules, and walking through the completed website that contains a home page, interior page, blog section, contact page, and search results.

5
Prepping Our Project

One of the most important things that will help you learn how to become better frontend developers is taking a look at a design mockup and dissecting how you would implement it within Drupal. This would mean asking ourselves questions along the way, such as how the homepage is put together, how a user interacts with a webpage, and how we are going to implement a specific functionality. In this chapter, we will do exactly that as we begin with a fully working HTML mockup that we can review within the browser and then convert it into a Drupal 8 theme, piece by piece. To give us a better idea of what we will be covering, let's review the following:

- We will start by reviewing our completely designed mockup with a Homepage, Interior page, Landing page, Blog posts, a Contact Us page with a Google map and web form, and other user interactions that we will need to build.

- Once we have a better understanding of what we are building, we will take a backup of the database and restore it onto our Drupal 8 instance. This will allow us to have a baseline starting point from which to build a theme.

- Finally, we will finish up with creating our new theme structure, including defining the metadata, creating our regions, and implementing one of several CSS and JavaScript libraries.

While we work through each section, we have the ability to refer to the Chapter05 exercise files folder. Each folder contains a start and end folder with files that we can use to compare our work when needed. This also includes database snapshots that will allow us to all start from the same point when working through various lessons.

Before we get started, let's open up the Mockup folder located in our exercise files and the index.html page using Google Chrome web browser. The Mockup contains a fully functioning HTML website that we have been tasked with developing for our client. We will be reviewing this mockup throughout the remaining chapters to compare against our final Drupal 8 theme, so let's get started.

Walking through the design mockup

Whether we are working for a digital agency or simply freelancing, in most cases, we will already have purchased a theme or designed one from scratch that has been built in pure HTML, CSS, and JavaScript. Having a theme already available to us makes our job as a frontend developer much easier in identifying what needs to be built. As we begin to review each page of our design, we will be taking notes about specific functionality that we will later revisit when creating our new theme. We will clearly point out such items as regions, page layouts, blocks of content, and how we would best implement CSS and JavaScript.

Homepage layout

If we haven't already done so, let's open up the homepage of our mockup, as shown in the following image, and navigate as any other user visiting our site would.

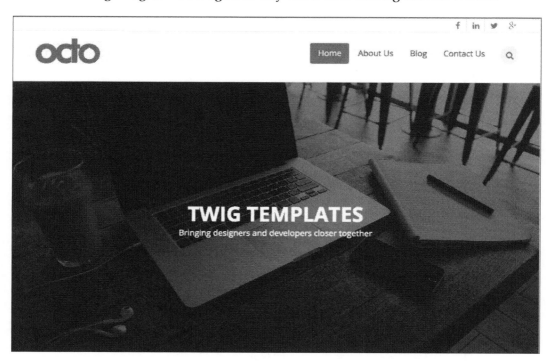

At first glance, our mockup seems to contain some very standard components, such as a header with a logo, menu, full page slider, and some social network icons. However, there are several hidden characteristics that we may have missed unless we click around our homepage.

The first item to point out is the search icon in the main menu. Clicking on this icon reveals a hidden search input that allows the user to search content, as shown in the following image:

We know that Drupal 8 provides the user with the ability to search database content as well as providing us with a search block that will need to account for in our theme.

The second item is a Parallax function where the background image moves at a slower rate than the text overlaid on it as we scroll. If we happened to click on the arrow icon at the bottom of the page instead of scrolling, we also discover that we are automatically taken to another section of the homepage. One thing to note is that the scrolling effect is smooth and not sudden. This Parallax method, as well as the smooth scroll effect, will require us to implement some custom JavaScript or libraries that assist in providing this type of user interaction.

Our third item is the fixed header containing the logo, main menu, and search element. When a user begins to scroll down the page, the header becomes fixed to the top of the viewport. This feature allows the end user to navigate anywhere within the website without having to scroll back to the top of any long-form content pages.

As we continue further down the homepage layout, we come to another section of content, as shown in the following image:

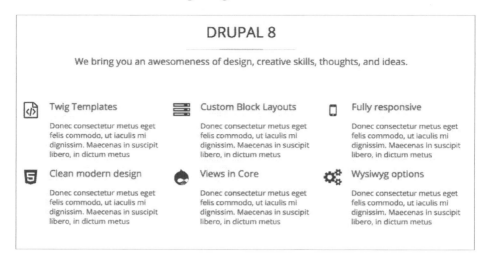

This section of content should be of no concern as it contains some simple markup with headings and blocks of text, but we will need to make a note of the icons being used. We will look at implementing these icons using Font-Awesome, a CSS toolkit that allows for iconic fonts.

Finally, our homepage consists of a footer and subfooter with three small blocks of content containing various text blocks and a form element, as shown in the following image:

One thing to note is that our header and footer areas will be consistent throughout the mockup. Keeping this in mind, we will take a look at how to implement this in our theme without having to repeat the content from page to page.

Defining homepage regions and user interaction

One last exercise we need to consider based on our homepage is what visible regions we have that can contain content. Starting from the top of our homepage and ending at the bottom of our document, we should be able to identify the following regions:

- Top Header with social network icons
- Header with logo, menu, and hidden search element
- Headline section with static background and vertically sliding text
- Before Content section to display the content before the main content
- Content section with various blocks of content
- Footer with three separate blocks of text and form elements
- Sub footer with the left and right sections containing content

We will need to define these regions within our theme, along with any others we discover as we review the internal pages of our mockup.

Finally, let's review the notes we took that pertain to user experience and functionality that may be new to us and that we will need to implement when building our homepage. Such items are:

- Search icon that when clicked shows and hides the search block to user
- Parallax background effect
- Slider text on the top of a fixed background image
- Smooth scrolling when the user clicks on the navigation link in slider
- Font icons

With our review of the complete homepage, it's now time to move on to the interior pages and investigate what else our mockup has in store for us.

Basic page layout

Let's begin reviewing the **About Us** section of our mockup by clicking on the corresponding menu item in the header. As we begin to review our first interior page, we will note that our basic page layout includes a page title that spans across the width of our page, as shown in the following image:

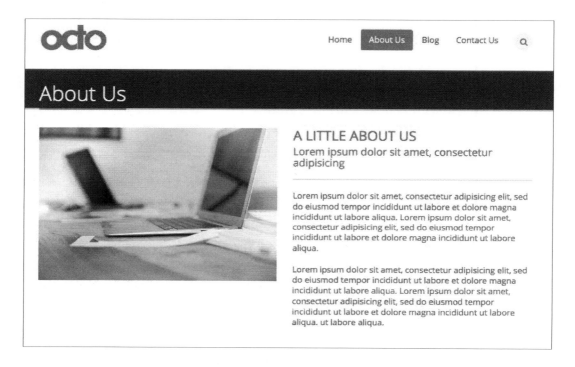

This basic page differs from our homepage and is our first clue that we will need to consider one or more alternative page layouts for our interior pages.

After scrolling a little further down our page, we also find a section of content displaying team members that consists of a heading, subheading, and four blocks of identical content, highlighting each team member.

If we hover our mouse over each of the team member images, we will note a visual effect where the image fades from gray to full color. We will need to keep this in mind while identifying the fields that make up this piece of content and how we may need to manipulate the HTML markup to achieve this technique.

Our basic page is a simple one-column layout, which does not introduce any new layouts we may need to define as of yet, and which should not be too challenging to develop. It is also typical of most of the pages that a frontend developer or themer will face while creating themes.

Defining interior regions

Starting from the top of our interior page and ending at the bottom, we should be able to identify the following new regions:

- A title bar with a page title
- The After Content section to display content blocks below main content

We will need to define these regions within our theme along with any others we discover as we continue to review pages of our mockup.

Landing page layout

One of the more complex page layouts in our mockup is that of the Blog section. If we navigate to the Blog landing page by clicking on the **Blog** menu item in our header, we will be presented with a very rich looking page, as shown in the following screenshot:

Landing pages often display a listing of content with related or highlighted information to accompany it. Our blog page is no different, and it consists of a teaser of content previewing each blog post and repeating down the page. We are also presented with a two-column layout with the content region to the left and a sidebar to the right. This page gives us our second layout to consider when creating our Twig templates.

Some other regions of content are the **Categories** listing and tabbed block of **Popular** and **Recent** blog posts that reside in the right sidebar. This content is just an extension of the blog post itself with a listing of taxonomy terms and a teaser. Drupal 8 will be able to handle vocabulary terms, View modes, and Views listing of content, all without having to worry about any contributed modules.

Blog detail layout

Because landing pages only generally provide us with a listing of content, let's quickly review the blog content in more detail beginning with browsing an individual blog post. We can accomplish this by clicking on the **Post Two** blog post title, which should bring us to the Post content type detail page.

It looks like the two-column page layout is being continued from our landing page to our detail page. This will make it very easy for us to develop a Twig template that both our teaser and full content views can use. We also have repeating sidebar content on our detail page as well. This is a great indication of blocks of content that we will need to make sure is reusable, another great feature of Drupal 8 since blocks can now be reused.

Before we move on to the View of our contact page, we need to keep in mind two different features of the Blog detail page. The first is a slider present when a post has multiple images, which is indicated by the two blue navigational dots.

Upon closer inspection, we can view each image by clicking on either of the two dots. We will need to make another mental note when it comes to this image field and consider how we can determine if there are multiple images and how to apply the slideshow effect to them.

The other item of interest is towards the bottom of our Blog post, and it consists of a commenting feature, as shown in the following image:

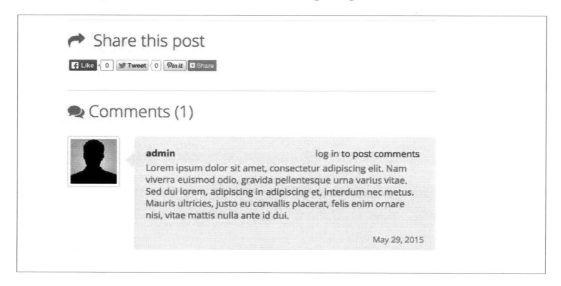

This new commenting region allows users not only to leave feedback about a post, but also the ability to share a post using social networks, as is apparent with the **Share this post** heading being displayed above the comment region. We will look at how to theme comments in Drupal 8 in more detail later in *Chapter 8, Theming Our Blog Listing Page*.

Contact page

Our second to last navigational page to review is the **Contact Us** page. Traditional contact pages consist of general business hours, e-mail addresses, and other methods to contact the user of the website. However, if we navigate to the contact page by clicking on the **Contact Us** link in the menu, we will be presented with the following image:

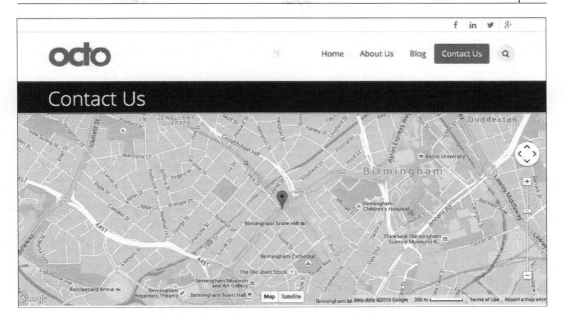

The **Contact Us** page shows a full-width one-column layout with a gorgeous Google Map highlighting the location of our office with a map marker. The map is fully functional, and it allows the end user to navigate wherever they would like in the world. The Google Maps API allows us to add this type of user interaction very easily to a page with very little JavaScript. Drupal 8 makes this even easier with their new way to handle JavaScript libraries. We will keep this in mind when developing this Twig template.

Adding a little more personalization to our contact page, this web form allows any user to contact us.

GET IN TOUCH WITH US

Lorem ipsum dolor sit amet, consectetur adipiscing elit. Nullam imperdiet ante in metus lobortis, vitae sagittis lorem viverra. In felis leo, posuere a lorem in, vestibulum hendrerit lectus. Vestibulum eget sapien dignissim, vestibulum lectus vitae, pretium mi.

Your name *

Your email address *

Subject *

Message *

Being fully responsive, our web form will function on all mobile devices and is a great example of customization versus just a typical e-mail address being displayed. We have various examples of form elements within our mockup that will be developed while creating our Drupal 8 theme.

However, what would a website be without giving our end user an ability to search for content?

Search results

The final page of our mockup ties back into our search block in the header of our website, allowing us to display the content of our website based on a user query. Drupal 8 provides us with this mechanism to index content and allows us to then display the search results. We can find a mockup of the search results page located in the exercise files Mockup folder titled search.html, as shown in the following image:

One thing we will find though is that the search results are very limited without extending the functionality with other third-party search services such as Apache Solr, which provides for a much more robust search experience. Still, we will take a look at how to customize the search results page for a cleaner look and feel.

So enough review of our mockup, let's get busy creating a Drupal 8 theme based on the design we just previewed. This would be the time where we put on some good music and do the tedious work of installing Drupal 8, configuring content types, creating blocks and views, and populating our site with content so we have something to actually theme. However, let's skip all that tedious work and just start with a database snapshot.

Restoring our database snapshot

Before we get started, let's open up the `Chapter05/start` folder located in our exercise files and restore the database snapshot by dropping the tables in our current Drupal 8 instance and importing the `drupal8.sql` file. Information on how to restore database snapshots was covered in *Chapter 1, Setting Up Our Development Environment*.

After restoring our database snapshot, we can browse our Drupal 8 instance by navigating to the homepage in our browser. We should see the typical **Bartik** theme being displayed with four pages containing content to match our mockup, including **Home**, **About Us**, **Blog**, and **Contact Us**.

At this point, we will need to log in to Drupal using the User login link, which has replaced the Drupal 7 login block. Once at the **Log in** screen, we enter admin's username and admin's password.

While we are using a very simple username/password combination to develop, I would advise you to use something stronger and more secure before moving any Drupal instance to a production web server. For more security features in Drupal 8, check out this article: `https://dev.acquia.com/blog/drupal-8/10-ways-drupal-8-will-be-more-secure/2015/08/27/6621`.

All of the content we need to recreate our mockup exists in the database, and as we begin to theme each section of our site, we will simply reference that content. If there is anything new or different with how content was created or configured, we will stop to briefly discuss it. For now, we will dive right into discussing the benefits of creating a custom theme and then proceed to setting up our theme folders.

Creating a custom theme

Previously, we looked at creating both a starter theme and a subtheme and, while each has its own benefit, we will often want to have the flexibility to develop on the fly. This means that we do not have to worry about managing a set of files already developed. This may sound contradictory to everything we have heard earlier, but taking an agile approach to theming allows for designers to create rich designs outside the boundaries of Drupal. With the introduction of Twig templates, we pretty much broke the mold on having to architect the layout of Drupal in a specific way. So, gone are the days of telling a designer that we can't implement their ideas.

As we create our custom theme, we will have the freedom to use whatever frontend tools are in the wild combined with the ability to implement both CSS and JS Frameworks using libraries, templates, and custom CSS/JS.

Setting up theme folders

By now, setting up a theme should be second nature. We practiced this numerous times in *Chapter 4, Getting Started – Creating Themes*. But, in case we need a refresher, we can refer to that chapter for any outstanding questions.

We can begin by navigating to the `themes` folder and create a new folder named `octo`. This new folder will contain all of the files we will be using to develop our theme:

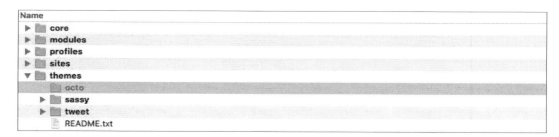

Next, we will create five additional subfolders within our main `themes` folder that will contain our CSS, Images, JavaScript, Twig templates, and any third-party vendor libraries such as Twitter Bootstrap. To ensure that we are all able to follow along without any naming conflicts, please make sure to name the five subfolders as follows:

We will be referencing these subfolders throughout the development of our theme with each folder containing the following files:

- `css`: This contains custom style sheets.
- `img`: This contains images used by the style sheets.
- `js`: This contains custom JavaScript.
- `templates`: This contains Twig templates.
- `vendor`: This contains JavaScript libraries.

Adding a screenshot

Go ahead and copy `screenshot.png` from the `Chapter05/start/themes/octo` folder and place it within the `themes/octo` folder. Drupal will use this screenshot within the Appearance page to help visually identify our theme.

Creating our configuration file

Any new theme must contain an `*.info.yml` file to define metadata, style sheets, libraries, and regions so that Drupal 8 recognizes that there is a new theme available to be installed. Let's begin by opening up our favorite text editor and creating a new file named `octo.info.yml`.

Our new configuration file will contain the following required metadata to start with:

```
name: Octo
type: theme
description: 'A responsive Drupal 8 theme.'
core: 8.x
base theme: false
```

Make sure to save our changes and clear Drupal's cache. This will ensure that the theme registry picks up our changes.

Installing our theme

Navigate to /admin/appearance and locate our new theme on the Appearance page. If we look within the **Uninstalled themes** section, we will see the **Octo** theme available to install, as shown in the following screenshot:

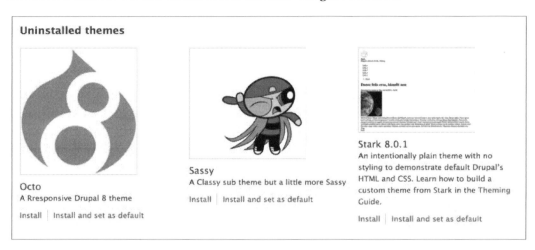

To install our theme, click on the **Install and set as default** link. With our new theme now installed, we can browse the homepage by clicking on the **Back to site** link in the **admin** menu. We will see that the original Bartik theme styling has been replaced with the non-styled look of our Octo theme, as shown in the following screenshot:

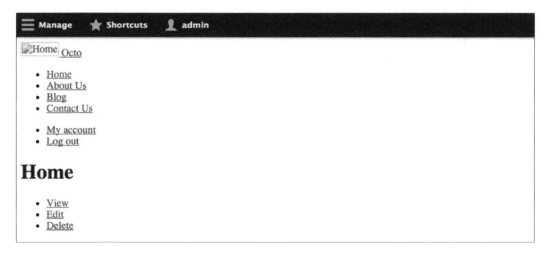

Setting up our regions

Currently, our theme is using the default Drupal 8 regions as we have not specified any within our configuration file. This would be fine if the content in our Mockup worked nicely with those regions, but as we discovered earlier, there are definitely some regions outside of the default that will need to be defined.

For example, Drupal 8 provides only a single Footer region, and we will clearly need more than one region in our footer to accomplish the three blocks of content, as well as the two additional blocks of content that fall below our footer.

Let's edit our `octo.info.yml` file and define the specific regions we will need to place blocks of content needed by our homepage and interior pages. Begin by adding a new block of metadata to define regions with the following:

```
regions:
  header_top: 'Header Top'
  header: 'Header'
  primary_menu: 'Primary menu'
  secondary_menu: 'Secondary menu'
  page_top: 'Page top'
  page_bottom: 'Page bottom'
  highlighted: Highlighted
  headline: 'Headline'
  breadcrumb: Breadcrumb
  before_content: 'Before Content'
  content: Content
  sidebar_first: 'Sidebar first'
  sidebar_second: 'Sidebar second'
  after_content: 'After Content'
  footer_first: 'Footer first'
  footer_second: 'Footer second'
  footer_third: 'Footer third'
  footer_bottom_left: 'Footer Bottom Left'
  footer_bottom_right: 'Footer Bottom Right'
```

Make sure to save any changes to our `octo.info.yml` file and then clear Drupal's cache. Finally, we will want to confirm that our newly defined regions are available to be used by navigating to `/admin/structure/block` and looking at the Block layout page to verify that our regions are now available, as shown in the following image:

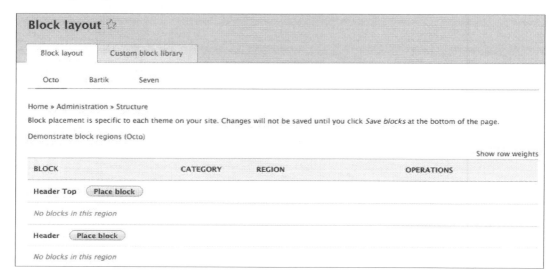

So far, we are progressing very nicely with adding our required metadata and regions that our theme will need, sort of a wash, rinse, and repeat pattern; with options like adding configuration information, clearing cache, and verifying changes being available. How about taking a look at adding some assets that we will need before we start tackling different page sections of our site?

Setting up our assets

Drupal 8 definitely manages assets in a different way than we were used to in Drupal 7. With the introduction of `Yaml` configuration and asset libraries, we now have a separation of how CSS and JavaScript is referenced and used. Of course, we should be experts by now, but to recap, the process contains two steps.

1. First, we need to create a `*.libraries.yml` file, which will allow us to organize our theme's CSS, JavaScript, and dependencies.

2. Second, we will need to add the library reference to our theme's configuration file.

We will be using the Twitter Bootstrap library again with our theme. To ensure that we all use the same version of Bootstrap, we have provided a copy within the exercise files.

Begin by copying the Bootstrap folder contained in the `Chapter05/start/themes/octo/vendor` folder and place it within the `themes/octo/vendor` folder.

With Bootstrap accessible by our theme, we can create a new file named `octo.libraries.yml` and save it within the root of our theme. Next, we will want to add the following metadata to our `octo.libraries.yml` file:

```
bootstrap:
  version: 3.3.6
  css:
    theme:
      vendor/bootstrap/css/bootstrap.min.css: {}
      vendor/bootstrap/css/bootstrap-theme.min.css: {}
  js:
    vendor/bootstrap/js/bootstrap.min.js: {}
  dependencies:
    - core/jquery
```

The metadata we added basically starts with a variable name for how we want to access the library from our configuration file such as `octo/bootstrap`. Next, we need to make sure that we reference the version of the library we are adding followed by the path to the CSS, JS, and any dependencies. When dealing with YAML files, it is important to make sure that you have the proper indentations or else we may experience errors.

Now that we have our `octo.libraries.yml` file in place and have added a reference to Bootstrap, we need to open up our `octo.info.yml` file and add a pointer to our library in order for Drupal to recognize any assets that need to be loaded into our theme.

Open up the `octo.info.yml` file, and add the following prior to our `regions` section:

```
libraries:
  - octo/bootstrap
```

Make sure to save our changes and then clear Drupal's cache. If everything was successful, we should be able to navigate back to our homepage and note the Bootstrap CSS affecting out page elements. We can also confirm this by inspecting the page with Google Chrome and see in fact that Bootstrap is being loaded properly, as shown in the following screenshot:

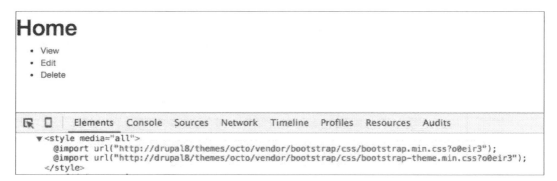

Adding additional assets

Now that we have a sense of how libraries are added to our theme, we will need to add additional assets including our images, CSS, and JavaScript files that we will be using to create our theme throughout the remaining lessons.

Begin by opening the `Chapter05/start/themes/octo` folder and copying the contents of the `css`, `img` and `js` folders and placing them into their respective folders inside the `themes/octo` folder, as shown in the following screenshot:

With our base assets in place, we will need to open back up our `octo.libraries.yml` file within our editor and add a global library entry that points to our new files.

Open up `octo.libraries.yml` and add the following entry directly below the bootstrap entry:

```
base:
  version: VERSION
  css:
    theme:
      css/styles.css: {}
  js:
    js/octo.js: {}
  dependencies:
    - core/jquery
```

It's important to remember that the formatting and order of these entries is crucial in making sure that we don't experience any Drupal errors, so feel free to look at the completed `octo.libraries.yml` file located in the `Chapter05/end/themes/octo` folder as a reference. Just to clarify, we want to make sure that Twitter Bootstrap loads first, then our base styling and scripts.

Once we have completed adding the new entry, make sure to save the file, then open up `octo.info.yml`, and add the following reference to our `base` library so that it reads as follows:

```
libraries:
  - octo/bootstrap
  - octo/base
```

Save the file and don't forget to clear Drupal's cache, this will ensure that our changes take effect. Now if we browse back to our homepage and inspect the markup, we will see that the new references have been added to our page and our styling has changed again:

Home

- View
- Edit
- Delete

```
  Elements   Console   Sources   Network   Timeline   Profiles   Resources   Audits
▼ <style media="all">
    @import url("http://drupal8/themes/octo/vendor/bootstrap/css/bootstrap.min.css?o0eikg");
    @import url("http://drupal8/themes/octo/vendor/bootstrap/css/bootstrap-theme.min.css?o0eikg");
    @import url("http://drupal8/themes/octo/css/styles.css?o0eikg");
  </style>
```

We will be adding additional assets to our octo.libraries.yml file as we address each page of our site that needs additional functionality, so it is important to be comfortable with this process.

Handling default files

One last thing we need to make sure that we take care of before finishing this chapter is considering how Drupal handles default files. That is, files that we upload such as a logo, an image field on a content type, or any inline images that we would place directly in the content of our page.

Since we are using database snapshots to save time on having to recreate content, we want to make sure that any images that the database may be referencing are available to us and we don't encounter broken image paths.

We can take care of this by copying the contents of our files folder located within the Chatper05/start/sites/default/files folder and placing them into the sites/default/files folder of our Drupal 8 instance. If prompted to replace or overwrite files, go ahead and say yes to ensure that we have all the files needed.

Once we are done, our sites/default/files folder should contain subfolders with images organized based on the upload date, inline images, and styles for image derivatives, as shown in the following screenshot:

We have now completed adding all the assets and initial libraries that our new custom theme will need—a great start to strengthen our theming skills.

Summary

The process of reviewing HTML mockups in preparation to convert it into a Drupal 8 theme takes time and patience. We need to make sure that we explore a website in great detail to spot possible layouts, regions, and user interactions that may require custom JavaScript and libraries. In this lesson, we accomplished the following:

- We broke down our HTML mockup page by page to enable us to better define what regions, layouts, and libraries we may need to create and configure for Drupal 8

- Having a clear starting point for everyone to begin theming from is important, and we used the database snapshots to ensure that we didn't have to work through the tedious process of entering content

- Finally, we began configuring our new theme by setting up our `octo.info. yml` file with regions and references to asset libraries that we set up within our `octo.libraries.yml` file

In the next chapter, we will dive into setting up our homepage layout to match the homepage of our mockup. We will begin creating Twig templates for our HTML wrapper and homepage as well as work further with libraries and assets.

6
Theming Our Homepage

Any good design draws the user in with a visually exciting homepage, whether it is a clean, minimal navigation menu, great-looking photographs, or clear, concise information that keeps the user engaged. We are tasked with providing all of those features and more, though the thought of implementing a homepage with all these items may seem overwhelming at first. We will soon realize that they are just a series of steps that will become the norm for any Drupal 8 project. In this chapter, we will walk through implementing the following:

- We will start with the obvious task of applying our website logo and working with the new site branding block. This will be followed by creating our first Twig template to handle our HTML wrapper and any assets and functionality that should be globally applied.

- Next, we will address converting our mockup's homepage markup into a Twig template with various regions to hold content.

- We will start with static content and then slowly convert it into dynamic content with blocks for our search block, menu, and other regions.

- Because aggregating data is such an integral part of Drupal with Views now in core, we will discover how to replicate content to use with the theming of our homepage slider.

As we work through each section, we have the ability to refer back to the Chapter06 exercise files folder. Each folder contains the start and end folders with files that we can use to compare our work when needed. This also includes database snapshots that will allow us to all start from the same point when working through various lessons.

Creating our HTML wrapper

In order to start addressing the markup of our homepage, we need to look at creating our first Twig template. The `html.html.twig` template is a little different than most templates, as it contains the basic structure or wrapper for a Drupal page that the rest of our templates will inherit. This template contains your standard HTML5 markup containing `html`, `head`, `title`, and `body` elements along with any other variables that Drupal 8 needs to output content.

We can begin by navigating to `core/modules/system/templates` and copying the `html.html.twig` Twig template to our `themes/octo/templates` folder. One thing to keep in mind as we start working with the Twig templates is that we will always copy a template from core to our themes folder to ensure that we don't accidentally modify any core files.

Next, we can open `html.html.twig` and review the markup in our editor. We have the following code:

```
<!DOCTYPE html>
<html{{ html_attributes }}>
  <head>
    <head-placeholder token="{{ placeholder_token|raw }}">
    <title>{{ head_title|safe_join(' | ') }}</title>
    <css-placeholder token="{{ placeholder_token|raw }}">
    <js-placeholder token="{{ placeholder_token|raw }}">
  </head>
  <body{{ attributes }}>
    <a href="#main-content" class="visually-hidden focusable">
      {{ 'Skip to main content'|t }}
    </a>
    {{ page_top }}
    {{ page }}
    {{ page_bottom }}
    <js-bottom-placeholder token="{{ placeholder_token|raw }}">
  </body>
</html>
```

The markup is similar to any other HTML document, with the addition of Twig variables and filters to output attributes, title, regions, and placeholders for CSS/JS. For example, `<css-placeholder token="{{ placeholder_token|raw }}">` outputs any CSS files that we added to our `*.libraries.yml` file and have referenced from within our themes configuration. Then, the `{{ page }}` variable will output the contents of any `page.html.twig` templates that it calls.

If we begin to compare the `html.html.twig` template to the markup of our homepage mockup, we can start to visualize how things come together.

Introducing web fonts

Our mockup takes full advantage of Google Fonts by adding it to the head of our document. The external reference allows our CSS to render the typography on various pages. The only problem is that currently we are not including the web fonts in our Drupal theme. Because we cannot download Google Fonts and use them locally, they need to be externally hosted. But how do we add externally hosted files to a `*.libraries.yml` file?

The answer is actually quite simple. We need to specify the file type as external, and adding an external asset is something new we have yet to discuss. So, we can walk through the steps involved:

1. Open `octo.libraries.yml`.

2. Add the following entry:

```
webfonts:
  version: VERSION
  css:
    theme:
      //fonts.googleapis.com/css?family=Open+Sans:300,400,
        600,700,800|Roboto+Slab: { type: external }
```

3. Save `octo.libraries.yml`.

4. Open `octo.info.yml`.

5. Add the following library reference pointing to the entry of our new web fonts:

```
libraries:
  - octo/bootstrap
  - octo/webfonts
  - octo/base
```

6. Save `octo.info.yml`.

Make sure to clear Drupal's cache and refresh our homepage. If we inspect the page, we should see our external reference to Google Fonts being loaded directly after Twitter Bootstrap. Now that our HTML wrapper is complete, we can move on to creating our homepage template.

Creating our homepage

The next item we will move on to is creating the main homepage template. By default, Drupal uses the `page.html.twig` template to render any regions we have defined within our configuration. Because we broke out our Mockup into functional areas, we have a sense of what each region will contain. Our job is to recreate the homepage, which will require us to follow these basic theming techniques.

1. First, we will take advantage of Drupal's file name suggestions to create our homepage template.

2. Then, we will replace the contents of our template with the contents of our Mockups homepage.

3. Finally, we will need to review the output of our new template.

Using page templates

If we inspect the homepage, it is currently using the core `page.html.twig` template to output content. But if we take advantage of the FILE NAME SUGGESTIONS provided, we are presented with a couple of additional choices for displaying content.

```
<!-- THEME DEBUG -->
<!-- THEME HOOK: 'page' -->
<!-- FILE NAME SUGGESTIONS:
   * page--front.html.twig
   * page--.html.twig
   x page.html.twig
-->
<!-- BEGIN OUTPUT from 'core/modules/system/templates/page.html.twig' -->
<div class="layout-container">...</div>
<!-- END OUTPUT from 'core/modules/system/templates/page.html.twig' -->
```

The reason we are interested in alternative templates for our homepage is due to the fact that as we navigate from page to page, we have clear layout changes. Our homepage has a completely different layout than our interior page, with the exception of any global elements. Knowing this, it would make sense to create a separate homepage template to manage our content.

We can begin by following these steps:

1. Navigate to `core/modules/system/templates` and copy `page.html.twig`.

2. Place the copy within our `themes/octo/templates` folder.

3. Rename `page.html.twig` to the suggested name of `page--front.html.twig`.

Make sure to clear Drupal's cache and refresh our homepage. If we inspect the page again, we will note that we have an indicator next to `page--front.html.twig` under the `FILE NAME SUGGESTIONS`, and the output is now pointing to our `themes` folder.

Working with static content

When working with a mockup, the easiest way to start any theming project is by simply replacing the Twig templates contents with the static content from our design.

1. Open `page--front.html.twig` and delete the entire contents.

2. Navigate to `Mockup/index.html` and copy the markup between the opening and closing `body` element minus the JavaScript references and paste it into `page--front-html.twig`.

3. Save `page--front-html.twig`.

Make sure to clear Drupal's cache and refresh the homepage within our browser. We should now have a working copy of the homepage mockup; well, sort of.

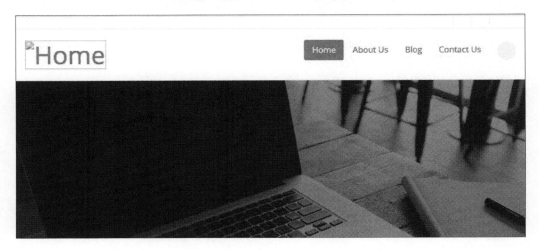

If it was only that simple, we would all be Drupal rock stars. What we do have though is a good starting point for which we can begin to replace static content with dynamic content. Also, we can validate the following:

- Our `page--front.html.twig` template is only being used on the homepage, or else our Error page would look the same once we navigated to any other page.

- Our CSS, JavaScript, and assets are being included properly or else our homepage would look horrible.

Implementing our Header Top region

The first item we will need to address is replacing the static content in our Header Top region. Referring back to the Mockup, we have a menu of social icons that display within this region. Also, if we look closely, each social icon is using the Font Awesome library. Tackling the next section will require the following techniques:

1. First, we will create a custom block to display our Social Icons menu and then assign it to the Header Top region so that it is available to render.

2. Next, we will add the Font Awesome library for our social icon to use.

3. Finally, we will modify our static content to display our Header Top region.

Creating our Social Icons block

Creating blocks of content is fairly simple, and we will be doing this often as we recreate each section of our theme. We will start by navigating to the **Block layout** page at `/admin/structure/block` and following these nine steps:

1. Click on the **Place block** button in the **Header Top** region.

2. Click on the **Add custom block** button.

3. Enter a **Block description** of `Social Icons`.

4. Select **HTML No Editor** from the **Text format** dropdown.

5. Add the markup located in the `Chatper06/start/content/SocialIcons.txt` file to the **Body** field, as shown in the following image:

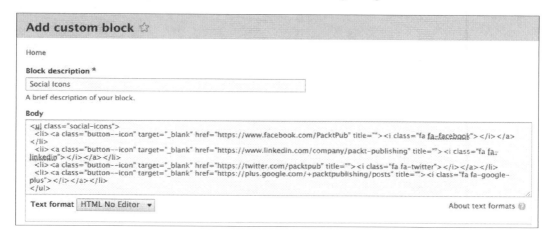

6. Click on the **Save** button to proceed to the **Configure block** screen.

7. Uncheck the **Display title** checkbox.

8. Choose **Header Top** from the **Region** field.

9. Click on the **Save block** button, as shown in the following image:

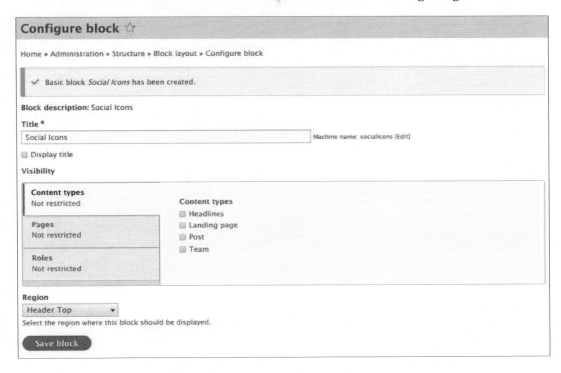

We now have our Social Icons block created and assigned to our Header Top region. Next, we need to add the Font Awesome icon library.

Installing Font Awesome library

Font Awesome is an icon font implementation that allows scalable vector icons to be referenced the same way you would a font family. Our social icons as well as other sections of our theme will take advantage of Font Awesome to display various icons. We can find detailed information regarding Font Awesome at `https://fortawesome.github.io/Font-Awesome`. To ensure that we all use the same version of Font Awesome, we will need to navigate to the `Chapter06/start/themes/octo/vendor` folder and copy the `font-awesome` folder to our `themes/octo/vendor` folder.

Once the files are accessible by Drupal, we can follow these remaining steps to add Font Awesome to our theme:

1. Open `octo.libraries.yml`.
2. Add the following entry:

```
font-awesome:
  version: 4.3.0
  css:
    theme:
      vendor/font-awesome/css/font-awesome.min.css: {}
```

3. Save `octo.libraries.yml`:
4. Open `octo.info.yml`:
5. Add the following library reference pointing to our new web fonts entry:

```
libraries:
  - octo/bootstrap
  - octo/webfonts
  - octo/font-awesome
  - octo/base
```

6. Save `octo.info.yml`:

Make sure to save our changes and clear Drupal's cache for our changes to take effect. Finally, we will need to add the Header Top region to our homepage before being able to see our Social Icons menu.

Refactoring Header Top region

Currently, our `page--front.html.twig` template is not outputting our Header Top region. We will need to refactor our markup to replace the static content with the output of the `{{ page.header_top }}` region.

Current markup

```
<div class="header-top">
  <div class="container">
    <div id="block-socialicons" class="block">
      <ul class="social-icons">
        <li><a class="button--icon" target="_blank"
            href="https://www.facebook.com/PacktPub" title="">
            <i class="fa fa-facebook"></i></a></li>
        <li><a class="button--icon" target="_blank"
            href="https://www.linkedin.com/company/
            packt-publishing" title="">
            <i class="fa fa-linkedin"></i></a></li>
```

```
        <li><a class="button--icon" target="_blank"
            href="https://twitter.com/packtpub" title="">
            <i class="fa fa-twitter"></i></a></li>
        <li><a class="button--icon" target="_blank"
            href="https://plus.google.com/+packtpublishing/posts"
            title=""><i class="fa fa-google-plus"></i></a></li>
      </ul>
    </div>
  </div>
</div>
```

New markup

```
<div class="header-top">
  <div class="container">
    {{ page.header_top }}
  </div>
</div>
```

Make sure to save our changes, clear Drupal's cache and then refresh the browser. If all was successful, our Header Top region should now be identical to the mockup:

Implementing our Header region

The second item we will need to address is replacing the static content in our Header region. Referring back to the mockup, we have a logo, menu, and search form, each with their respective functionality. Tackling this next section will require quite a few more steps:

- First, we will address the logo that has been moved into the brand new site branding block. We will upload a new logo, assign the block to our header region, and work with block templates.

- Next, we will use Twig to print our Header region within our homepage to view any blocks assigned to it.

- Then, we will work with the search form block and create both the block template and the input template while introducing some new Twig techniques to work with variables. We will also add our first custom JavaScript to enable the toggle functionality.

- We will also take a look at our main menu and work with menu templates to modify the markup to match our design.

- Finally, we will add our custom script to make our header region sticky, so that as our user scrolls down the page, the header remains within our view.

Adding a logo

Currently, our website is not displaying a site logo. This is in part due to the fact that we have yet to upload a logo for our theme. We can address this by navigating to /admin/appearance/settings in our browser, as shown in the following image:

We can upload a new image by following these four steps:

1. Uncheck **Use the default logo supplied by the theme**.
2. Click on the **Choose File** button under the **Upload logo image** field.
3. Select the logo.png file located in the Chapter06/start/themes/octo/img folder.
4. Click on the **Save configuration**.

We should now see that the path to custom logo displays as `logo.png` with the path to our file being `public://logo.png` or `sites/default/files/logo.png`, as shown in the following image:

If for some reason the path to the image is different but the logo still displays properly, it may be due to us uploading a logo in the previous chapter.

Enabling Site branding

In Drupal 8, the Site logo, Site name, and Site slogan have been moved into a brand new Site branding block. We will need to place this block into the Header region, so that it will display later once we add the region to our `page--front-html.twig` template.

Begin by navigating to `/admin/structure/block` and locate the **Disabled** region section. We will see the **Site branding** block currently disabled. We can place the **Site branding** block into the **Header** region by following these steps:

1. Select **Header** from the **Region** dropdown.
2. Click on the **Save blocks** button.

Now that the block is assigned to our Header region, we can continue with configuring it by clicking on the **Configure** button to the right of the **Site branding** block:

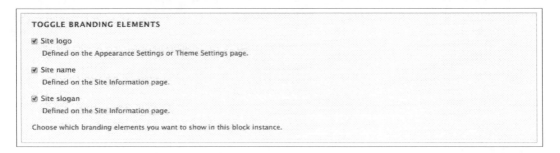

Located under the **TOGGLE BRANDING ELEMENTS**, we have the option of enabling or disabling specific page elements. In our case, we only want the Site logo to be displayed:

1. Uncheck **Site name**.
2. Uncheck **Site slogan**.
3. Click the **Save block** button.

Now that we have our logo uploaded and our site branding block assigned to a region, we need to add the Header region to our homepage template.

Printing our Header region

Within our `page--front.html.twig` template, we want to be able to see any blocks of content that we assign to the Header region. In order to do this, we will need to add the `{{ page.header }}` variable.

1. Open `page--front.html.twig`.
2. Add the Twig variable `{{ page.header }}` directly below the `header-nav` container so that our markup looks like the following:

   ```
   <div class="header-nav container">
       {{ page.header}}
   ```

3. Save `page--front.html.twig`.

Make sure to save our changes, clear Drupal's cache, and then refresh the browser. Currently, we are displaying two logos, which we will address next by moving our static markup in a new block template.

Creating Block templates

In an attempt to clean up our page template, we will create a block template for our site branding block. However, we first need to know the location of the Twig template that Drupal is using to output our logo. When we inspect the page, we should see the following:

```
<!-- THEME DEBUG -->
<!-- THEME HOOK: 'block' -->
<!-- FILE NAME SUGGESTIONS:
   * block--octo-branding.html.twig
   x block--system-branding-block.html.twig
   * block--system.html.twig
   * block.html.twig
-->
<!-- BEGIN OUTPUT from 'core/modules/system/templates/block--system-branding-block.html.twig' -->
<div id="block-octo-branding" class="contextual-region">...</div>
<!-- END OUTPUT from 'core/modules/system/templates/block--system-branding-block.html.twig' -->
```

Now that we know the path to `block--system-branding-block-html-twig`, we can grab a copy and place it within our themes templates folder:

1. Navigate to `core/modules/system/templates` and copy the `block--system-branding-block.html.twig` template to our `themes/octo/templates` folder.

2. Open `block--system-branding-block.html.twig` and delete the current markup.

3. Replace the content with the following markup:

```
<div class="navbar-header">
  <button type="button" class="navbar-toggle"
    data-toggle="collapse" data-target=".navbar-main">
    <i class="fa fa-bars"></i>
  </button>

  {% if site_logo %}
    <h1 class="logo">
     <a href="{{ url('<front>') }}"
     title="{{ 'Home'|t }}" rel="home" id="logo">
       <img src="{{ site_logo }}" alt="{{ 'Home'|t }}" />
     </a>
    </h1>
  {% endif %}
</div>
```

4. Save `block--system-branding-block.html.twig`.

5. Open `page--front.html.twig`.

6. Delete the navbar-header section.

7. Save `page--front.html.twig`.

Make sure to save our changes, clear Drupal's cache, and then refresh the browser. Our header is coming along nicely, and should look like the following image:

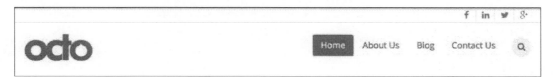

There are a lot of different Twig variables, filters, and conditional logic happening with the markup for our `block--system-branding-block.html.twig` template, so let's take a moment to explain.

- First, we are using Twig conditional logic `{%...%}` to test whether the site logo exists, and if so, print the markup between.

- Second, we are replacing the `href` value with `{{ url('front') }}`, which outputs the current URL path to our homepage.

- Third, we are using a Twig translation filter `{{ 'value|t' }}` to translate the values in the `title` and `alt` attributes.

- Finally, we are using a Twig variable `{{ site_logo }}` to grab the path to our logo.

If for some reason our header does not look like what we are expecting, we can always take a look at the `Chapter06/end/themes/octo/templates` folder and compare our Twig templates with the completed ones.

Implementing our search form block

The next item we will move on to is replacing the search functionality within our page header. Referring back to the mockup, we have a hidden search form that can be toggled to display by the end user. Tackling this next section will require multiple theming techniques.

1. First, we will need to assign Drupal's search for block to the Header region.

2. Next, we will need to create a Twig template for the search block and move the markup out of our homepage and into the template.

3. Finally, we will need to add the proper JS to enable the toggling of the search field.

Placing our search form block

Currently, we do not have a search form block available to us within our Block layout. We will need to locate the block and place it within our Header region.

1. Navigate to `/admin/structure/block`.

2. Locate the **Header** region.

3. Click on the **Place block** button.

4. Locate the **Search form** block from the **Place block** dialog.

5. Click on the **Place block** button.

6. Uncheck the **Display title** checkbox.

7. Click on the **Save block** button from the Block layout page.

Our Header region should now contain two blocks: one for site branding and the other for our search form.

If we navigate back to our homepage, we should see our search form block displayed to the right of our logo. We will want to refactor our `navbar-search` markup by adding it to the search form block being output by Drupal.

Creating a search form block template

If we inspect the search form block using Chrome's developer tools, we will identify that Drupal is using the general `block.html.twig` template. We want to be more specific with our naming convention as we will be modifying the markup in this block. Based on the FILE NAME SUGGESTIONS, we can create a new block named `block--search-form-block.html.twig`. Follow these steps:

1. Navigate to `core/modules/block/templates` and copy the `block.html.twig` template to our `themes/octo/templates` folder.

2. Rename `block.html.twig` to `block--search-form-block.html.twig`.

3. Replace the content with the following markup:

```
<div class="navbar-search">
  <div class="search-icons">
    <a class="open-form"><i class="fa fa-search"></i></a>
    <a class="close-form"><i class="fa fa-times"></i></a>
  </div>
  <div class="search-block-form">
    {{ content }}
  </div>
</div>
```

4. Save `block--search-form-block.html.twig`.

Our search form block is now in place, but we still need to remove the navbar-search section from our page--front-html.twig template so that we don't have duplicate markup.

1. Open page--front.html.twig.

2. Delete the navbar-section of the markup:

```
<div class="navbar-search">
   ...content...
</div>
```

Make sure to save our changes, clear Drupal's cache and then refresh the browser. Our search form block is now in place and styled similarly to our mockup. However, if we click on the search icon, nothing will happen. We are currently missing the custom JavaScript to enable this functionality.

Adding custom JavaScript

Initially, when we added our base styling to our octo.libraries.yml file, we also referenced a custom JavaScript file that is located in our themes/octo/js folder titled octo.js. If we open this file, we will see the shell to add jQuery that is initiated once the page has finished loading. We will be adding any custom script within this function:

```
! function($) {
    $(document).ready(function() {

    });
}(jQuery);
```

As this is not meant to be a JavaScript lesson, we will not be going into detail about any scripts we added to this function. We will, though briefly, discuss the intention of each script.

In order for our search form to be unhidden and hidden, it relies on the click event of the search icon being triggered. We can add the following script to our function to enable this interaction:

```
//-- Search icon
(function() {
  $(".open-form").click(function(){
    $(".open-form").hide();
    $(".close-form").css("display","block");
    $(".search-block-form").show();
    $(".search-block-form input").focus();
```

```
      return false;
   });
   $(".close-form").click(function(){
      $(".close-form").hide();
      $(".open-form").css("display","block");
      $(".search-block-form").hide();
      return false;
   });
})();
```

We can also find the completed `octo.js` file within the `Chapter06/end/themes/octo/js` folder to compare with our file. Make sure to save the file, clear Drupal's cache, and then refresh our homepage. If we click on the search icon, we should see our search form being displayed, as shown in the following image:

We are not quite done; the input element is not displaying over the menu. We can clearly see the outline of the input and the placeholder attribute, which prompts the user what to enter into our input, is missing. We can fix this by adding one additional Twig template for the input element.

Creating an input element template

If we inspect the markup for the search input, we can identify that the Twig template being used by Drupal is `input.html.twig`. As is the case with all input elements, we may find that this is not sufficient. Using the FILE NAME SUGGESTIONS, we can create a new input template titled `input--search.html.twig`:

1. Navigate to `core/modules/system/templates` and copy the `input.html.twig` template to our `themes/octo/templates` folder.

2. Rename `input.html.twig` to `input--search.html.twig`.

3. Replace the content with the following markup:

```
{% set classes = ['form-control',] %}

<input{{attributes.addClass(classes).setAttribute
   ('placeholder','Enter your search terms...') }} />
   {{ children }}
```

Make sure to save our changes, clear Drupal's cache, and then refresh the browser. Now if we click on the search icon, everything should look and function exactly like our mockup.

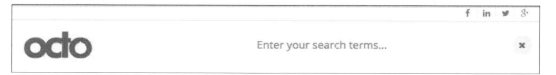

Therefore, we once again are introducing some new Twig functionality that should be explained in a little more detail.

First, we are using adding a new CSS class named `form-control` that is specific to Twitter Bootstrap. We are then setting a Twig variable named `classes` with that value, and then using the Twig function `attributes.addClass()` to pass the value to Drupal.

Second, we are using a second Twig function `setAttribute()`, which allows us to add the `placeholder` attribute with a value of **Enter your search terms**.

As we are starting to see, the new Twig functionality in Drupal is very powerful and allows us to achieve most theming requirements directly in a Twig template without the need to use the Theme layer.

Working with menus

When dealing with our main menu, we are using Drupal's Main navigation menu block. This block is already assigned to our Primary menu region, which makes it very easy to access within our `page--front.html.twig` template:

1. Open `page--front.html.twig`.
2. Add the `{{ page.primary_menu }}` variable to our page directly below the `{{ page.header }}` variable.
3. Save `page--front.html.twig`.

Make sure to save our changes, clear Drupal's cache, and refresh the browser. We will now see the Main navigation block being displayed to the right of our logo, as shown in the following image:

Taking a closer look, it's clear that the unordered list for our menu is missing the following classes, `nav nav-pills nav-main`, which is causing the menu items to not display inline or show with the Bootstrap pill formatting that our static menu is displaying.

Creating a menu template

If we inspect the markup for the main menu, we can identify the Twig template being used by Drupal is `menu.html.twig`. Using the FILE NAME SUGGESTIONS, we can create a more specific template titled `menu--main.html.twig`.

1. Navigate to `core/modules/system/template` and copy `menu.html.twig` to the `themes/octo/templates` folder.

2. Rename `menu.html.twig` to `menu--main.html.twig`.

3. Now we will need to open our new template, locate the first unordered list, and add the missing CSS classes by replacing the following markup:

   Current markup

   ```
   <ul{{ attributes }}>
   ```

   New markup

   ```
   <ul{{ attributes.addClass('nav nav-pills nav-main') }}>
   ```

Make sure to save our changes, clear Drupal's cache, and refresh the browser. We will now see the Main navigation block displaying inline similar to our static menu.

Creating System Menu block template

Similar to how we handled the markup for our site branding, it would be much easier to manage the `navbar-main` wrapper within the block that outputs our menu. This will allow us to also remove the `navbar-main` markup completely from our homepage template.

If we inspect the markup for the main menu, we can identify the block template being used by Drupal is `block--system-menu-block.html.twig`. Knowing the fact that there will only ever be a single main menu, we can feel confident using this same template for our needs:

1. Navigate to `core/modules/system/template` and copy `block--system-menu-block.html.twig` to the `themes/octo/templates` folder.

2. Replace the content with the following markup:

   ```
   <div class="navbar-main navbar-collapse collapse">
     {{ content }}
   </div>
   ```

3. Save `block--system-menu-block.html.twig`.

4. Open `page--front.html.twig`.

5. Modify the `header-nav` section to look like the following:

```
<div class="header-nav container">
  {{ page.header}}
  {{ page.primary_menu }}
</div>
```

6. Save `page--front.html.twig`.

Make sure to clear Drupal's cache and then refresh the homepage. Our menu is now complete and functional. Finally, we need to add our custom script that will turn our header into a sticky header.

Creating a sticky header

One of the more common UI improvements seen around the Web is the implementation of sticky headers. Our mockup implements this with a little bit of CSS and some custom JavaScript.

First, the markup for our header region contain a class of `header` that will be used to add an additional class of `sticky` once the user has scrolled down the page a certain number of pixels.

Second, we can use the **Document Object Model (DOM)** with JavaScript to determine how far the user has scrolled past a specific element in our markup. We can use the reverse to then remove the `sticky` class once they have scrolled back to the top of the page.

1. Open `octo.js` located in the `themes/octo/js` folder.

2. Add the following script block:

```javascript
//-- Sticky Header
(function() {
  var mainnav = $('.header');
  if (mainnav.length) {
    var elmHeight = $('.header-top').outerHeight(true);
    $(window).scroll(function() {
      var scrolltop = $(window).scrollTop();
      if (scrolltop > elmHeight) {

        if (!mainnav.hasClass('sticky')) {
          mainnav.addClass('sticky');
        }
```

```
        } else {
          mainnav.removeClass('sticky');
        }
      })
    }
  })();
```

Make sure to save our changes, clear Drupal's cache and then refresh the browser. If we begin to scroll down the page, we will see the Header region stick to the top of our browser. Scrolling back up to the top, our Header region then returns to normal.

We have successfully completed the header of our homepage. Complete it with logo, dynamic main menu, and search functionality.

Implementing our Headline Region

The third item we will need to address is replacing the static content in our Headline region. Referring back to the mockup, we have a responsive slider, parallax content, and a jump to the menu icon. Tackling the next section will introduce some new steps:

1. First, we will address the Headline slider, which will require us to build a view to aggregate Headline content using a block display.

2. Next, we will assign the new block to our Headline region and refactor the markup.

3. Finally, we will add a JS library for FlexSlider to enable the responsive slider.

Creating our Headline View and Block

Drupal 8 has taken the popular Views module and integrated it into the core module system. We can take advantage of Views to aggregate the content that our Headline slider needs.

To get started, we will need to navigate to /admin/structure/views and click on the **Add new view** button from the **Views** Admin screen, where we will add the following information:

- **VIEW BASIC INFORMATION**:
    1. **View name**: Headlines.
    2. Check the **Description** box.
    3. **Description**: A listing of Headlines.

- **VIEW SETTINGS**: Show: Content of type: Headlines sorted by: **Newest first**

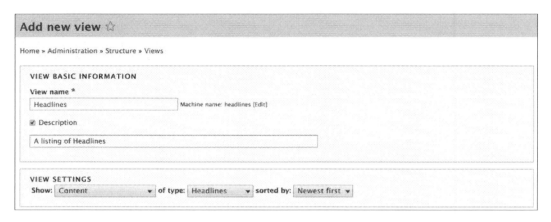

- **BLOCK SETTINGS**:
    1. Check the **Create a block** checkbox.
    2. **Block title**: Headlines.

- **BLOCK DISPLAY SETTINGS**:
    1. **Display format: HTML List of: titles**.
    2. **Items per block**: 3.
    3. Click on the **Save and edit** button.

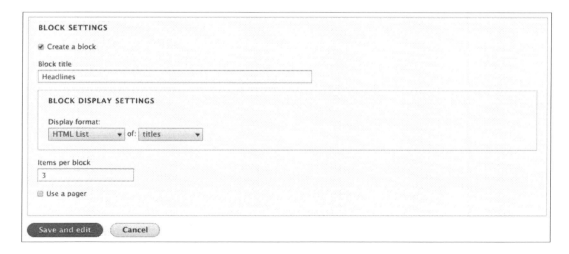

Now that our Headlines view has been created, we will need to add an additional field and adjust the format settings before we can use our new block. With the view still open, we will need to make the following adjustments to the **Block: Style options**.

1. Click on the **Settings** link next to the **Format: HTML List** link under the **FORMAT** section.
2. Change the **Wrapper class** from **item-list** to flexslider.
3. Add a **List class** named slides.
4. Click on the **Apply** button.

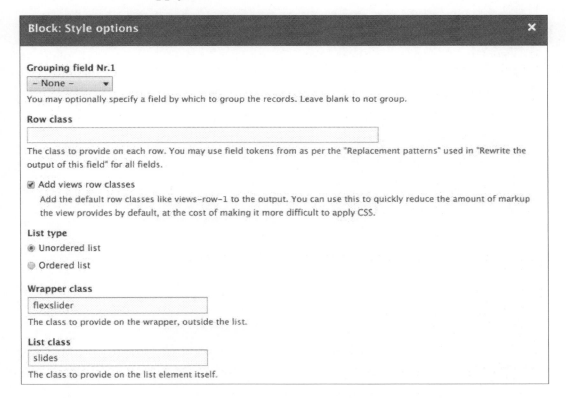

Next, we will need to make adjustments to the **Block: Row style options**:

1. Click on the **Settings** link next to the **Show: Fields** link under the **FORMAT** section.
2. Uncheck the **Provide default field wrapper elements** checkbox.

3. Click on the **Apply** button.

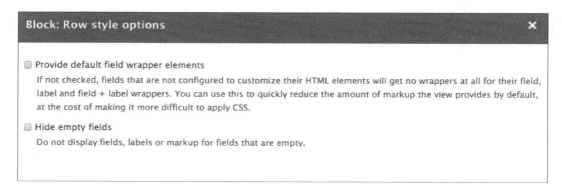

We now need to add an additional field for our Headlines view that will display the subheading under the main heading of our content. We can accomplish this by performing the following steps:

1. Click on the **Add** button in the **Fields** section.
2. From the **Add fields** dialog, enter subheading in the **Search** field
3. Check the checkbox next to **Sub Heading**.
4. Click on the **Apply (all displays)** button.
5. From the **Configure field: Content: Sub Heading** dialog, expand the **STYLE SETTINGS** and uncheck **Add default classes** checkbox.
6. Click on the **Apply** button and then on the **Save** button to make sure that our changes to the Headlines view have been saved.

One last field configuration we will need to make is to the Title field. We need to have it displayed as an H2 heading for styling and SEO purposes.

1. Click on the **Content: Title** link in the **FIELDS** section.
2. Expand the **STYLE SETTINGS** section.
3. Check the **Customize field HTML** checkbox.
4. Select **H2** from the **HTML Element** field.
5. Uncheck the **Add default classes** checkbox.
6. Click on the **Apply (all displays)** button.

At this point, make sure to save the View, and then we can move on to the next step of placing our block.

Adding our Headlines Block

We can start by navigating to /admin/structure/block and following these steps:

1. Click on the **Place block** button in the **Headline** region.
2. Locate the **Headlines** block.
3. Click on the **Place block** button.
4. Uncheck the **Display title** checkbox.
5. Click on the **Save block** button.

We now have our Headlines block placed into the Headline region for us to be able to output from our homepage template.

Printing our Headline region

Within our page--front.html.twig template, we want to be able to display our Headlines block. In order to do this, we will need to add the {{ page.headline }} variable.

1. Open page--front.html.twig.
2. Add the Twig variable {{ page.headline }} directly below the headline container and delete the remaining markup between the opening and closing headline container so that our markup looks like the following:

```
<div class="headline">
  {{ page.headline }}
</div>
```

3. Save page--front.html.twig.

Make sure to save our changes, clear Drupal's cache, and refresh the browser. Feel free to review the `page--front.html.twig` template located in the `Chapter06/end/themes/octo/templates` folder to compare the markup if needed. If everything was done properly, our Headline region should be displaying three headlines, as shown in the following image:

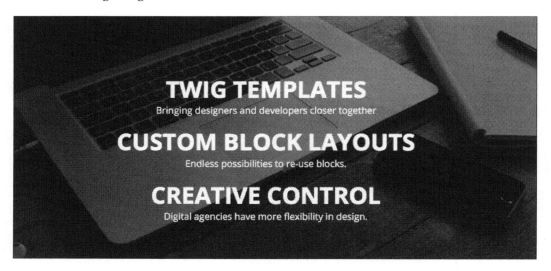

Configuring FlexSlider library

FlexSlider is a fully responsive jQuery slider developed by Woo Themes. The slider is very easy to implement and has numerous configuration options. We can find detailed information regarding FlexSlider at `https://www.woothemes.com/flexslider`.

To ensure that we use the same version of FlexSlider, we will need to navigate to the `Chapter06/start/themes/octo/vendor` folder and copy the `flexslider` folder to our `themes/octo/vendor` folder. Once the files are accessible by Drupal, we can follow these remaining steps to add FlexSlider to our theme:

Open `octo.libraries.yml` and add the following entry:

```
flexslider:
  version: 2.5.0
  css:
    theme:
      vendor/flexslider/flexslider.css: {}
  js:
    vendor/flexslider/jquery.flexslider-min.js: {}
  dependencies:
    - core/jquery
```

Make sure to save our changes and clear Drupal's cache for our changes to take effect. Next, we need to consider how we will be using the FlexSlider library. If we were going to use it globally, then we could add it to our `octo.info.yml` file. However, because we will only be using it on our homepage, we can take advantage of the `{{attach library() }}` function.

Attaching a library using Twig

In order to attach a library using Twig, we will need to follow these steps:

1. Open `page--front.html.twig`.

2. Add the following Twig function to the top of our template:

    ```
    {{ attach_library('octo/flexslider') }}
    ```

Make sure to save our changes and clear Drupal's cache for our changes to take effect. If we now inspect our homepage, we will see the FlexSlider library loading. However, if we go to any of the interior pages and inspect the markup, we will see that the FlexSlider library is absent. Being able to attach libraries only where needed is helpful, as it makes sure unnecessary CSS or scripts are not loaded.

Enable FlexSlider

In order for us to enable FlexSlider, we have one last step. We need to add the configuration for our slider to our `octo.js` so that it knows which markup to use for the slides:

Open `octo.js.` and add the following script block:

```
//-- Flexslider
(function() {
  $('.flexslider').flexslider({
    direction: "vertical",
    controlNav: false,
    directionNav: false
  });
})();
```

Make sure to save our changes and clear Drupal's cache for our changes to take effect. If we browse our homepage, we will see our Headline slider is now fully functional, as shown in the following image:

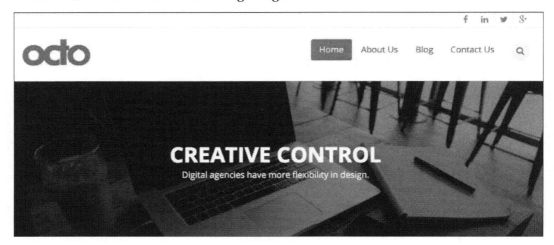

We have almost completed our Headline region. There are two more pieces of UI to implement, one of these is what is known as the Parallax effect.

Implementing Parallax

Parallax is a scrolling effect where the background image scrolls at a slower speed than the foreground of the page. The effect creates a subtle 3D effect. In order for us to implement this, we just need to add a small script block to our `octo.js` file, which targets our markup that has a class of `intro` and then uses data attributes on that section to manage the speed of the effect and how far to scroll.

Open `octo.js` and add the following script block:

```
//-- Parallax
(function() {
  $(window).scroll(function(e){
    var bg = $('.intro');
    var yPos = -($(window).scrollTop() / bg.data('speed'));
    var coords = '50% '+ yPos + 'px';
    bg.css({ backgroundPosition: coords});
  })
})();
```

Make sure to save our changes and clear Drupal's cache. If we browse our homepage, we will see the Parallax effect within the Headline region. As we begin to scroll down the page, we will see that our Headline background image scrolls at a slower speed.

Adding a scroll effect

A subtle yet nice touch to our homepage is the addition of an animated scroll effect. At the bottom of our Headline region we have a link, which when clicked by a user smoothly scrolls the page to the next section. The markup is already in place and uses IDs for JavaScript to trigger the effect and to know where to scroll the page to. All we need to do is add the library and the script, and attach the library to our homepage.

Begin by navigating to the `Chapter06/start/themes/octo/vendor` folder and copy the `jquery-scrollTo` folder to our `themes/octo/vendor` folder. Once the files are accessible by Drupal, we can follow these remaining steps to add the library:

Open `octo.libraries.yml` and add the following entry:

```
scroll-to:
  version: 2.1.1
  js:
    vendor/jquery-scrollTo/jquery.scrollTo.min.js: {}
  dependencies:
    - core/jquery
```

Make sure to save our changes and clear Drupal's cache for our changes to take effect.

Enabling the scroll script

In order for us to enable jQuery Scroller, we need to initialize it within our `octo.js` so that we know which element should be triggered when the user clicks on the link.

Open `octo.js` and add the following script block:

```
//-- Scroll to
(function() {
  $('#goto-section2').on('click', function(e){
    e.preventDefault()
    $.scrollTo('#section2', 800, { offset: -220 });
  });
})();
```

Make sure to save our changes and clear Drupal's cache for our changes to take effect. Finally, all that is left is attaching the library to our homepage.

Attaching ScrollTo library using Twig

In order to attach our library using Twig, we will need to follow these steps:

1. Open `page--front.html.twig`.
2. Add to the top of our template the following Twig function:

   ```
   {{ attach_library('octo/ scroll-to) }}
   ```

Make sure to save our changes and clear Drupal's. If we browse our homepage and click on the link at the bottom of our Headline region, we will now see the animated smooth scrolling functioning perfectly.

We definitely covered a lot of different techniques when refactoring our Headline region, but we now need to move on to our Before Content region.

Implementing our Before Content region

The fourth item we will need to address is replacing the static content in our Before Content region. Referring back to the mockup, we have two blocks of content that will require us to follow these steps to implement.

1. First, we will create the Our Services block and Our Features block and assign it to the Before Content region.
2. Finally, we will refactor the markup and print the Before Content region using Twig variables.

Creating our Services block

Creating blocks of content is fairly simple and we should already be comfortable with the process.

We will start by navigating to the **Block layout** page at `/admin/structure/block` and following these steps:

1. Click on the **Place block** button in the **Before Content** region.
2. Click on the **Add custom block** button.
3. Enter a **Block description** of our services.
4. Select **HTML No Editor** from the **Text format** dropdown.
5. Add the markup located in the `Chatper06/start/content/OurServices.txt` file to the **Body** field.

6. Click on the **Save** button to proceed to the **Configure block** screen.
7. Uncheck the **Display title** checkbox.
8. Select the **Pages** vertical tab within the **Visibility** section.
9. Enter a value of `<front>` in the **Pages** text area.
10. Choose **Show for the listed pages** under **Negate the condition**.
11. Choose **Before Content** from the **Region** field.
12. Click on the **Save block** button.

We have one block completed, now let's add the second block.

Creating our Features block

Creating blocks of content is fairly simple, and we should already be comfortable with the process.

We will start by navigating to the **Block layout** page at `/admin/structure/block` and following these steps:

1. Click on the **Place block** button in the **Before Content** region.
2. Click on the **Add custom block** button.
3. Enter a **Block description** of our features.
4. Select **HTML No Editor** from the **Text format** dropdown.
5. Add the markup located in the `Chatper06/start/content/ OurFeatures.txt` file to the **Body** field.
6. Click on the **Save** button to proceed to the **Configure block** screen.
7. Uncheck the **Display title** checkbox.
8. Select the **Pages** vertical tab within the **Visibility** section.
9. Enter a value of `<front>` in the **Pages** text area.
10. Choose **Show for the listed pages** under **Negate the condition**.
11. Choose **Before Content** from the **Region** field.
12. Click on the **Save block** button.

With our two blocks completed and assigned to the Before Content region, we need to make sure that they are ordered correctly. From the Block layout page, make sure that Our Services is followed by Our Features within the Before Content region. Now it's time to refactor our static markup and print the region to our `page--front. html.twig` template.

Refactoring Before Content region

Currently, our `page--front.html.twig` template is not outputting our Before Content region. We will need to refactor our markup to add a new Twig variable that contains our two blocks `{{ page.before_content }}`.

Begin by opening `page--front.html.twig` and locating the section wrapper, and replace all the content between with our new Twig variable.

Current markup

```
<section id="section2" class="section">
  <div class="container">
    ... content ...
  </div>
</section>
```

New markup

```
<section id="section2" class="section">
  <div class="container">
    {{ page.before_content }}
  </div>
</section>
```

Make sure to save our changes, clear Drupal's cache and then refresh the browser. If all was successful, our Before Content region should now be identical to the Mockup.

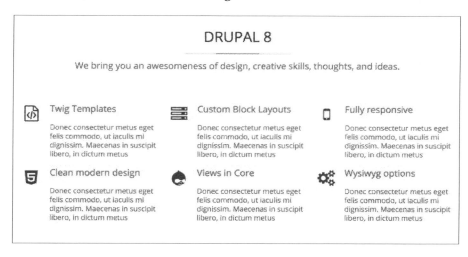

Finally, we are at the end of our homepage, with the only piece left to refactor being our Footer region, which consists of several custom blocks.

Implementing the footer

Our footer is a little different to what we have been implementing so far. The footer consists of multiple regions and custom blocks to easily match our mockup, and will mean us following these steps:

1. First, we will need to create five custom blocks for our Newsletter, About Us, Contact Us, Copyright, and Social Icons content. Once the blocks are created, they will need to be assigned to their respective regions.

2. Finally, we will need to refactor the markup in our footer to accommodate the various Twig variables to print out each region.

Creating our custom blocks

We will begin with creating the five custom blocks as well as assigning them to the regions they need to be placed in. This will be somewhat repetitive, but is needed in order for us to complete our footer. We will start by navigating to the **Block layout** page at /admin/structure/block and following these steps.

Newsletter block:

1. Click on the **Place block** button in the **Footer first** region.
2. Click on the **Add custom block** button.
3. Enter a **Block description** of Newsletter.
4. Select **HTML No Editor** from the **Text format** dropdown.
5. Add the markup located in the Chatper06/start/content/ Newsletter.txt file to the **Body** field.
6. Click on the **Save** button to proceed to the **Configure block** screen.
7. Choose **Footer first** from the **Region** field.
8. Click on the **Save block** button.

About Us block:

1. Click on the **Place block** button in the **Footer second** region.
2. Click on the **Add custom block** button.
3. Enter a **Block description** of About Us.
4. Select **HTML No Editor** from the **Text format** dropdown.
5. Add the markup located in the Chatper06/start/content/AboutUs.txt file to the **Body** field.
6. Click on the **Save** button to proceed to the **Configure block** screen.

7. Choose **Footer second** from the **Region** field.

8. Click on the **Save block** button.

Footer Contact block:

1. Click on the **Place block** button in the **Footer third** region.

2. Click on the **Add custom block** button.

3. Enter a **Block description** of Footer Contact.

4. Select **HTML No Editor** from the **Text format** dropdown.

5. Add the markup located in the `Chatper06/start/content/FooterContact.txt` file to the **Body** field.

6. Click on the **Save** button to proceed to the **Configure block** screen.

7. Enter a title of Contact Us in the **Title** field.

8. Choose **Footer third** from the **Region** field.

9. Click on the **Save block** button.

Copyright block:

1. Click on the **Place block** button in the **Footer Bottom Left** region.

2. Click on the **Add custom block** button.

3. Enter a **Block description** of copyright.

4. Select **HTML No Editor** from the **Text format** dropdown.

5. Add the markup located in the `Chatper06/start/content/Copyright.txt` file to the **Body** field.

6. Click on the **Save** button to proceed to the **Configure block** screen.

7. Uncheck the **Display title** checkbox.

8. Choose **Footer Bottom Left** from the **Region** field.

9. Click on the **Save block** button.

Social Icons block:

1. Click on the **Place block** button in the **Footer Bottom Right** region.

2. Click on the **Place block** button next to the Social Icons block. We don't need to recreate this block since blocks are now reusable.

3. Uncheck the **Display title** checkbox.

4. **Footer Bottom Right** should already be selected for us from the **Region** field.

5. Click on the **Save block** button.

We have successfully added all five blocks and assigned them to their respective regions. Now we just need to refactor the markup for each region, and we should be all set.

Refactoring our main footer

We will be refactoring the markup for each section of our main footer by replacing the static markup with the Twig variable for each region. We should be comfortable with this process by now, so let's start.

Begin by opening `page--front.html.twig` and locating the `main-footer` section of our markup. Within the main footer, we will see individual sections of content for each of the blocks we just created.

Footer first

Locate the following markup and replace the content between with the Twig variable that represents the page region.

Current markup

```
<div class="col-md-4">
    ... content ...
</div>
```

New markup

```
<div class="col-md-4">
  {{ page.footer_first }}
</div>
```

Footer second

Locate the following markup and replace the content between with the Twig variable that represents the page region.

Current markup

```
<div class="col-md-4">
    ... content ...
</div>
```

New markup

```
<div class="col-md-4">
  {{ page.footer_second }}
</div>
```

Footer third

Locate the following markup and replace the content between with the Twig variable that represents the page region.

Current markup

```
<div class="col-md-4">
    ... content ...
</div>
```

New markup

```
<div class="col-md-4">
  {{ page.footer_third }}
</div>
```

With our markup now refactored, if we look at the `main-footer` section of our homepage, the complete markup should look like the following:

```
<div class="container main-footer">
  <div class="row">
    <div class="col-md-4">
      {{ page.footer_first }}
    </div>

    <div class="col-md-4">
      {{ page.footer_second }}
    </div>

    <div class="col-md-4">
      {{ page.footer_third }}
    </div>

  </div>
</div>
```

Make sure to save our changes and then clear Drupal's cache. If we browse our homepage, we should see our static content has been replaced with the three custom blocks.

Now, let's refactor the two remaining blocks of content by locating the `footer-copyright` section of our markup. Within the footer copyright, we will see individual sections of content for the two blocks we just created.

Footer bottom left

Locate the following markup and replace the content between with the Twig variable that represents the page region.

Current markup

```
<div class="col-md-8">
    ... content ...
</div>
```

New markup

```
<div class="col-md-8">
  {{ page.footer_bottom_left }}
</div>
```

Footer bottom right

Locate the following markup and replace the content between with the Twig variable that represents the page region.

Current markup

```
<div class="col-md-4">
    ... content ...
</div>
```

New markup

```
<div class="col-md-4">
  {{ page.footer_bottom_right }}
</div>
```

With our markup now refactored, if we look at the `footer-copyright` section of our homepage, the complete markup should look like the following:

```
<div class="footer-copyright">
  <div class="container">
    <div class="row">
      <div class="col-md-8">
        {{ page.footer_bottom_left }}
      </div>
      <div class="col-md-4">
        {{ page.footer_bottom_right }}
      </div>
    </div>
  </div>
</div>
```

Make sure to save our changes and then clear Drupal's cache. If we browse our homepage, we should see our static content has been replaced with the two custom blocks. Our footer is complete, and should look like the following image:

Summary

When we first started our homepage, it seemed to be a daunting task filled with deciding how we should convert our mockup into a dynamic rendition of blocks, regions, Twig templates, and variables. We learned through repetition that such a daunting task is actually not that complicated after all. In this chapter, we accomplished the following:

- We worked with site branding by adding our logo, creating Twig templates for blocks, and refactoring markup.
- We learned best practices to add assets with libraries, custom scripts, and scripts to our website and individual pages.
- We discovered how to develop the aggregated content using Views, create Block layouts from Views, and format the output of Views content for use with JavaScript libraries.

In the next chapter, we will continue our theming by taking a look at creating an interior page template, carrying over any global regions such as our Header and Footer, and will continue working with various Twig templates.

7

Theming Our Interior Page

One of the great features of Drupal 8 is the new Twig templating engine. Simply by using the recommended file name suggestions, we saw how easy it was to theme our homepage by creating a `page--front.html.twig` template. However, we are not able to use this same template for our interior pages as Drupal only renders our homepage template on the front page of our website.

Instead, we will need to create a new Twig template that all of our interior pages can use when a user is navigating our website. By default, Drupal outputs content using the `page.html.twig` template. In this chapter, we will look at using the `page.html.twig` template, along with discussing strategies to address the following:

- We will begin with reviewing the About Us page mockup and identify any additional components that may require custom blocks, new regions, and Twig templates.

- Then, we will take a look at reusing regions such as our header and footer as they are considered global components that will be needed across all of our interior pages.

- Drupal 8 has moved the page title into a new Page title block. We will take a closer look at how we can use this block to recreate our Title Bar region.

- Using regions to control page flow is important in order to manage the content, and in Drupal we will look at printing out different regions while outputting any block content that has been assigned to them.

- Sometimes, we have the need to manipulate our main content's markup to add additional styling. You will learn how to not only print the content region but also take advantage of Node templates.

- Finally, Views play such an integrated part of any theme, so we will take another look at Drupal Views to display the content. You will learn how to use Twig variables to override fields as well as display the content by creating block displays.

Although we will work through each section, we can refer back to the `Chapter07` exercise files folder. Each folder contains a `start` folder and an `end` folder with files that we can use to compare our work when needed. This also includes database snapshots that will allow us all to start from the same point when working through various lessons.

Reviewing the About Us mockup

In order for us to identify page elements, we will be recreating them for the About Us page and need to take a closer look at our mockup. The About Us page can be found in the `Mockup` folder located in our exercise files. Begin by opening up the `about-us.html` file within the browser, as shown in the following image:

There are several page elements that we will need to recreate, and we can identify the following:

1. First is the header, which we created previously on our homepage. We will need to add this region to our interior pages as well to ensure that our users can navigate from page to page and use the global search functionality.

2. Second is the page title, which spans across the top of all our interior pages. This is a common element in Drupal that helps the user to identify which page they are currently on.

3. Third is the main content region. Any nodes or custom blocks can output content in this region. We will need to make sure that we account for the content assigned to this region and manage how it flows within our page.

As we continue to scroll down the page, we come across additional content, as shown in the following image:

4. The Team Member listing represents the content that is repeated, and anytime we see repeating content, we should consider building this using Drupal 8 views. This view will be specific to our About Us page, so we will look at creating a view block for this section and control the visibility accordingly.

5. Finally, we will need to include our page footer. Once again, we already created this region on our homepage, so we will need to make sure that we include it within our interior page template as well.

We identified five specific page sections that need to be developed and themed. Most of the sections are global to all pages, with the exception of our team member listing. Now that we have a plan for what we will be developing, let's get started by creating our interior page template.

Creating our interior page template

Drupal provides us with multiple ways to address templating a specific page. As we saw when we created our homepage, we can take advantage of Twig debugging to identify which templates are being output. The same is true for our interior pages. If we navigate to the About Us page and inspect the markup we can identify that Drupal is using the default `page.html.twig` template, as shown in the following image:

```
<!-- THEME DEBUG -->
<!-- THEME HOOK: 'page' -->
<!-- FILE NAME SUGGESTIONS:
   * page--node--2.html.twig
   * page--node--%.html.twig
   * page--node.html.twig
   x page.html.twig
-->
<!-- BEGIN OUTPUT from 'core/modules/system/templates/page.html.twig' -->
▶ <div class="layout-container">…</div>
<!-- END OUTPUT from 'core/modules/system/templates/page.html.twig' -->
```

This template is clearly different than the `page--front.html.twig` template we created earlier, which explains why some of our page elements are missing. However, this is a good example of how we can use different Twig templates to control the markup.

Begin by following these steps:

1. Navigate to the `core/modules/system/templates` folder and copy `page.html.twig`.

2. Place the copy within our `themes/octo/templates` folder.

Make sure to clear Drupal's cache and refresh the About Us page. If we inspect the page again, we will note that our new template is being used. We can now begin to modify the markup safely.

Adding our Global Header

Our website has several global components that were present on our home page that don't currently exist on our interior pages. One such item is the Global Header, which consists of the Utility menu, Logo, Main menu, and Search form block.

To add this section to our template, all we need to do is simply copy the `header` markup from the `page--front.html.twig` template.

1. Open `page.html.twig` and delete the entire contents.

2. Open `page--front.html.twig` and copy the following markup:

    ```
    <header class="header" role="banner">
      <div class="header-top">
        <div class="container">
          {{ page.header_top }}
        </div>
      </div>

      <div class="header-nav container">
        {{ page.header}}
        {{ page.primary_menu }}
      </div>
    </header>
    ```

3. Paste the markup into `page.html.twig`.

> One more very important item to keep in mind is that we will need to also add the page content region to our template. Failure to add the `{{ page.content }}` region will result in not being able to log in to the Drupal Admin or see any content that Drupal assigns to this region.

4. Add the following Twig variable to the bottom of our template:

    ```
    {{ page.content }}
    ```

5. Save `page.html.twig`.

Make sure to clear Drupal's cache and refresh the About Us page within our browser. Our header is now in place and functioning as we would expect.

Implementing our page title

Every content type we develop in Drupal includes a title field, which is used to identify the node currently being displayed. In Drupal 8, the title field warrants its own block called Page title. This new block provides us with the flexibility to place the page title into any region and have it display wherever it is needed in our layout.

In order for us to implement the page title displayed within our mockup, we will need to complete a series of steps:

1. First, we will copy the static markup from our mockup into our interior page template and preview the results.

2. Second, we will configure our theme to add a new Title Bar region that we can use to assign content to.

3. Next, we will need to assign the Page title block to our new region and then output it within our `page.html.twig` template.

4. Finally, we will refactor the static Page title markup using Twig to create a new block template.

Working with static HTML

When implementing any section of content within our theme, this will often begin with copying static HTML. Having actual working HTML within our template file ensures that our content displays the way we are expecting. The other advantage of copying static HTML into our template is that it allows us to easily replace the markup with dynamic content. Let's begin by following these steps:

1. Open `page.html.twig`.

2. Navigate to `Mockup/about-us.html` and copy the following markup. Don't forget to include the opening and closing main layout section, as shown here:

    ```html
    <main role="main" class="main">

        <section class="page-top">
          <div class="container">
            <h1>About Us</h1>
          </div>
        </section>

      </main>
    ```

3. Paste the markup into the `page.html.twig` template.

4. Save `page.html.twig`.

Make sure to clear Drupal's cache and refresh the About Us page within our browser. We should now see the static page title being displayed.

We may also note the Page title block being displayed below our static title. By default, Drupal assigns the Page title block to the Content region. In order for us to replace our static title with Drupal's Page title block, we will need to add a new region.

Adding new regions

When we first created our theme, we added regions for Drupal to use when assigning blocks of content. While we may have thought we accounted for all the regions our theme would need, we neglected to add one for our page title.

We can add new regions to our theme at any time by modifying our configuration file. In order to add a new Title Bar region, we will need to navigate to our themes/ octo folder and follow these steps:

1. Open the octo.info.yml file.

2. Add the following to our regions section:

   ```
   title_bar: 'Title Bar'
   ```

3. Save octo.info.yml.

Make sure to clear Drupal's cache and then navigate to the Block layout page located at /admin/structure/block. We should now see that the new region has been added.

Reassigning the Page title block

With our new region added, we can focus on reassigning the Page title block by following these steps:

1. Locate the **Page title** block in the **Content** region.
2. Select **Title Bar** from the **Region** dropdown.
3. Click on the **Save blocks** button.

If for any reason the Page title block is missing from the Block layout screen, we can add it by using the **Place block** button next to the region we want to place it in. Now we need to print our new region so that we can view the Page title block within our template.

Printing the Title Bar region

In order for our `page.html.twig` template to display the Page title block, we need to print the Title Bar region. The Twig variable that represents the region's name can always be found by looking in our themes `octo.info.yml` file.

1. Open `page.html.twig`.
2. Add the Twig variable `{{ page.title_bar }}` directly below the `main` element so that our markup looks like the following:

   ```
   <main role="main" class="main">
     {{ page.title_bar}}
   ```

3. Save `page.html.twig`.

Make sure to clear Drupal's cache and then refresh the browser. Our About Us page is now displaying two page titles—one dynamic and one static, as shown in the following image:

We can fix the duplicated page titles by moving our static markup into the Page title block template that Drupal is outputting. This will give us the freedom to then remove the static markup completely from our `page.html.twig` template while maintaining the styling that is currently being displayed.

Creating a block template

If we inspect the page title on the About Us page, we will see that Drupal is using the default `block.html.twig` template. We can take advantage of FILE NAME SUGGESTIONS to create our own block template specific to the Page title and then refactor the markup into it by following these steps:

1. Navigate to `core/modules/block/templates` and copy the `block.html.twig` template to our `themes/octo/templates` folder.

2. Rename `block.html.twig` to `block--page-title-block.html.twig`.

3. Replace the content with the following markup:

```
<section class="page-top">
  <div class="container">
    {{ content }}
  </div>
</section>
```

4. Save `block--page-title-block.html.twig`.

5. Open `page.html.twig`.

6. Delete the `page-top` section.

7. Save both templates.

Make sure to clear Drupal's cache and then refresh the browser. As we navigate from page to page, we should see a single page title being displayed and updating to display the current page's title. Time to move on to our main content section.

Implementing our main page structure

Our main page structure can be considered anything below the global header and page title and anything above the global footer. In our case, the main page structure for our About Us page consists of three regions—Before Content, Content, and After Content. Currently, we are already printing the main content region, but we have yet to add our structural layout or the other two regions.

Begin by opening `page.html.twig`, located in our `themes/octo` folder, and replace the following markup section with the new markup.

Current markup

```
<main role="main" class="main">
  {{ page.title_bar }}
</main>

{{ page.content }}
```

New markup

```
<main role="main" class="main">
  {{ page.title_bar }}
  {{ page.before_content }}
  <div id="content" class="content full">
    <div class="container">
      <div class="row">
        <div class="col-md-12">
          {{ page.content }}
        </div>
      </div>
    </div>
  </div>
  {{ page.after_content }}
</main>
```

Make sure to save our changes and then clear Drupal's cache to ensure the theme registry has picked up our new layout.

While reviewing the markup earlier, we are adding the Before Content region followed by the structural markup for our main content and then our After Content region. These two new regions will allow our layout to be flexible enough to add block content above and below our main content area. We will be using both these regions as we continue to implement our theme.

In the meantime, let's preview our About Us page in the browser and compare it to our mockup. We want to make sure that we haven't lost any styling during our refactoring of markup.

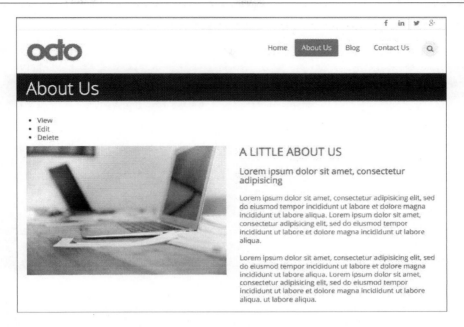

In comparing our About Us page side by side with the mockup, we will note that our h3 and h4 elements are missing some CSS. Upon closer inspection, our design is expecting our Landing page content type to include a CSS class of landing. Including this CSS class would ensure that our h3 has the adequate bottom margin and our h4 would be colored gray and include the bottom border separating the Headings from the content.

So how would we go about adding a CSS class to our About Us page? Actually, we can create a Twig template for any specific node or content type using the same methods we have for any other page.

Creating a Node template

If we inspect the About Us page, we can determine exactly what Twig template we should use. By default, Drupal will use the `node.html.twig` template. However, we can create our own copy of the template based on the multiple file name suggestions. This will result in all of our Landing Page content types using this new template:

```
<!-- THEME DEBUG -->
<!-- THEME HOOK: 'node' -->
<!-- FILE NAME SUGGESTIONS:
   * node--2--full.html.twig
   * node--2.html.twig
   * node--landing-page--full.html.twig
   * node--landing-page.html.twig
   * node--full.html.twig
   x node.html.twig
-->
<!-- BEGIN OUTPUT from 'core/modules/node/templates/node.html.twig' -->
<article data-history-node-id="2" data-quickedit-entity-id="node/2" role="article" class="contextual-region"
```

Begin by navigating to the `core/modules/node/templates` folder and following these steps:

1. Copy the `node.html.twig` template to our `themes/octo/templates` folder.

2. Rename `node.html.twig` to `node--landing-page.html.twig`.

3. Replace the content with the following markup:

   ```twig
   {% set classes = ['landing'] %}

   <article{{ attributes.addClass(classes) }}>
       <div{{ content_attributes }}>
       {{ content }}
     </div>
   </article>
   ```

4. Save `node--landing-page.html.twig`.

In the earlier-mentioned markup, we are adding the minimal structure that our landing page content type needs to output any fields that have been enabled. We also take advantage of Twig to create a variable named classes that allows us to add CSS class names to any existing classes that Drupal may be adding using the `attributes.addClass()` function. This is a simple technique, but one that will be used often to add CSS classes to our markup.

Make sure to clear Drupal's cache and then refresh the browser. If we take a look at the About Us page again, we will see that our H3 and H4 headings are styled to match our mockup.

Implementing our Team members section

The next area of our About Us page we will need to create is the display of our Team members listing. We will be taking an existing Drupal content type named Team and using Views to display the four team members.

In order for us to implement the Team members section, we will need to complete a series of steps as follows:

1. First, we will review the structural markup for our team members section in preparation for creating a new Drupal View.

2. Next, we will look at various methods to theme View content as we complete our Team Members display.

3. Finally, we will assign our custom View block to a new region and limit the page visibility to our About Us page.

Prepping our Team Member View

The Views module provides multiple ways of creating block displays, whether we are simply outputting the fields of a content type as an unordered list or relying on rendering a specific content type directly. In any case, it is best to start off by breaking down how the Team Members block is structured within our mockup and then creating our view based on those needs.

Let's start by reviewing the visual display and then break down the structural markup. Navigate to the exercise files and open up the `about-us.html` file found in the Mockup folder as shown here:

Visually, we can determine that our view will require the following content:

- Header
- Subheader
- Four-column layout, with each column representing a team member

However, if we inspect the markup of an individual Team member, we will get a better idea of what fields a team member will need to display.

Markup

```
<div class="col-md-3 col-sm-6 views-row">

    <div class="img-round img-grayscale-hover">
      <a href="#" class="img-link">
        <span class="img-border">
          <img src="img/team-one.jpg" width="250" height="250"
            alt="Stephen Maturin">
        </span>
      </a>
    </div>

    <h6><span>Stephen Maturin</span></h6>

    <p>Technical Architect</p>

    <a class="button--icon" href="https://www.facebook.com/
    PacktPub"><i class="fa fa-facebook"></i></a>

    <a class="button--icon" href="https://twitter.com/
    packtpub"><i class="fa fa-twitter"></i></a>

    <a class="button--icon" href="https://plus.google.com/
    +packtpublishing/posts"><i class="fa fa-google-plus"></i></a>

</div>
```

Based on the markup mentioned earlier, each team member content type will need to display the following fields:

- Team Photo
- Title
- Position
- Social icons

Now that we have identified both our visual and structural markup and fields, we can begin creating our new Team Member view.

Creating our Team Member View

To get started, we will need to navigate to /admin/structure/views and click on the **Add new view** button. From the **Views** Admin screen, we will add the following information:

- **VIEW BASIC INFORMATION**:
    1. **View name:** Team Members
    2. Check the **Description** box
    3. **Description:** A listing of Team Members
- **VIEW SETTINGS: Show: Content of type: Team sorted by: Newest first**

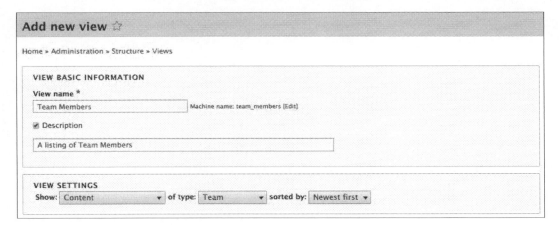

- **BLOCK SETTINGS**:
    1. Check the **Create a block** checkbox.
    2. **Block title:** Team Members Listing

- **BLOCK DISPLAY SETTINGS**:
    1. **Display format: Unformatted list of: fields**.
    2. **Items per block**: 4.
    3. Click on the **Save and edit** button.

Now that our Team Member view has been created, we will need to add additional fields and adjust the format settings before we can use our new block. With the view still open we will need to add the following fields:

1. Click on the **Add** button next to the **FIELDS** section.
2. Enter the term photo in the **Search** field to filter our choices.
3. Click on the **Team Photo** checkbox.
4. Click on the **Apply (all displays)** button.

Next, we will need to configure the Team Photo field.

1. Click on the **STYLE SETTINGS** section link.

2. Uncheck the **Add default classes** checkbox.

3. Click on the **Apply (all displays)** button.

With our Team Photo field added, we will need to repeat the steps mentioned earlier to add the remaining fields.

Job Position

1. Click on the **Add** button next to the **FIELDS** section.
2. Enter the term Job Position in the **Search** field to filter our choices.
3. Click on the **Job Position** checkbox.
4. Click on the **Apply (all displays)** button.
5. Click on the **STYLE SETTINGS** section link.
6. Uncheck the **Add default classes** checkbox.
7. Click the **Apply (all displays)** button.

Facebook link

1. Click on the **Add** button next to the **FIELDS** section.
2. Enter the term Facebook link in the **Search** field to filter our choices.
3. Click on the **Facebook link** checkbox.
4. Click on the **Apply (all displays)** button.
5. Click on the **STYLE SETTINGS** section link.
6. Uncheck the **Add default classes** checkbox.
7. Click on the **Apply (all displays)** button.

Twitter link

1. Click on the **Add** button next to the **FIELDS** section.
2. Enter the term Twitter link in the **Search** field to filter our choices.
3. Click on the **Twitter link** checkbox.
4. Click on the **Apply (all displays)** button.
5. Click on the **STYLE SETTINGS** section link.
6. Uncheck the **Add default classes** checkbox.
7. Click on the **Apply (all displays)** button.

Google Plus link

1. Click on the **Add** button next to the **FIELDS** section.

2. Enter the term `Google Plus link` in the **Search** field to filter our choices.

3. Click on the **Google Plus link** checkbox.

4. Click on the **Apply (all displays)** button.

5. Click on the **STYLE SETTINGS** section link.

6. Uncheck the **Add default classes** checkbox.

7. Click on the **Apply (all displays)** button.

With all of our fields now added to our view, we can click on the **Save** button to make sure that we don't lose any of our work. Our fields should now look like the following image:

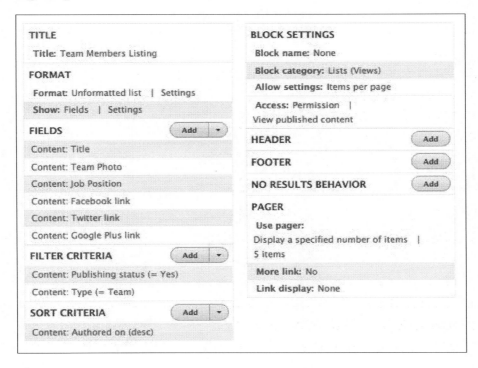

We will be modifying our view quite frequently as we begin theming it, but in the meantime, let's assign our new block to the After Content region we created earlier. This will give us a better idea of what it currently looks like before proceeding.

Managing our Team Members listing block

Any time we create a new block display using views, we can easily assign it to any region from the Block layout page. Begin by navigating to /admin/structure/ block and follow these nine steps:

1. Locate the **After Content** region.
2. Click on the **Place block** button.
3. Locate the **Team Members** block.
4. Click on the **Place block** button.
5. Uncheck the **Display title** checkbox.
6. Select the **Pages** tab under **Visibility**.
7. Enter the path /about into the **Page** text field.
8. Make sure that the **Show for the listed pages** checkbox is selected.
9. Click on the **Save block** button.

With our Team Members block assigned to the After Content region, we can now navigate back to the About Us page and preview the display:

User Experience
Facebook
Twitter
Google Plus

We clearly have to do something to match our Team Members block to our mockup. If we compare the mockup to our About Us page, we can see that it doesn't yet match. We can address this, starting with adding some CSS directly to our View.

Formatting Views with CSS

The first noticeable thing is that our four team members are stacked on the page vertically versus displaying nicely in four columns across the page. In order to resolve this, we need to simply add the Twitter Bootstrap column classes to our view's rows. We can achieve this by navigating to `/admin/structure/views/view/team_members` and following these four steps:

1. Click on the **Settings** link next to **Unformatted list** within the **FORMAT** section.

2. From the **Block: Style options** dialog, select the **Row class** text field and enter a value of col-md-3 col-sm-6.

3. Click on the **Apply** button.

4. Click on the **Save** button.

Navigate back to the About Us page, and our Team Members block should be displaying in their proper columns, as shown in the following image:

If we inspect the Team Members block, we can see that our view rows are now outputting the CSS class we added:

```
<!-- THEME DEBUG -->
<!-- THEME HOOK: 'views_view_unformatted' -->
<!-- BEGIN OUTPUT from 'core/modules/views/templates/views-view-unformatted.html.twig' -->
<div class="col-md-3 col-sm-6 views-row">…</div>
<div class="col-md-3 col-sm-6 views-row">…</div>
<div class="col-md-3 col-sm-6 views-row">…</div>
<div class="col-md-3 col-sm-6 views-row">…</div>
<!-- END OUTPUT from 'core/modules/views/templates/views-view-unformatted.html.twig' -->
```

So far so good, but we still need to clean up how the Team Members block and fields are being output. Fortunately, we can add CSS classes to our overall view as well as rewrite the fields output to better match our mockup.

Adding CSS classes to Views

So far we have been working with the basic settings of a View. We can actually achieve more complex settings, such as contextual filters, relationships, and other miscellaneous settings within the Views UI. In the case of our Team Members view, we need to globally add a single CSS class name. While you may think we would need to create a Twig template to achieve this, we can actually add a CSS class from the admin by navigating to /admin/structure/views/view/team_members and following these steps:

1. Click on the **ADVANCED** field set to expand the options within it.
2. Locate the **OTHER** section.
3. Click on the **None** link next to **CSS class:**.
4. Enter a value of team into the **CSS class name(s)** text field.
5. Click on the **Apply (all displays)** button.
6. Click on the **Save** button.

If we navigate back to the About Us page and inspect the Team Members block, we will see that our view now has the new class added to it.

```
<!-- THEME DEBUG -->
<!-- THEME HOOK: 'views_view' -->
<!-- BEGIN OUTPUT from 'core/modules/views/templates/views-view.html.twig' -->
<div class="team contextual-region js-view-dom-id-8206c0105827ad9ce1d4dd058e8e8c7550896824e2b22cac452a4d
<!-- END OUTPUT from 'core/modules/views/templates/views-view.html.twig' -->
```

Using Twig variables to rewrite field content

Another feature widely used when theming Views is the ability to rewrite field content. Every field we add to a view can be rewritten to easily modify the markup, and with Twig now part of Drupal 8 we can use this syntax to achieve the markup that our view needs.

One important item to remember when using this technique is that by default Drupal will provide field wrapper elements to each field. This unfortunately adds additional and unneeded div elements around every field. We will want to turn this setting off by navigating to /admin/structure/views/view/team_members and completing the following:

1. Locate the **FORMAT** section.
2. Click on the **Settings** link next to **Show: Fields**.
3. Uncheck the **Provide default field wrapper elements** checkbox.
4. Click on the **Apply** button.

Now that we have turned off the default field wrapper elements, we can proceed to rewriting each field starting with Team Photo.

Content: Team Photo

1. Click on the **Content: Team Photo** link under the **FIELDS** section.

2. Choose the **Team (250x250)** image style from the **Image style** dropdown.

3. Expand the **REWRITE RESULTS** section.

4. Check the **Override the output of this field with custom text** checkbox.

5. Expand the **REPLACEMENT PATTERNS** section to view the replacement patterns we can use to rewrite our markup.

6. Enter the following markup in the **Text** field:

    ```
    <div class="img-round img-grayscale-hover">
      <a href="#" class="img-link">
        <span class="img-border">
          {{ field_team_photo }}
        </span>
      </a>
    </div>
    ```

7. Click on the **Apply (all displays)** button to complete the field rewrite.

8. Click on the **Save** button to save our view.

To validate that our field has been rewritten, navigate back to the About Us page and our Team Members' photographs should now be displaying, as shown in the following image:

If we inspect the markup of the page, we can see how simple rewriting the field output of views can be. Let's finish rewriting our fields by navigating to /admin/ structure/views/view/team_members and following these remaining steps.

Content: Title field

1. Click on the **Content: Title** link under the **FIELDS** section.

2. Uncheck the **Link to the Content** checkbox.

3. Expand the **REWRITE RESULTS** section.

4. Check the **Override the output of this field with custom text** checkbox.

5. Expand the **REPLACEMENT PATTERNS** section to view the replacement patterns we can use to rewrite our markup.

6. Enter the following markup in the **Text** field:
   ```
   <h6><span>{{ title }}</span></h6>
   ```

7. Click on the **Apply (all displays)** button.

8. Click on the **Save** button to save our view.

Content: Job Position field

1. Click on the **Content: Job Position** link under the **FIELDS** section.

2. Expand the **REWRITE RESULTS** section.

3. Check the **Override the output of this field with custom text** checkbox.

4. Expand the **REPLACEMENT PATTERNS** section to view the replacement patterns we can use to rewrite our markup.

5. Enter the following markup in the **Text** field:
   ```
   <p>{{ field_job_position }}</p>
   ```

6. Click on the **Apply (all displays)** button.

7. Click on the **Save** button to save our view.

Content: Facebook link field

1. Click on the **Content: Facebook link** link under the **FIELDS** section.

2. Expand the **REWRITE RESULTS** section.

3. Check the **Override the output of this field with custom text** checkbox.

4. Expand the **REPLACEMENT PATTERNS** section to view the replacement patterns we can use to rewrite our markup.

5. Enter the following markup in the **Text** field:

```
<a class="button--icon"
  href="{{ field_facebook_link__uri }}">
  <i class="fa fa-facebook"></i></a>
```

6. Click on the **Apply (all displays)** button to complete the field rewrite.
7. Click on the **Save** button to save our view.

Content: Twitter link field

1. Click on the **Content: Twitter link** link under the **FIELDS** section.
2. Expand the **REWRITE RESULTS** section.
3. Check the **Override the output of this field with custom text** checkbox.
4. Expand the **REPLACEMENT PATTERNS** section to view the replacement patterns we can use to rewrite our markup.
5. Enter the following markup in the **Text** field:

```
<a class="button--icon"
  href="{{ field_twitter_link__uri }}">
  <i class="fa fa-twitter"></i></a>
```

6. Click on the **Apply (all displays)** button.
7. Click on the **Save** button to save our view.

Content: Google Plus link field

1. Click on the **Content: Google Plus link** link under the **FIELDS** section.
2. Expand the **REWRITE RESULTS** section.
3. Check the **Override the output of this field with custom text** checkbox.
4. Expand the **REPLACEMENT PATTERNS** section to view the replacement patterns we can use to rewrite our markup.
5. Enter the following markup in the **Text** field:

```
<a class="button--icon"
href="{{ field_google_plus_link__uri }}">
<i class="fa fa-google-plus"></i></a>
```

6. Click on the **Apply (all displays)** button.
7. Click on the **Save** button to save our view.

With the remaining fields rewritten using the proper Twig replacement patterns, we can navigate back to our About Us page and review the results, as shown in the following image:

Our Team Members block is coming together nicely. We do have one field that is out of order and that is our team members' names. Currently, they are appearing above our images, and we need to fix that by rearranging our View's fields.

Rearranging View fields

When we work with Views, we will often need to modify the fields that we have added, including rearranging them so that they display properly to match our design. We can easily accomplish this using the Views UI by navigating to `/admin/structure/views/view/team_members` and following these steps:

1. Click on the dropdown button next to the **FIELDS** section.
2. Choose **Rearrange** from the list.
3. Drag the **Content: Title** field below the **Content: Team Photo** field using the drag icons.
4. Click on the **Apply (all displays)** button.
5. Click on the **Save** button to save our view.

Now that we have our fields rearranged properly, we still need to add the header and subheader so that they appear above our block. Because we need the headings to be part of our view block, we can take a look at using the View header to add the markup and content required to match our mockup.

Adding a View header

Our best option to add this markup is to use the View header, which can be done by navigating to `/admin/structure/views/view/team_members` and following these steps:

1. Click on the **Add** button within the **HEADER** section of our views **BLOCK SETTINGS**.

2. Choose **Text area** from the **Add header** window, this will allow us to provide markup text for the area.

3. Click on the **Apply (all displays)** button.

4. Choose **Full HTML** from the **Text format** dropdown.

5. Enter the following markup in the **Content** field:

    ```
    <div class="view-header">
      <h2 class="block-title">Meet our awesome team</h2>
      <hr>
      <p class="block-subtitle">We bring you an awesomeness of
      design, creative skills, thoughts, and ideas.</p>
    </div>
    ```

6. Click on the **Apply** button.

7. Click on the **Save** button to save our view.

If we view our About Us page, we see that our header and tagline are now being displayed. We are almost finished with this section.

The only visual element still missing is the gray background that helps separate our Team Members block from the rest of our content. Also, if we were to resize the page and check for any responsive qualities, we would note that something is just not quite right. In fact, upon further investigation, our After Content region does not include the `container` class that enables Twitter Bootstrap to apply its media queries properly.

Refactoring the After Content region

Adding markup to any regions requires us to either create or modify an existing Twig template. As we have seen before, all we need to do is inspect our page markup to determine where the template resides and what file name suggestion we should use:

```
<!-- THEME DEBUG -->
<!-- THEME HOOK: 'region' -->
<!-- FILE NAME SUGGESTIONS:
   * region--after-content.html.twig
   x region.html.twig
-->
<!-- BEGIN OUTPUT from 'core/modules/system/templates/region.html.twig' -->
▶<div>…</div>
<!-- END OUTPUT from 'core/modules/system/templates/region.html.twig' -->
```

Begin by following these steps:

1. Navigate to `core/modules/system/templates` and copy the `region.html.twig` template to our `themes/octo/templates` folder.

2. Rename `region.html.twig` to `region--after-content.html.twig`.

3. Replace the content with the following markup:

```
{% set classes = ['region','region-' ~ region|clean_class,] %}

{% if content %}
  <div{{ attributes.addClass(classes) }}>
    <div class="container">
      {{ content }}
    </div>
  </div>
{% endif %}
```

4. Save `region--after-content.html.twig`.

Make sure you clear Drupal's cache and then refresh the browser. If we preview the About Us page, we will now see our completed Team Members section. By using Twig to create a template for our After Content region, we enabled the markup to be responsive with the `container` class as well as using the `classes` variable to display the name of the region for our global styling to take effect.

In order for us to complete the interior page structure, we need to add back our global footer. Let's take a look at doing that now.

Adding our global footer

Our website has several global components that were present on our homepage that don't currently exist on our interior pages. One such item is the global header, which consists of the utility menu, logo, main menu, and search form block.

To add this section to our template, we need to simply copy the `footer` markup from the `page--front.html.twig` template:

1. Open `page.html.twig` and delete the entire contents.

2. Open `page--front.html.twig` and copy the following markup:

```
<footer id="footer" role="contentinfo">

    <div class="container main-footer">
        <div class="row">
          <div class="col-md-4">
            {{ page.footer_first }}
          </div>

          <div class="col-md-4">
            {{ page.footer_second }}
          </div>

          <div class="col-md-4">
            {{ page.footer_third }}
          </div>

        </div>
          </div>

    <div class="footer-copyright">
      <div class="container">
        <div class="row">
```

```
        <div class="col-md-8">
            {{ page.footer_bottom_left }}
        </div>

        <div class="col-md-4">
            {{ page.footer_bottom_right }}
        </div>

      </div>
    </div>
  </div>

</footer>
```

3. Paste the markup into `page.html.twig`.

4. Save `page.html.twig`.

Make sure you clear Drupal's cache and refresh the About Us page within your browser. Our footer is now in place, and it is functioning as we would expect.

We have successfully completed theming our About Us page and in the process created our interior page template. The remaining pages we will be creating can take advantage of our new `page.html.twig` template, but before we wrap up this lesson I want to address one more item.

Fixing JavaScript errors

When we created our homepage, we attached a couple of JavaScript libraries directly to our `page--front.html.twig` template. However, since we are loading our theme's custom scripts file globally, this can sometimes create unnecessary JavaScript errors.

If we inspect our About Us page, we will see one such error caused by our script trying to configure the FlexSlider library, which only exists on our homepage.

```
  ⚙ ▼ Uncaught TypeError: $(...).flexslider is not a function                  octo.js?v=8.0.2:49
      (anonymous function) @ octo.js?v=8.0.2:49
      (anonymous function) @ octo.js?v=8.0.2:56
      j                     @ jquery.js:3099
      k.fireWith            @ jquery.js:3211
      n.extend.ready        @ jquery.js:3417
      I                     @ jquery.js:3433
```

While we are not covering the fundamentals of JavaScript and how to write proper syntax, it is important to point out this issue. This can be a common error when using JavaScript with the different techniques used to theme Drupal 8. So, let's take a quick look at how to fix this to have this as part of our theming tools moving forward.

Begin by navigating to `themes/octo/js` and opening the `octo.js` file. From here, we can follow these steps to resolve the JavaScript error:

1. Locate the **Flexslider** function call.

2. Wrap the function in a conditional structure that will look to see if the `flexslider` library exists before configuring it. The revised structure should look like the following:

```
//-- Flexslider
  (function() {

    if (typeof $.fn.flexslider === 'function'){

      $('.flexslider').flexslider({
        direction: "vertical",
        controlNav: false,
        directionNav: false
      });

    }

  })();
```

3. Save `octo.js`.

The simple `typeof` operator can be used with any JavaScript library we may be referencing within our theme to ensure that we don't initialize a library unnecessarily. If we clear Drupal's cache and then reload our About Us page, we will no longer have any JavaScript function errors.

Summary

We covered a lot of different techniques while recreating our About Us page. From reviewing the mockup to working with various Twig templates, our theming skills have improved. Let's take a moment to recap what we accomplished in this chapter:

- We began with reviewing our About Us mockup to help identify the different page elements we would need to consider when creating our interior page template.

- Next, we added back any global regions to our template so that users would be able to navigate to the various pages of our website.

- The page title plays a very important part in identifying where a user is within our site, so you learned how to work with the Page title block, create a block template, and refactor markup to match our design.

- Our Team Members section required you to learn different techniques to create and format fields using Drupal's View module. We rewrote fields using Twig, added View headers to create introductory text, and followed up by adding CSS classes to various sections.

- Finally, we looked at a common JavaScript error and how to resolve loading libraries unnecessarily.

In the next chapter, we will continue our theming by taking a look at setting up our Blog Landing page, working with various display modes associated with content types, and using those display modes with Views.

8
Theming Our Blog Listing Page

The blog section of our website will be by far be the most complex to set up, as we will be taking advantage of the Twig template layer to modify the HTML markup from the Node level all the way down to the field level. What does this mean? It simply means we will be breaking our mockup down into small chunks, whether it be the blog teaser, a listing of blog categories, or even the simple blog image itself.

In this chapter, we will look at creating multiple Twig templates that our Blog listing page will use, as well as the following:

- We will begin by reviewing our Blog listing page as displayed in our mockup and identifying the areas we will need to theme.
- Next, we will create our Blog listing page, along with a teaser view of our content that will link to the Blog detail page.
- Our Blog listing also contains three custom blocks of content, which will require us to dive a little deeper into using Drupal views, custom blocks, and Twig templates to create categories, popular blogs, and a recent blogs list.
- We will also take a look at how we can deal with multiple field items to create a slideshow of images that will be used both on our Blog listing and Blog detail pages.
- Finally, we will focus on how to work with comments and the theme layer to display them properly.

While we work through each section, we have the ability to refer back to the Chapter08 exercise files folder. Each folder contains a start and end folder with files that we can use to compare our work when needed. This also includes database snapshots that will allow us all to start from the same point when working through various lessons.

Reviewing the Blog Listing mockup

In order to assist us in identifying page elements that we will be recreating for the blog page, it would make sense to open up our mockup and review the layout and structure. The Blog page can be found in the Mockup folder located in our exercise files. Begin by opening up the blog.html file within the browser, as shown in the following image:

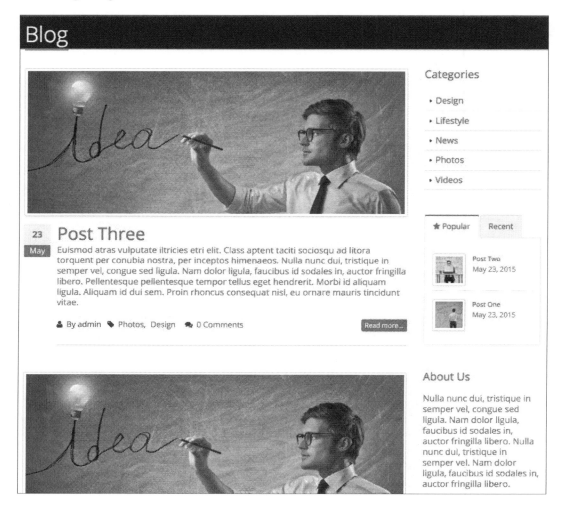

If we look at our mockup and break it down into manageable parts, we will notice several components that we will need to create using our existing post content type:

- The first is the blog teaser in the main content area, which consists of one or more images, post metadata, title, text, and some taxonomy terms that help identify the type of post we are viewing. Since this is repeated content, we will take advantage of Drupal views and custom view modes to recreate this section.

- The second is the **Categories** listing in the right-hand sidebar, which displays the category of posts available on our website. This is a simple HTML list that we can recreate using Drupal views.

- The third is a tabbed component to display **Popular** and **Recent** blog posts. While this looks a little more complex, we will use some advanced Drupal views techniques to recreate it.

- The fourth is a custom block with some **About Us** text and should be simple to develop.

So we have identified four specific page components for our blog listing page. We will concentrate on creating these various items of our site and, once complete, we should be able to compare our blog listing page with our mockup.

Creating our blog listing

Our blog listing is a shortened representation of our Blog detail page, with just enough information to tease our users into reading more. To help us identify what fields we will need to display for our blog listing, we should review each individual post on our mockup. We can visually identify that we will need to display the following fields:

- Image
- Post date
- Title
- Teaser
- Author
- Tags (taxonomy)
- Comments

While all of these fields make up our post content type, there are also additional fields such as Thumbnail and Full content that are not being displayed. So how would we go about presenting the same data to users differently, based on the layout? We could hide fields using CSS, or add PHP conditions, but there is a much easier method for creating different display modes.

Adding a new display mode

One feature of Drupal 8 that provides us with the flexibility to present content differently based on specific requirements is **display modes**. By default, Drupal provides each content type or node with a handful of displays for enabling fields based on a default view or teaser view. We can see a listing of all the current display modes associated with content by navigating to /admin/structure/display-modes/view, as shown in the following image:

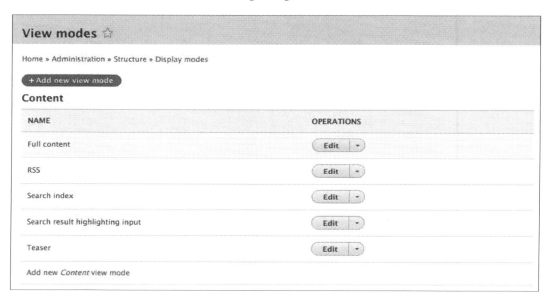

However, we are not limited to just these displays. We can create different displays for both Node forms and Node views. In fact, let's create a new view mode for our blog listing by following these steps:

1. Click on the **Add new Content view mode** link.

2. Enter the value Listing in the **Name** text field.

3. Click on the **Save** button.

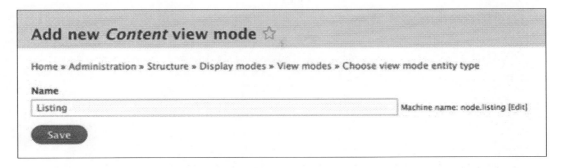

Now that we have created our new View mode, we can use it with any content type that we choose. In the case of our post content type, we will utilize it to manage what fields will be displayed when using the listing display.

Managing the display

The ability to manage a content types display has actually been around since Drupal 6. Once known as build modes, we can now utilize our new display by navigating to `/admin/structure/types/manage/post/display` and enabling the custom display settings as shown:

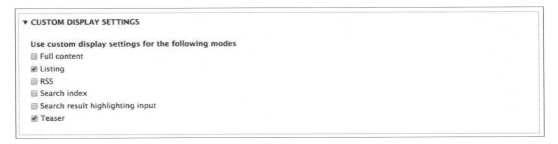

1. Click on the **CUSTOM DISPLAY SETTINGS** fieldset to expand it.
2. Check the **Listing** checkbox under **Use custom display settings for the following modes**.
3. Click on the **Save** button.

Our new listing display should now be available to select along the top of our **Manage display** screen. Selecting **Listing** will display a new view mode that we can use to specify which fields will be enabled.

Enabling fields

Fields can be dragged, dropped, and rearranged by simply clicking on the drag icon next to each field name. Any fields located under the **Disabled** section will not be displayed when the Listing view mode is used. For our blog listing page, we only want to display the **Image**, **Teaser**, and **Tags** fields. Go ahead and drag these into place, as shown in the following image:

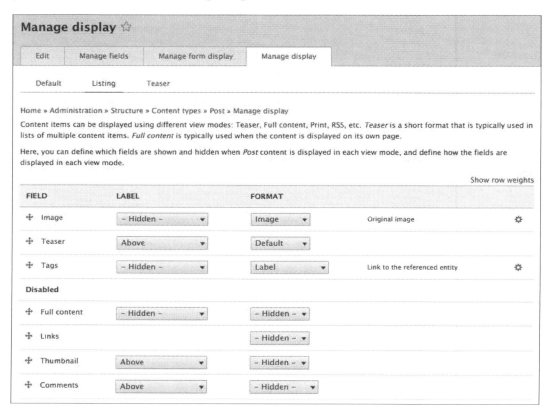

Once we have rearranged the fields as needed, we can click on the **Save** button to lock in our changes.

Managing the display of fields is not just about selecting which fields are enabled or disabled. We also have the ability to specify how the label of each field will be presented, as well as how each field will be formatted.

Field label visibility

The label for each field can have one of four states. The label can display above or inline with the field, as well as be hidden or visually hidden. Visually hiding a label does not prevent the label itself from being available for screen readers, and is great for accessibility requirements.

For our three fields, we will want them to all be hidden from our display, so we can follow these steps to hide each field:

1. Click on the **LABEL** dropdown next to the **Image** field and choose **Hidden**.
2. Click on the **LABEL** dropdown next to the **Teaser** field and choose **Hidden**.
3. Click on the **LABEL** dropdown next to the **Tags** field and choose **Hidden**.
4. Click on the **Save** button.

Formatting fields

Each field can also be formatted so that it is displayed differently, based on the formatting options. This allows us to have finer control over how text is displayed, how content is referenced, and what size an image is displayed at. Based on the formatting options, there may be additional settings that can be applied.

For example, if we click on the gear icon to the right of our image field, we will be presented with options to select various image styles and even enable the image to link to the node itself:

Currently, our fields do not require formatting, but it is important to know where to manage this functionality when the need arises.

Creating a Post Listing view

So now that we have a new listing display for our post content type, you may be asking how do we actually use it? Just like any content that we want to aggregate, we will start with creating a Drupal view. But unlike previous views that we created, which used fields, we will be creating a view that uses the Content Types display mode.

To get started, we will need to navigate to `/admin/structure/views` and click on the **Add new view** button. From the **Views** admin screen, we will add the following information:

- **VIEW BASIC INFORMATION**:
    1. **View name**: Post Listing.
    2. Check the **Description** box.
    3. **Description**: A listing of all Posts.

- **VIEW SETTINGS**: Show: **Content of type**: **Post sorted by**: **Newest first**
- **BLOCK SETTINGS**:
    1. Check the **Create a block**.
    2. **Block title**: Post Listing.

- **BLOCK DISPLAY SETTINGS**:
    1. **Display format**: **Unformatted list of**: **teasers**.
    2. **Items per block**: 3.
    3. Click on the **Save and edit** button.

All of these steps are similar to the Team Member view we created in *Chapter 7, Theming Our Interior Page*. Instead of displaying fields though, we are displaying the Teaser view mode to begin with and will modify our format to use the Listing display mode next.

Using Content Display modes with views

Our Post Listing view is currently using the Teaser view mode of our Post content type. This varies from the typical fields display that we have created so far. Using a view mode from a content type is more flexible because it allows us to manage the display of our fields from the content type itself, without the need to modify our view in the future.

If we preview our view, we will get a glimpse of what fields our post's teaser display has enabled:

In order for us to utilize the Listing view mode for our Post content type, we will need to modify the format currently being used. We can change this by following these steps:

1. Select the **Teaser** link under the **FORMAT** section.
2. Choose **Listing** from the **View mode** dropdown.
3. Click on the **Apply** button.
4. Click on the **Save** button to save the changes.

If we preview the results, we will see our display has changed and we are now showing only the fields we enabled previously on the Listing view mode.

Now that we have our Post Listing view created, we can manage the block display and place it on our Blog listing page.

Managing our Post Listing block

Any time we create a new block display using views, we can easily assign it to any region from the Block layout page. Begin by navigating to `/admin/structure/block` and follow these steps:

1. Locate the **Content** region.
2. Click on the **Place block** button.
3. Locate the **Post Listing** block.
4. Click on the **Place block** button.
5. Uncheck the **Display title** checkbox.
6. Select the **Pages** tab under **Visibility**.
7. Enter the path `/blog` into the **Page** text field.
8. Make sure the **Show for the listed pages** checkbox is selected.
9. Click on the **Save block** button.
10. Click on the **Save blocks** button at the bottom of the **Block layout** page.

Make sure the Post Listing block is the last block displayed in our content region. If not, then reorder the blocks accordingly and click on the **Save blocks** button at the bottom of the Block layout screen.

Navigate back to the Blog listing page by browsing to `/blog` or by selecting the Blog link in the main menu. We can see that our Post listing block is now displaying on the page in a single column, as shown in the following image:

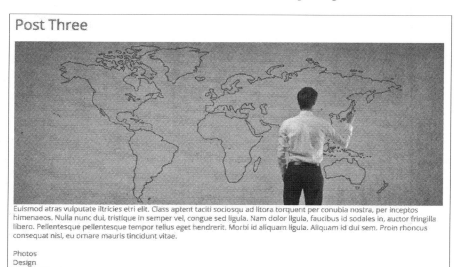

Post Three

Euismod atras vulputate iltricies etri elit. Class aptent taciti sociosqu ad litora torquent per conubia nostra, per inceptos himenaeos. Nulla nunc dui, tristique in semper vel, congue sed ligula. Nam dolor ligula, faucibus id sodales in, auctor fringilla libero. Pellentesque pellentesque tempor tellus eget hendrerit. Morbi id aliquam ligula. Aliquam id dui sem. Proin rhoncus consequat nisi, eu ornare mauris tincidunt vitae.

Photos
Design

If we refer back to our mockup ,we can see that while most of the content we need is being displayed, we are still missing the post date, author, and comment count. Also our structure and styling still needs some work. This is where creating a Twig template specific to our nodes display mode will allow us to modify our markup and add any missing variables that our page may need.

Implementing our Node template

Creating a node template is not foreign to us; our process begins the same way we would create any Twig template. We begin by inspecting the markup of our page to identify which template is currently being used and the various file name suggestions available to us. Since our Post Listing block is referencing the listing view mode of our post content type, we can create a new Twig template called `node--post--listing.html.twig`.

Begin by grabbing a copy of the `node.html.twig` template from `core/modules/node/templates` and placing it into our `themes/octo/templates` folder. We will then rename the file to `node--post--listing.html.twig` so that we only affect the markup for this particular content types display. Next, we will need to replace the current markup within our template with the following new markup:

New markup

```
<article{{ attributes }}>
  {{ content }}
</article>
```

Make sure to save the template, clear Drupal's cache, and refresh the Blog page. At first glance, nothing has changed, but we are now using a custom Twig template to display our content. We will be walking through building up our template until it resembles our mockup by discussing the following techniques:

- First, we will use Twig to add additional CSS classes to our `article` element. This will allow us to apply formatted styling to each individual post that is being repeated on the page.

- Next we will work with the `{{ content }}` variable to print individual fields. This will give us the opportunity to add additional HTML markup for both formatting and structure to each post.

- We will learn how to work with field level templates to account for multiple content within a single field. This will enable us to create the image slider for each post when it has more than one image uploaded, as well as add additional markup to individual fields so that taxonomy tags display correctly.

- Twig filters play an important role in theming and we will learn how to use them to format dates. This will allow us to display the post date properly, based on the design.

- Finally, we will dive into the Theme layer to preprocess variables needed to help identify the path for each page and to retrieve the comment count if one exists for each post.

Adding CSS classes to Twig

Adding additional CSS classes to our markup is not new for us. We implemented this technique in the previous lesson when we developed our `node--landing-page.html.twig` template in *Chapter 7, Theming Our Interior Page*. In fact, Drupal 8 provides us with various ways to work with its attributes, with everything from adding classes to removing classes. We are only touching the surface of how we can use this technique. For even more information, we can refer to the documentation at Drupal.org, located at `https://www.drupal.org/node/2513632`.

For our post listing,, we need to add two CSS classes to our `article` element. We can accomplish this by setting a `classes` variable within our template and then using the `{{ attributes.addClass() }}` function to inject the two new classes into the attributes.

Open up `node--post--listing.html.twig` and replace the markup with the following:

New markup

```
{% set classes = ['post', 'post--listing'] %}

<article{{ attributes.addClass(classes) }}>
  {{ content }}
</article>
```

Make sure to save the template, clear Drupal's cache, and refresh the blog page. We should see a slight change in our styling with the introduction of a bottom border separating each post.

Working with content variables

So far, our node template is just printing out the `{{ content }}` variable, which contains all the fields we have enabled for the listing display mode. In some cases this may suffice, but we can actually print the individual fields that the `{{ content }}` variable contains by referencing the field using dot syntax notation. Having this flexibility allows us to add structural markup for each field.

Let's give this a try by opening `node--post--listing.html.twig` and modifying our markup to print the image field for our post:

New markup

```
{% set classes = ['post', 'post--listing'] %}

<article{{ attributes.addClass(classes) }}>
    {{ content.field_image }}
    {{ content }}
</article>
```

Make sure to save the template, clear Drupal's cache, and refresh the blog page. We should see our post image is now duplicated for each post. Why is this? Well, if we refer back to our markup, we are telling Drupal to output `{{ content.field_image }}`, which prints the image field. But we are also following that by printing all of the content using `{{ content }}`.

Using the without filter

Any time we are developing a Twig template and start printing individual fields for a content type, we will want to prevent the same field from being printed again when the `{{ content }}` variable is called. Twig provides us with the `without` filter to assist us in accomplishing this.

To test this, open up `node--post--listing.html.twig` and modify the markup to reflect the following:

New markup

```
{% set classes = ['post', 'post--listing'] %}

<article{{ attributes.addClass(classes) }}>
    {{ content.field_image }}
    {{ content|without('field_image') }}
</article>
```

Make sure to save the template, clear Drupal's cache, and refresh the Blog page. We now only have a single instance of our image field displayed. Using the `without` filter and passing the field name as a value has successfully prevented the field from printing a second time. We will continue using this technique, as well as printing the individual fields for our Post Listing block as we theme our node.

Creating our post image slider

If we refer back to our mockup of the blog page by opening the `blog.html` page located in our `Mockup` folder, we will notice that our post can contain one or more images. However, when more than one image exists, we present the image in a slider for the user to see all post images:

In order for us to implement this functionality, we will need to know exactly how many images our image field contains. While we can't access this information from the node level, we can implement this from the field level by creating a field template specifically for the field.

Working with field templates

If we browse back to our Drupal instance and navigate to the blog page, we can inspect the image field and locate which Twig template is currently being used by Drupal:

```
<!-- THEME DEBUG -->
<!-- THEME HOOK: 'field' -->
<!-- FILE NAME SUGGESTIONS:
   * field--node--field-image--post.html.twig
   * field--node--field-image.html.twig
   * field--node--post.html.twig
   * field--field-image.html.twig
   * field--image.html.twig
   x field.html.twig
-->
<!-- BEGIN OUTPUT from 'core/modules/system/templates/field.html.twig' -->
▶<div data-quickedit-field-id="node/11/field_image/en/listing">…</div>
<!-- END OUTPUT from 'core/modules/system/templates/field.html.twig' -->
```

Drupal provides multiple **FILE NAME SUGGESTIONS** for us to choose from, but since we don't know if we will reuse this field with another content type later, we will be as specific as possible and create `field--node--field-image--post.html.twig` by following these steps:

1. Navigate to the `core/modules/system/templates` folder and copy the `field.html.twig` template.

2. Place `field.html.twig` into our `themes/octo/templates` folder and rename it `field--node--field-image--post.html.twig`.

3. Open `field--node--field-image--post.html.twig` and replace the markup with the following:

```
{% if items|length > 1 %}
  <div class="post-image">
    <div class="owl-carousel">
      {% for item in items %}
        <div class="img-thumbnail">
          {{ item.content }}
        </div>
      {% endfor %}
    </div>
  </div>
{% else %}
  <div class="single-post-image post-image">
    {% for item in items %}
      <div class="img-thumbnail">{{ item.content }}</div>
    {% endfor %}
  </div>
{% endif %}
```

Make sure to save the template and clear Drupal's cache. Before we preview the blog page let's take a moment to discuss what exactly is happening in this new template.

1. First, we are using a Twig filter `{% if items|length > 1 %}` to test the length of the items variable to see if our image field contains multiple images. If it does, we will print the markup for that condition, but if not, we will print the markup contained in the `{% else %}` condition.

2. Second, since any field item can contain multiple items, we need to loop `{% for item in items %}` through the items and print `{{ item.content }}`.

3. Finally, the remaining markup adds the necessary structure and CSS classes for the next step of the process, which is adding the Owl Carousel library to our theme.

If we now browse to the blog page, we will see that our field images are styled to include a rounded border, a light box shadow, and some necessary padding.

Adding the Owl Carousel library

In order to add the slider functionality to multiple images, we will be implementing Owl Carousel, which can be found at `http://owlgraphic.com/owlcarousel/`. Owl Carousel provides us with a responsive touch enabled slider that we can apply to our post images. We will be grabbing a copy of the library from our exercise files, adding the library to our theme, configuring it within our `octo.libraries.yml` file, and then using Twig to attach the library to our node templates.

Begin by navigating to the `Chapter08/start/themes/octo/vendor` folder and copying the `owl-carousel` folder to our `themes/octo/vendor` folder. Once the files are accessible by Drupal, we can add the reference to our library by following these remaining steps:

1. Open `octo.libraries.yml`.

2. Add the following entry:

    ```
    owl-carousel:
      version: 1.3.3
        css:
          theme:
            vendor/owl-carousel/owl.carousel.css: {}
            vendor/owl-carousel/owl.theme.css: {}
        js:
          vendor/owl-carousel/owl.carousel.min.js: {}
        dependencies:
          - core/jquery
    ```

3. Save `octo.libraries.yml`.

Before we can preview the new functionality, we still have a few steps left to complete. Next, we will need to attach the library to our Blog listing page. As we will not want this library to load on every page, using the `{{ attach_library() }}` function will be our preferred method.

Begin by opening `node--post--listing.html.twig` and then adding the following Twig function to the top of our template:

```
{{ attach_library('octo/owl-carousel') }}
```

It is very important to make sure that we are using single quotes to surround the path to our library, otherwise the slightest typo will cause the library to not be loaded. Now make sure to save the template and then we can move on to initializing Owl Carousel.

Begin by opening `octo.js` and adding the following script to the bottom of our file directly below our `Scroll to` function:

```
//-- Owl Carousel
(function() {

  if (typeof $.fn.owlCarousel === 'function'){
    $('.owl-carousel').owlCarousel({
      slideSpeed : 300,
      paginationSpeed : 400,
      singleItem:true
    });
  }

})();
```

Make sure to save `octo.js` and then let's review exactly what our new function is doing:

1. First, we are conditionally checking if the Owl Carousel function exists. This ensures we avoid any JavaScript errors on other pages where our library is not loaded.

2. Next, we are initializing Owl Carousel and passing three parameters to it: one for how fast an image should slide, one for pagination, and then finally we tell it how many images we want to display.

With our library added, attached to our template, and initialized, we can now clear Drupal's cache and refresh our Blog listing page. We will now see that any posts that contain multiple images display as a slider. This provides some nice responsive functionality for our users.

Using Twig filters for dates

The next section of our post listing we need to address is the post date. By default, Drupal will print dates in the form of a Unix timestamp. In most cases, we will want to convert these dates into a more user friendly format. Luckily, we can take advantage of another Twig function, `date()`, to convert dates easily.

Begin by opening `node--post-listing.html.twig` and adding the following markup directly after where we are printing the post image:

New markup

```
<div class="post-date">
  <span class="day">{{ node.createdtime }}</span>
  <span class="month">{{ node.createdtime }}</span>
</div>
```

Make sure to save the template, clear Drupal's cache, and then refresh the Blog listing page. We will now see exactly what the Unix timestamp looks like when printed. While our theming is now being applied, we need to convert the timestamp into day and month:

 Euismod atras vulputate iltricies etri elit. Class aptent taciti sociosqu ad litora torquent per conubia nostra, per inceptos himenaeos. Nulla nunc dui, tristique in semper vel, congue sed ligula. Nam dolor ligula, faucibus id sodales in, auctor fringilla libero. Pellentesque pellentesque tempor tellus eget hendrerit. Morbi id aliquam ligula. Aliquam id dui sem. Proin rhoncus consequat nisl, eu ornare mauris tincidunt vitae.

Let's now use the `date()` function and apply it to `node.createdtime` to display the day and month format of our timestamp.

Open `node--post-listing.html.twig` and modify our post-date markup to reflect the following:

New markup

```
<div class="post-date">
  <span class="day">{{ node.createdtime|date('d') }}</span>
  <span class="month">{{ node.createdtime|date('M') }}</span>
</div>
```

Make sure to save the template, clear Drupal's cache, and then refresh the Blog listing page. By adding the simple Twig function to our timestamp, we now have the correct formatting and styling:

 Euismod atras vulputate iltricies etri elit. Class aptent taciti sociosqu ad litora torquent per conubia nostra, per inceptos himenaeos. Nulla nunc dui, tristique in semper vel, congue sed ligula. Nam dolor ligula, faucibus id sodales in, auctor fringilla libero. Pellentesque pellentesque tempor tellus eget hendrerit. Morbi id aliquam ligula. Aliquam id dui sem. Proin rhoncus consequat nisl, eu ornare mauris tincidunt vitae.

Our post listing is starting to come together. Next, we will add the title of our post along with the teaser field, before moving on to our metadata.

Printing title and teaser

Working with Node titles when theming can sometimes be a mystery, unless you have a good understanding of what Drupal is doing behind the scenes. The title field is one of the few required fields that each Content type must contain. The challenge is that while it's considered a field, it doesn't truly function like other fields. We do not have access to manage the Node title in the admin, as we can with the rest of our fields. While we could extend the functionality by using modules such as `https://www.drupal.org/project/title`, we will manage the Node title directly within our Twig template.

Open `node--post-listing.html.twig` and add the following markup directly after our `post-date` section:

New markup

```
<div class="post-content">

  {{ title_prefix }}
  <h2{{ title_attributes }}>
    <a href="{{ url }}" rel="bookmark">{{ label }}</a>
  </h2>
  {{ title_suffix }}

  {{ content.field_teaser }}

</div>

{{ content|without('field_image','field_teaser') }}
```

Make sure to save the template, clear Drupal's cache, and then refresh the Blog listing page. Our post title and teaser should now be displayed:

We are familiar with printing individual fields and removing them from the main content flow. What is new though is how we print the title. Within a node template, the title is referred to as `{{ label }}` and the `{{ url }}` variable points to the path of the individual post. We utilize these two variables to create our title within a h2 heading and a link. We also have some extraneous variables, such as `{{ title_prefix }}` and `{{ title_suffix }}`, which are utilized by contributed modules to inject markup before or after our title.

Creating our post metadata

We are getting close to completing the theming of the post listing. We are still missing the post metadata, which consists of the author, the categories that a post has been tagged with, and the comment count.

We will begin with adding the structural markup for our post-meta content, including printing the author associated with each post:

1. Open `node--post--listing.html.twig`.

2. Add the following markup directly below the teaser variable:

```
<div class="post-meta">

  <span class="post-meta-user">
    <i class="fa fa-user"></i> By {{ author_name }}
  </span>

</div>
```

Make sure to save the template, clear Drupal's cache, and then refresh the blog listing page. Our post author is now displayed, with a link to the user profile. Since we are using the default author information for the node, and not a specific field, we have the ability to print that information using the `{{ author_name }}` variable:

Now we need to address the tags field, which displays any categories associated with a post. The tags field, as we will see in a moment, can contain one or more values, which will require us to modify the markup on the field level:

1. Open `node--post--listing.html.twig`.

2. Add the following markup within our `post-meta` section, directly below our `post-meta-user` markup:

```
<span class="post-meta-tag">
  <i class="fa fa-tag"></i> {{ content.field_tags }}
</span>
```

3. Make sure to exclude the `field_tags` variable from the main content variable.

Make sure to save the template, clear Drupal's cache, and then refresh the Blog listing page. We should now see our post categories displayed only once per post. However, our tags are displayed stacked on top of each other, instead of inline as our design requires. If we inspect the page markup for our tags, we will see that each category has a `div` element wrapped around it, causing them to be block level elements.

Field templates and taxonomy

In order for us to modify the markup for our taxonomy tags, we will need to create a field level template. Using the file name suggestions provided by Twig, we can create our own template by following these steps:

1. Navigate to the `core/modules/system/templates` folder and copy the `field.html.twig` template.

2. Place a copy of the template in our `themes/octo/templates` folder.

3. Rename the file `field--field-tags.html.twig`.

4. Replace the markup with the following:

```
<ul>
   {% for item in items %}
      <li{{ item.attributes.addClass('field-item') }}>
            {{ item.content }}
      </li>
   {% endfor %}
</ul>
```

Make sure to save the template, clear Drupal's cache, and then refresh the Blog listing page. Based on the markup we added, we have replaced the block level elements with an unordered list, and each taxonomy tag is now a list item:

Our post listing is starting to take shape, but you may have noticed that we are not returning the number of comments that each post contains. How do we remedy this when there is no comment count variable available to the Node template?

Handling comments in Drupal 8

One of the new things introduced in Drupal 8 is the comment field. Previously, when you created or edited a content type, you would simply enable Comments by turning them on or off. Well, comments are now their own field and must be added to a content type like any other field that you want to create.

If we navigate to /admin/structure/comment, we will get a glimpse of the **Default comments** configured by Drupal.

Comment types are similar to Content types, as they are fieldable and multiple comment types can be created. Feel free to inspect the comment type in more detail, but be aware that this is the comment type we are using with our Post content type.

In fact, if we navigate to /admin/structure/types/manage/post/fields, we will see that we have a field called field_comments which is of **FIELD TYPE Comments**. The comment field was added to our Post content type and provided to us with the database snapshot.

If we were to add this field to our Listing display, it would not return a comment count, but instead display the Comment form. Based on our design, that does not help us. However, knowing the field name for our comments will allow us to do some advanced theming within the Drupal 8 theme layer to retrieve the comment count, place it within a variable and print it within our Twig template.

Creating a theme file

The *.theme file is a PHP file that contains theme hooks for preprocessing variables. We will create a theme file specific to our theme that we can use to grab the comment count, based on each individual post, and then return the count to our Twig template as a variable that can be printed.

Let's begin by creating a new file called octo.theme and saving it to our themes/ octo folder.

Next, we will add the following PHP code:

```php
<?php

function octo_preprocess_node(&$variables) {
  $node = $variables ['elements']['#node'];
  $id = $node->id();

  // Create comment count variable for template
  $count = _octo_comment_count($id);
  $variables['comment_count'] = _octo_plural($count, 'Comment',
  'Comments');
}
```

The `octo_preprocess_node(&$variables)` function is known as a theme hook and is an adaptation of `theme_preprocess_node`. Within this function, we are passing by reference any variables accessible to the Node using `&$variables`. Since everything in Drupal is an array, we can traverse the `$variables` array to retrieve the Node ID, which we use to pass to a custom function that returns the number of comments for each node.

Next, we will add the two custom functions directly below our preprocess function:

```php
function _octo_comment_count($id) {
  $count = db_query("SELECT comment_count FROM
  comment_entity_statistics WHERE entity_id = :id",
  array(':id' => $id))->fetchField();

  return empty($count) ? '0' : $count;
}


function _octo_plural($count, $singular, $plural) {
  if ( $count == 1 )
    return $count . ' ' . $singular;
  else
    return $count . ' ' . $plural;
}
```

Our first custom function returns the comment count for a specific node ID, which is passed to the function from our preprocess function. This custom function uses `db_query` to select the count from the `comment_entity_statistics` table in Drupal.

Our second custom function allows us to pluralize the count and return a more formatted count to our preprocess function, which we in turn will assign to our `comment_count` variable for use in our Twig template.

Once finished, make sure to save our file and clear Drupal's cache.

Printing our comment count

Now that we have utilized the theme layer to create a new variable containing the comment count for each node, we can print the variable to our template by following these steps:

1. Open `node--post--listing.html.twig`.

2. Add the following markup directly after our `post-meta-tag` section:

```
<span class="post-meta-comments">
  <i class="fa fa-comments"></i>
  <a href="{{ url }}/#comments">{{ comment_count }}</a>
</span>
```

Make sure to save the template, clear Drupal's cache, and then refresh the Blog listing page. Based on the markup we added, we now have our comment count displayed for each post:

 Post Three

Euismod atras vulputate iltricies etri elit. Class aptent taciti sociosqu ad litora torquent per conubia nostra, per inceptos himenaeos. Nulla nunc dui, tristique in semper vel, congue sed ligula. Nam dolor ligula, faucibus id sodales in, auctor fringilla libero. Pellentesque pellentesque tempor tellus eget hendrerit. Morbi id aliquam ligula. Aliquam id dui sem. Proin rhoncus consequat nisl, eu ornare mauris tincidunt vitae.

👤 By admin 🏷 Photos, Design 💬 0 Comments

Adding a read more link

We have almost completed the theming of our Post listing. We have one more component to add, and that is our read more link. We have all the elements we need to create this link, so let's start by following these steps:

1. Open `node--post--listing.html.twig`.

2. Add the following markup directly after our `post-meta-comments` section:

```
<a href="{{ url }}" class="button button--primary button--xs
pull-right">Read more...</a>
```

Make sure to save the template, clear Drupal's cache, and then refresh the Blog listing page. The main content area of our Post listing is now finished. It is time to move on to the sidebar and our three blocks of content, which contain Categories, Popular content, and our About block.

Creating a Categories block

The content of each of our posts has been assigned one or more tags to identify what category the post belongs to. This type of identification gives our end users another way to easily navigate content. On our mockup, the right-hand sidebar contains a custom block with an unordered list of categories. We will utilize views to create a block display of taxonomy terms by following these steps.

To get started, we will need to navigate to /admin/structure/views and click on the **Add new view** button. From the **Views** admin screen, we will add the following information:

- **VIEW BASIC INFORMATION**:
    1. **View name**: Categories.
    2. Check the **Description** box.
    3. **Description**: Post categories.

- **VIEW SETTINGS**: Show: **Taxonomy terms of type**: **Tags sorted by**: **Unsorted**.
- **BLOCK SETTINGS**:
    1. Check **Create a block**.
    2. **Block title: Categories**.

- **BLOCK DISPLAY SETTINGS**:
    1. **Display format: Unformatted list of: Fields**.
    2. **Items per block**: 5.
    3. Click on the **Save and edit** button.

Now that our Categories view has been created, we will need to adjust the format settings. With the view still open, we will need to adjust the following fields:

- **FORMAT SETTINGS**:
    1. Click on the **Settings** link next to **Format: Unformatted list**.
    2. Uncheck the **Add views row classes** checkbox from the **Block: Style options** window and click on the **Apply** button.
    3. Click on the **Settings** link next to **Show: Fields**.
    4. Uncheck the **Provide default field wrapper elements** checkbox from the **Block: Row style options** window and click on the **Apply** button.

We now need to adjust the settings of our Taxonomy term field to exclude any extraneous CSS. With the view still open, we will need to adjust the following field:

- **FIELDS**:
    1. Select **Taxonomy term: Name**.
    2. Expand **STYLE SETTINGS**.
    3. Uncheck **Add default classes**.
    4. Click on the **Apply (all displays)** button.

Make sure to click on the **Save** button in the main view window to save the changes we just made, and then look at the results in the **Preview** window.

Managing our Categories block

Any time we create a new block display using views, we can easily assign it to any region from the Block layout page. Begin by navigating to /admin/structure/block and then follow these nine steps:

1. Locate the **Sidebar second** region.
2. Click on the **Place block** button.
3. Locate the **Categories** block.
4. Click on the **Place block** button.
5. Select the **Pages** tab under **Visibility**.
6. Enter the path /blog into the **Page** text field.
7. On a second line, add another path to /blog/*.
8. Make sure the **Show for the listed pages** checkbox is selected.
9. Click on the **Save block** button.

With our Categories block assigned to the Sidebar second region, we will now need to add the Sidebar second region to our `page.html.twig` template before we can preview it.

Implementing responsive sidebars

So far, we have only been dealing with a one column layout. All of our blocks have been assigned to regions before, after, or within our main content. Now we are faced with our first block that is associated with a sidebar. The challenge is to make sure that when content is added to a sidebar, our main content region adjusts accordingly.

For this next section, we will be modifying our `page.html.twig` template to conditionally look for the existence of sidebars and alter the column classes of our content region.

Begin by opening `page.html.twig` and adding the logic and markup for the sidebar first region. This markup will be added directly below the `<div class="row">` section, but above the content wrapper:

New markup

```
{% if page.sidebar_first %}
  <aside class="layout-sidebar-first" role="complementary">
    <div class="col-md-3">
      {{ page.sidebar_first }}
    </div>
  </aside>
{% endif %}
```

The markup we added conditionally checks to see if any blocks are assigned to the Sidebar first region. If any blocks are present, it will then print the included markup and blocks within the region.

When a sidebar is available to print, we need to be able to adjust our main content region's grid measurements accordingly. We can use similar logic to test and then create a new column class that can be used for our content region.

Add the following markup directly after our Sidebar first region:

New markup

```
{% if page.sidebar_second and page.sidebar_first %}
  {% set col_class = 'col-md-6' %}
{% elseif page.sidebar_second or page.sidebar_first %}
  {% set col_class = 'col-md-9' %}
```

```
{% else %}
  {% set col_class = 'col-md-12' %}
{% endif %}
```

The logic above checks for one or more sidebar regions and creates our new column class accordingly. We can then apply the new class to our content region by replacing the hardcoded column class with our new `col_class` variable:

```
<div class="{{ col_class }}">
  {{ page.content }}
</div>
```

Finally, we can add the conditional logic to print the Sidebar second region. This logic is similar to what we added for the Sidebar first region. Add the following markup directly below our main content region:

New markup

```
{% if page.sidebar_second %}
  <aside class="layout-sidebar-second" role="complementary">
    <div class="col-md-3">
      {{ page.sidebar_second }}
    </div>
  </aside>
{% endif %}
```

Make sure to save the template, clear Drupal's cache, and then refresh the Blog listing page. The main content area of our post listing is now adjusted to allow our Sidebar second region to display the Categories block:

If we look at our mockup, we can see that our Categories heading should be `<h4>` and the list of terms should be contained within an unordered list. How can we modify the markup for this block or view? Easy: we can create Twig templates for both the Block and the View to override the markup and add any classes that we need.

Theming a Block template

In the case of our Categories block, we can begin by navigating to the `core/modules/block/templates` folder and following these remaining steps:

1. Copy `block.html.twig` and place it into our `theme/octo/templates` folder.

2. Rename `block.html.twig` to `block--views-block--categories-block-1.html.twig` based on the template's suggestions.

3. Next, we will need to replace the current markup with the following new markup to convert the default `<h2>` to `<h4>`:

New markup

```
{% set classes = ['block'] %}

<div{{ attributes.addClass(classes) }}>
  {{ title_prefix }}

  {% if label %}
    <h4{{ title_attributes }}>{{ label }}</h4>
  {% endif %}

  {{ title_suffix }}

  {% block content %}
    {{ content }}
  {% endblock %}

</div>
```

Once finished, make sure to save the template, clear Drupal's cache, and then refresh the Blog listing page in the browser. Our Categories block heading is now displayed properly. We have managed to alter the heading of our Categories block, but we still need to modify the output of our categories to display as an unordered list, along with any additional CSS classes we may need. Time to add a Views template.

Drupal Views and Twig templates

Unlike most of Drupal's templates, Views do not provide a file name suggestion for overriding Twig templates. So how do we know exactly what to name our template? View templates can be created in a variety of ways, but the easiest way to remember this is by following this rule:

```
[base template name]--[view machine name].html.twig
```

So in the case of our Categories view, will want to create a new Twig template with the name `views-view-unformatted--categories.html.twig`.

Begin by navigating to the `core/modules/view/templates` folder and following these remaining steps:

1. Copy `views-view-unformatted.html.twig` and place it into our `theme/octo/templates` folder.

2. Rename `views-view-unformatted.html.twig` to `views-view-unformatted--categories.html.twig`.

3. Next, we will need to replace the current markup with the following new markup to convert the default `<div>` to `<ul>`:

   New markup

```twig
{% if title %}
    <h3>{{ title }}</h3>
{% endif %}

<ul class="nav nav-list primary pull-bottom">
{% for row in rows %}
    {%
    set row_classes = [
    default_row_class ? 'views-row',
    ]
    %}
    <li{{ row.attributes.addClass(row_classes) }}>
        {{ row.content }}
    </li>
{% endfor %}
</ul>
```

Once finished, make sure to save the template, clear Drupal's cache, and then refresh the Blog listing page. Our Categories block is now styled correctly and matches our design:

Managing popular versus recent content

The second block of content that we need to create for our Blog listing page is a little more complex to build and will provide us with experience of building and combining multiple views into a single view.

Creating our recent posts block

Our recent posts block will be a view that contains a listing of three of the most recent posts added to our site. We will take advantage of the Teaser display mode of our Post content type to present our view block.

To get started, we will need to navigate to /admin/structure/views and click on the **Add new view** button. From the **Views** Admin screen, we will add the following information:

- **VIEW BASIC INFORMATION**:
    1. **View name**: Recent Posts.
    2. Check the **Description** box.
    3. **Description**: A listing of recent posts.

- **VIEW SETTINGS: Show: Content of type: Post sorted by: Newest first.**

- **BLOCK SETTINGS**:
  1. Check **Create a block**.
  2. **Block title: Recent Posts**.

- **BLOCK DISPLAY SETTINGS**:
  1. **Display format: Unformatted list of: Teasers**.
  2. **Items per block**: 3.
  3. Click on the **Save and edit** button.

With our view now created, if we look at the **Preview** section, we will see our Post Teaser displayed with the title and thumbnail image. Since we are using the display mode of our post, we can manage the fields directly from the content type. Our Teaser display happens to be configured exactly how we will need it, so there is no need to change anything.

Make sure to click on the **Save** button to finalize our changes. We have the first part of our block created. Now we need to create our next view to display popular posts.

Creating our popular posts block

Popular posts, or anything popular for that matter, is all subjective. However, clients often want to see this type of information. We can accomplish this type of View block by utilizing the Comment statistics for each post. The number of comments each post has will determine which post will be displayed.

To get started, we will need to navigate to /admin/structure/views and click on the **Add new view** button. From the **Views** Admin screen, we will add the following information:

- **VIEW BASIC INFORMATION**:
  1. **View name**: Popular Posts.
  2. Check the **Description** box.
  3. **Description**: A listing of popular posts.

- **VIEW SETTINGS: Show: Content of type: Post sorted by: Newest first**.
- **BLOCK SETTINGS**:
  1. Check: **Create a block**.
  2. **Block title**: Popular Posts.

- **BLOCK DISPLAY SETTINGS**:
    1. **Display format: Unformatted list of: Teasers**.
    2. **Items per block**: 3.
    3. Click on **Save and edit** button.

With our view now created, if we look at the **Preview** section, we will see our Post Teaser displayed with the title and thumbnail image. However, we are only sorting the posts by the date they were authored versus the number of comments each post contains.

Sorting views by comment count

In order for us to determine the most popular posts, we will need to sort by the number of comments each post has. Begin by following these steps:

SORT CRITERIA:

1. Select the **Content: Authored on (desc)** link.
2. Click on the **Remove** link.
3. Click on the **Add** button.
4. Select **Comment count** from the **Add sort criteria** window.
5. Click on the **Apply (all displays)** button.
6. Choose **Sort descending** from the **Order** options.
7. Click on the **Apply (all displays)** button.

Make sure to click on the **Save** button in the main view window to save the changes. Now that we have our Popular Posts view complete, we need to combine it with our recent posts so that the two views act as one.

Attaching a view to the footer

One feature within views is the ability to create view footers. View footers can consist of custom text, other fields, or, as in our case, another view. We will use this feature to add our recent posts view by following these steps:

FOOTER:

1. Click on the **Add** button.
2. Scroll to bottom of the **Add footer** window and choose **View area**.
3. Click on the **Apply (all displays)** button.

4. Select **View: recent_posts - Display: block_1** from the **View to insert** dropdown.

5. Click on the **Apply (all displays)** button.

Make sure to click on the **Save** button in the main view window to save the changes. If we look in the preview window, we should now see both views being displayed. This is not so difficult once you understand how to use and manipulate Drupal views. Now that we have our two View blocks combined into a single Block, we can add it to our Blog listing page.

Managing our popular posts block

Any time we create a new block display using views, we can easily assign it to any region from the Block layout page. Let's begin by navigating to `/admin/structure/block` and following these steps:

1. Locate the **Sidebar second** region.

2. Click on the **Place block** button.

3. Locate the **Popular Posts** block.

4. Click on the **Place block** button.

5. Uncheck **Display title**.

6. Select the **Pages** tab under **Visibility**.

7. Enter the path `/blog` into the **Page** text field.

8. On a second line, add another path to `/blog/*`.

9. Make sure the **Show for the listed pages** checkbox is selected.

10. Click on the **Save block** button.

With our Popular Posts block assigned to the Sidebar second region, we will want to make sure it is second in the block order. Reorder the blocks if necessary and then click on the **Save blocks** button. If we navigate back to the Blog listing page, we will now see our new block displayed, but in desperate need of some styling.

Now for the fun part. We need to create a Twig template and modify the output of our View block so that we can place each view into its own tab. Let's take a look at how we can accomplish that.

Using Twig and Bootstrap tabs

The structure for Twitter Bootstrap tabs requires each block of content to be wrapped in a `<div>` element with a class of `tab-pane`. Also, each Tab pane must consist of an unordered list of items to display. We will start with converting both view blocks from an unformatted list to an unordered list, similar to what we did with our Categories block.

Recent Posts Twig template

Begin by navigating to the `core/modules/view/templates` folder and follow these remaining steps:

1. Copy `views-view-unformatted.html.twig` and place it in our `theme/octo/templates` folder.

2. Rename `views-view-unformatted.html.twig` to `views-view-unformatted--recent-posts.html.twig`.

3. Next, we will need to replace the current markup with the following:

    New markup

    ```twig
    {% if title %}
        <h3>{{ title }}</h3>
    {% endif %}

    <ul class="simple-post-list">
    {% for row in rows %}
        {%
        set row_classes = [
        default_row_class ? 'views-row',
        ]
        %}
        <li{{ row.attributes.addClass(row_classes) }}>
            {{ row.content }}
        </li>
    {% endfor %}
    </ul>
    ```

Once finished, make sure to save the template, clear Drupal's cache, and then refresh the page in the browser to verify that our Recent Posts block is now displayed as an unordered list. We will now repeat this step for the Popular Posts view.

Popular Posts Twig template

Begin by navigating to the `core/modules/view/templates` folder and follow these remaining steps:

1. Copy `views-view-unformatted.html.twig` and place it in our `theme/octo/templates` folder.

2. Rename `views-view-unformatted.html.twig` to `views-view-unformatted--popular-posts.html.twig`.

3. Next, we will need to replace the current markup with the following:

   New markup

```
{% if title %}
    <h3>{{ title }}</h3>
{% endif %}

<ul class="simple-post-list">
{% for row in rows %}
    {%
    set row_classes = [
    default_row_class ? 'views-row',
    ]
    %}
    <li{{ row.attributes.addClass(row_classes) }}>
        {{ row.content }}
    </li>
{% endfor %}
</ul>
```

Once finished, make sure to save the template, clear Drupal's cache, and then refresh the page in the browser to verify our Popular Posts block is now displayed as an unordered list. This next part will be a little trickier to accomplish, but will demonstrate that anything is possible with Twig templates.

Using Views-view templates

The main structure of views is contained within the `views-view.html.twig` template. We will need to modify this template to add some additional classes that will allow us to display each view within their own tab, as designed in the mockup. Like our previous view templates, the naming convention follows the same rules:

```
[base template name]--[view machine name].html.twig
```

So in the case of our Popular Posts view, will want to create a new Twig template with the name of `views-view--popular-posts.html.twig` that we can then modify the markup to accomplish our tabbed design.

Begin by navigating to the `core/modules/view/templates` folder and follow these remaining steps:

1. Copy `views-view.html.twig` and place it in our `theme/octo/templates` folder.

2. Rename `views-view.html.twig` to `views-view--popular-posts.html.twig`.

3. Next, we will need to replace the current markup with the following new markup:

New markup

```
<div class="tabs">

  <ul class="nav nav-tabs">
    <li class="active">
      <a href="#popularPosts" data-toggle="tab">
        <i class="fa fa-star"></i> {{ 'Popular'|t }}
      </a>
    </li>
    <li>
      <a href="#recentPosts" data-toggle="tab">
        {{ 'Recent'|t }}
      </a>
    </li>
  </ul>

  <div class="tab-content">

    {% if rows %}
      <div class="tab-pane active" id="popularPosts">
        {{ rows }}
      </div>
    {% elseif empty %}
      <div class="view-empty">
        {{ empty }}
      </div>
    {% endif %}
```

```
{% if footer %}
  <div class="tab-pane" id="recentPosts">
    {{ footer }}
  </div>
{% endif %}

    </div>

  </div>
```

Once finished, make sure to save the template, clear Drupal's cache, and then refresh the Blog listing page. Our Popular/Recent Posts block is now displaying in the tabbed interface, as shown in the following image:

By reviewing the markup, we can see that the way we constructed our view block allows for each independent view to be displayed in its own tab.

We are not quite done with our theming of this new block. As we can see from the page, our Post Teaser is missing some additional fields and formatting necessary to match our mockup. We will need to introduce another Twig template to handle the Teaser display mode and clean up our markup.

Creating a Post Teaser Twig template

Currently, the teaser display for our Post content type uses the default `node.html.twig` template. If we inspect the markup of our block, we can create a new Twig template with the recommended file name of `node--post--teaser.html.twig`.

Begin by navigating to the `core/modules/node/templates` folder and follow these remaining steps:

1. Copy `node.html.twig` and place it in our `theme/octo/templates` folder.

2. Rename `node.html.twig` to `node--post--teaser.html.twig`.

3. Next, we will need to replace the current markup with the following:

New markup

```
<div class="post-image">
  <div class="img-thumbnail">
    <a href="{{ url }}">
      {{ content.field_thumbnail }}
    </a>
  </div>
</div>

<div class="post-info">
  <a href="{{ url }}" class="tabbed-title">{{ label }}</a>
  <div class="post-meta">
    {{ node.createdtime|date('M d, Y') }}
  </div>
</div>

{{ content|without('field_thumbnail') }}
```

Once finished, make sure to save the template, clear Drupal's cache, and then refresh the Blog listing page. As we can see from the following image, our tabbed interface is identical to our mockup:

The markup we added is pretty straightforward. We are utilizing the content variable that each node has available to print out the thumbnail image, title, and post created date. We used these same techniques when we created the Post Listing template earlier.

There are quite a few steps involved in creating the final tabbed interface, but the ease of being able to create Twig templates makes modifying the markup simple.

Adding the About Us block

After all the complex Views, Blocks, and Twig templates, adding the About Us block to our sidebar will seem quite simple. The last block to complete our Blog Listing page already exists, so adding it will just be an exercise in managing custom block layouts.

Begin by navigating to /admin/structure/block and follow these steps:

1. Locate the **Sidebar second** region.
2. Click on the **Place block** button.
3. Locate the **About Us** block.
4. Click on the **Place block** button.
5. Select the **Pages** tab under **Visibility**.

6. Enter the path /blog into the **Page** text field.

7. On a second line, add another path to /blog/*.

8. Make sure the **Show for the listed pages** checkbox is selected.

9. Click on the **Save block** button.

With our About Us block assigned to the Sidebar second region, we will want to make sure it is third in the block order. Reorder the blocks if necessary and then click on the **Save blocks** button. We have one final piece of theming before our About Us block is complete.

Implementing the About Us template

In the case of our About Us block, we need to adjust the heading to display it similar to our Categories block. This will require us to replace the current <h2> with a <h4> heading.

Begin by navigating to the core/modules/block/templates folder and follow these remaining steps:

1. Copy block.html.twig and place it in our theme/octo/templates folder.

2. Rename block.html.twig to block--aboutus-2.html.twig, based on the template suggestions.

3. Next, we will need to replace the current markup with the following new markup to convert the default <h2> to <h4>:

New markup

```
{% set classes = ['block'] %}

<div{{ attributes.addClass(classes) }}>
  {{ title_prefix }}

  {% if label %}
    <h4{{ title_attributes }}>{{ label }}</h4>
  {% endif %}

  {{ title_suffix }}

  {% block content %}
    {{ content }}
  {% endblock %}

</div>
```

Once finished, make sure to save the template, clear Drupal's cache, and then refresh the Blog listing page in the browser. Let's give ourselves a big pat on the back as our page is now complete:

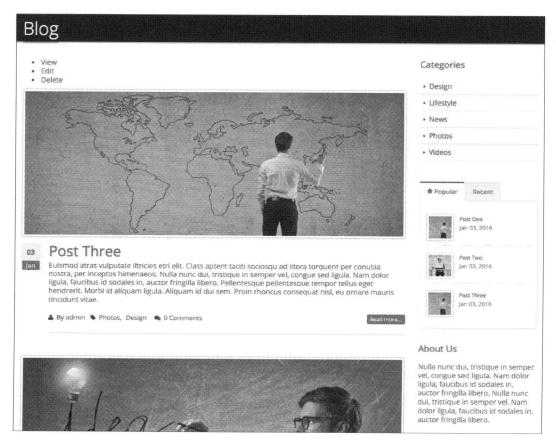

Summary

Let's give ourselves a big pat on the back. We learned a lot of new techniques for theming Drupal 8 in this chapter and our Blog listing page looks great. Quite a few different techniques were covered in a short period of time. We adopted best practices for theming different sections of our page, which will be used in almost any theme we create. Let's take a moment to recap what we have accomplished in this chapter:

- We began by reviewing our Blog Listing mockup to identify the key areas of our website that we will need to recreate.
- We learned how to effectively use Display modes to manage our content types fields, including how to hide labels and use field formatters.
- Field level Twig templates came in handy for modifying individual field markup, adding classes, using filters, and checking for multiple field items.
- Twitter Bootstrap gave us the flexibility to add slideshows and tabbed interfaces to our page content.
- We took a deeper look at using preprocessing and creating a *.theme file to create new variables accessible by our Twig templates.

In the next chapter, we will continue with our Post content by theming our Blog detail page, which will include focusing on the Comment field in more detail, additional preprocessing functions, and additional Twig templates.

9
Theming Our Blog Detail Page

Having completed the Blog listing page, we now need to focus on the development and theming of our Blog detail page. While not quite as complex as creating a listing page, we will need to have a better understanding of how content types interact with comments. In this chapter, we will take a look at creating a single `node.html.twig` template that our Blog detail page will use. This template will be based on the Full Content display mode and the introduction of the revamped comment system in Drupal 8. Let's review what tasks we will be accomplishing:

- We will begin with reviewing our Blog detail page as displayed in our mockup, and identify how specific fields will need to be presented for display.

- Next, we will create our Blog detail template, which will focus on the default display mode for our Post content type.

- We will take a more detailed look at how comments work in Drupal 8 as we enable them the comment form, display them, and thread them for a post.

- Finally, we will take a look at how to use the profile images that users have attached to their accounts to display in our page.

While we work through each section, we have the ability to refer back to the `Chapter09` exercise files folder. Each folder contains a `start` and `end` folder with files that we can use to compare our work when needed. This also includes database snapshots that will allow us all to start from the same point when working through various lessons.

Reviewing the Blog detail mockup

In order to assist us in identifying page elements we will be recreating for the Blog detail page, it would make sense to open up our mockup and review the layout and structure. The Blog page can be found in the `Mockup` folder located in our exercise files. Begin by opening up the `blog-detail.html` file within the browser, as shown in the following image:

The Blog detail mockup looks very similar to the Blog listing page, with the exception of a few new areas that were not present before:

- First, we have replaced the teaser content with the full content of the post.
- Second, we now have a new section below our main content that lists any comment threads, with a photo of the comment's author.
- Third, we have a comment form that allows users to leave their name, a subject, and a comment for each post.

Having identified these three different components, we can now take a quick look at what our Blog detail page currently looks like and discuss the best way to tackle each of these requirements.

Previewing our Blog detail page

Navigate to one of the Blog detail pages by clicking on the Post title from the main blog page or simply entering `/blog/post-one` in the browser:

We are in luck when it comes to our sidebar elements, as they are already positioned and themed the way they appear in the mockup. However, upon closer review we can see that we are missing some elements on our Blog detail page, or they are not themed the we may have expected. These issues may include:

- Post date
- Post title
- Post tags properly themed
- Comment thread
- Comment form

The challenge for us is to think how Drupal outputs each of these sections and address them individually as we build our Twig templates. Since we have Twig debugging enabled, we can determine that we should start with creating a new `node--post--full.html.twig` template.

Creating a Post Full template

While we know what our new Twig template should be named, we should also consider just how similar the Blog detail page is to each Post displayed on our Blog listing page. In fact, the only real differences are that our Blog detail displays the full content of our Post along with the Comments.

So instead of creating a brand new template, we can begin by duplicating the `node--post--listing.html.twig` template located in our `themes/octo/templates` folder and rename it `node--post--full.html.twig`.

Make sure to clear Drupal's cache and refresh the Blog detail page.

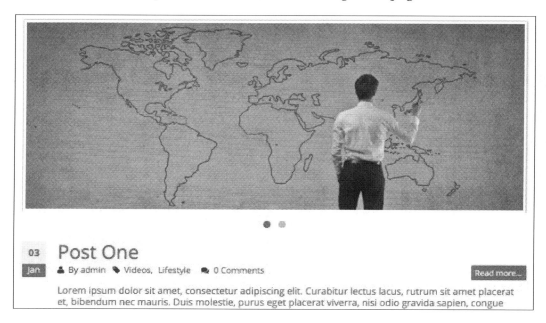

At first glance, we would think that most of our theming is completed for us. However, we actually have some components that need to be removed, such as the read more link and the teaser field. While some of these fields may not be displayed because they are being controlled from the Manager display admin, it is still good practice to remove these fields from our template.

Altering fields

We can begin by removing and replacing fields that we do not need. Begin by opening our Twig template, `node--post--full.html.twig`, and adjusting the markup in our `post-content` section:

New markup

```
<div class="post-content">
  {{ title_prefix }}
  <h2{{ title_attributes }}>
    <a href="{{ url }}" rel="bookmark">{{ label }}</a>
  </h2>
  {{ title_suffix }}

  <div class="post-meta">
    <span class="post-meta-user">
      <i class="fa fa-user"></i> By {{ author_name }}
    </span>

    <span class="post-meta-tag">
      <i class="fa fa-tag"></i> {{ content.field_tags }}
    </span>

    <span class="post-meta-comments">
      <i class="fa fa-comments"></i>
      <a href="{{ url }}/#comments">{{ comment_count }}</a>
    </span>

  </div>
</div>
```

Make sure to save the template, clear Drupal's cache, and refresh the Blog detail page. The read more link should now be gone and the page is starting to resemble our mockup:

One thing we may be asking ourselves is how is the full content of our Post being displayed if we are not printing it? We actually are printing it at the bottom of our template using the general {{ content }} variable. If we want to be more specific though, we can add the full content field directly to our template and exclude it from the general content variable by following these steps:

1. Open node--post--full.html.twig.

2. Modify the markup as shown here:

   New markup
   ```
   <div class="post-meta">
     ..existing markup..

     {{ content.field_full_content }}
   </div>

   {{ content|without('field_image','field_teaser', 'field_tags',
   'field_full_content') }}

   </article>
   ```

Make sure to save the template, clear Drupal's cache, and refresh the Blog detail page. We now have the first part of our blog detail page complete. What we are still missing though is the comment thread and comment form, which will allow users to interact with each post. Let's take a look at how to work with comments.

Working with comments

Drupal 8 introduced comments as a fieldable entity that can now be referenced by any other entity using the new comment field. So what exactly does that mean? This means you no longer manage comments as a configuration option from a content type. The benefit of moving comments into a fieldable entity is that it provides a wide range of flexibility. We can add additional fields if needed along with additional display modes to output comments.

In the case of our Post content type, we already created a relationship to comments to expedite our theming, but we should take a moment to review how that was done and then move on to printing comments in our Blog detail page.

Introducing Comment types

Comment types can be located by navigating to /admin/structure/comment and, as we can see by the interface in the following image, Comment types look very similar to Content types:

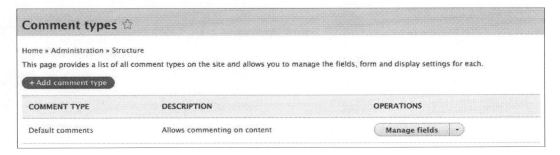

For our website, we are using the Default comments that Drupal creates as part of the default installation profile. It is just as simple to create additional Comment types the same way you would create any Content type. This comes in handy for providing multiple feedback mechanisms and provides us with various ways to display comments.

Reviewing Default Comment type fields and display

If we navigate to the **Manage fields** configuration by clicking on the **Manage fields** button, we will see that there is only a single text area field called Comment. This field allows the user to input the specific comment. We could easily add additional fields to capture more data, but this single field will suffice for our use.

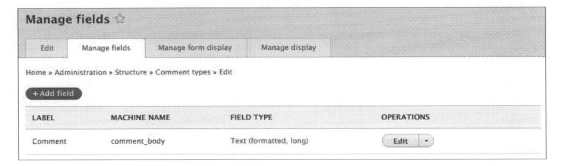

While this appears to be the only field, there are actually two additional default fields for author and subject that we may not be aware of until we navigate to the **Manage form display** screen by clicking on the **Manage form display** tab at the top of the page:

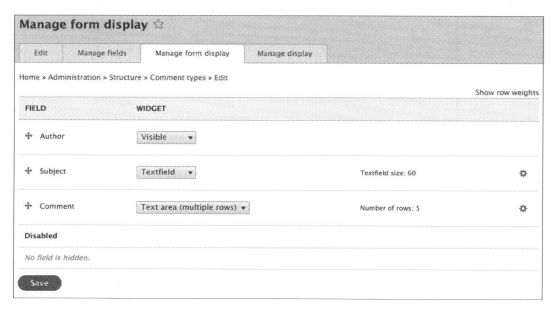

One thing to note is that the **Manage form display** interface handles the display of the comment form and any of its fields that are displayed when a user looks to add a comment to a Post. These fields can be reordered, disabled, or modified as needed.

This differs from the **Manage display** interface, which controls the display of the comments thread that users see when viewing a post. We can navigate to the **Manage display** screen by clicking on its tab:

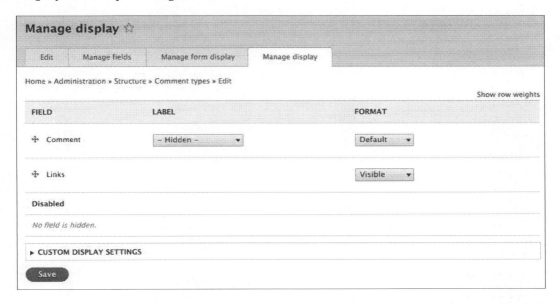

A very important field to point out on the **Manage display** screen is the **Links** field. If this field is disabled for any Comment type, we will have no links attached to each comment thread that allow for replying, editing, or deleting a thread, based on a user's permissions. Now that we have oriented ourselves with the new Comment type, we will need to enable it for our Post type.

Enabling Post Type Comments field

Currently our Blog detail page is not displaying a comment form and therefore no way to display comment threads. If we navigate to `/admin/structure/types/manage/post/display`, we will be taken to the **Manage display** screen for out Post type. If we take a closer look, we can see that the **Comment** field is disabled for our **Default** display mode:

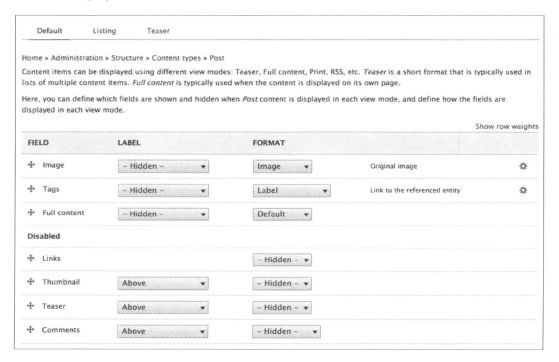

We can remedy that by dragging the **Comments** field out of the **Disabled** section and placing it directly under the **Full content** field:

Once complete, click the **Save** button. If we navigate back to `/blog/post-one`, we will see the default appearance of our Comment form:

One thing still missing is some actual comment threads, so let's take a moment and add a few comments by filling in the comment form for Post one. Make sure to fill in both the **Subject** and **Comment** fields. Once we hit the **Save** button, you should now see a new comment thread displayed directly above the comment form, as shown in the following screenshot:

A general rule of theming comments is that when someone replies to an existing comment, the reply is displayed directly below the original comment and indented so that you have a visual clue as to the thread developing. So that we can see what an actual thread looks like, let's reply to our first comment by clicking on the **Reply** link, filling in the required fields, and hitting the **Save** button. Our **Comments** section should now contain a comment thread:

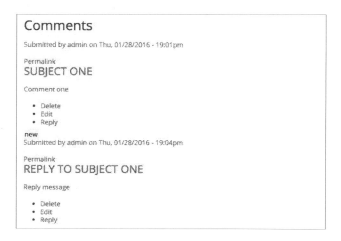

Perfect, we now have almost everything we need in place to theme the Comment section of our Blog detail page. We have a **Comments** thread, nested comments, and an **Add new comment** form. We will address each of these components individually in order to implement our required markup to match our mockup.

Creating a Field Comments template

Just like any other field attached to a content type, this has a corresponding field template that Twig uses to output the content. If we inspect the markup of our Comment section, we can determine which template is being used and where it is located:

```
<!-- THEME DEBUG -->
<!-- THEME HOOK: 'field' -->
<!-- FILE NAME SUGGESTIONS:
   * field--node--field-comments--post.html.twig
   * field--node--field-comments.html.twig
   * field--node--post.html.twig
   * field--field-comments.html.twig
   x field--comment.html.twig
   * field.html.twig
-->
<!-- BEGIN OUTPUT from 'core/modules/comment/templates/field--comment.html.twig' -->
<section data-quickedit-field-id="node/11/field_comments/en/full">...</section>
<!-- END OUTPUT from 'core/modules/comment/templates/field--comment.html.twig' -->
```

Using **FILE NAME SUGGESTIONS**, we can navigate to the `core/modules/` `comment/templates` folder and copy the `field--comment.html.twig` template to our `themes/octo/templates` folder. Next, we will need to replace the markup within our template with the following new markup:

New markup

```
<section id="comments" class="post-block post-comments">

  {% if comments and not label_hidden %}
    {{ title_prefix }}
    <h3{{ title_attributes }}>
      <i class="fa fa-comments"></i>{{ label }}
    </h3>
    {{ title_suffix }}
  {% endif %}

  {{ comments }}

  {% if comment_form %}
    <div class="post-block post-leave-comment">
      <h3{{ content_attributes }}>{{ 'Leave a comment'|t }}</h3>
      {{ comment_form }}
    </div>
  {% endif %}

</section>
```

Make sure to save the template, clear Drupal's cache, and refresh the Blog detail page for Post One. The formatting we just applied adds a few classes to our comments wrapper, as well as adding a Font Awesome icon to the Comments heading. We should also notice that the `field--comment.html.twig` template really breaks the entire comment block into three distinct regions:

- The Comment heading, indicated by the {{ label }} variable
- The Comment thread, indicated by the {{ comments }} variable
- The Comment form, indicated by the {{ comment_form }} variable

Now that we have identified the three key pieces of a comment block, we need to focus on the {{ comments }} variable itself as it contains our comment thread. Currently, our thread is not displaying as we would like. Each thread is hard to differentiate where it begins and ends, and we are missing the styling that would help it match our mockup. To remedy this, we can take advantage of another Twig template.

Theming the Comment thread

Drupal only provides two Twig templates for outputting the Comment section of our page. We have already addressed the Comment field template, so all that is left for us to target is the `comment.html.twig` template. It is this template that contains the markup for the thread that displays, and we can modify the markup to display the content exactly how we need it by following these steps.

Using the **FILE NAME SUGGESTIONS,** we can navigate to the `core/modules/comment/templates` folder and copy the `comment.html.twig` template to our `themes/octo/templates` folder. Next, we will need to replace the markup with our own, making sure to print the existing variables:

New markup

```
<article{{ attributes }}>

  <div class="comment">
    {{ user_picture }}

    <div class="comment-block">
      <div class="comment-arrow"></div>

      <div class="comment-by">
        <strong><span>{{ author }}</span></strong>
        <span class="pull-right">
          {{ content.links }}
        </span>
      </div>

      <div class="comment-content">
        {{ content.comment_body }}
      </div>

      <div class="comment-date">
        <span class="date pull-right">{{ created }}</span>
      </div>
    </div>

  </div>

  {% if parent %}
    <p class="visually-hidden">{{ parent }}</p>
  {% endif %}

</article>
```

Make sure to save the template, clear Drupal's cache, and then reload the Blog detail page in the browser. Our Comments thread should now be styled and indented as shown in the following image:

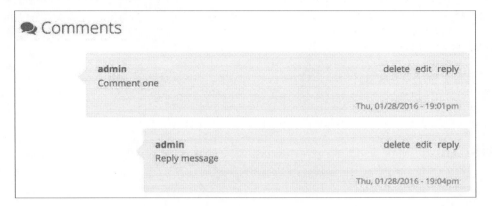

Obviously there is something still missing. The user image associated with the author of each comment is not being displayed. Also, our comment date is formatted using military time, which the majority of our users may not be familiar with. We can address both of these items fairly easily.

Enabling user photos for Comment threads

Right now, we have comment threads lacking a photo to identify the user that posted the comment. In most cases, this is due to a user not having uploaded a photo to their Drupal profile. In order for us to have an image for the `{{ user_picture }}` variable to print, we will need to upload our own photo.

Navigate to `/user/1/edit`, which will take us to our current profile page, keeping in mind that the user ID may be different, depending on how many users are in Drupal:

1. Locate the **Picture** field.
2. Click on the **Choose File** button.
3. Locate a photo or any image we want to represent ourselves, select it and then click on the **Open** button in the File dialog window.

4. We should now see a thumbnail image:

5. Click the **Save** button to complete this.

If we navigate back to the Blog detail page located at /blog/post-one, we will see the user photo displayed next to each comment:

Now that we have the user image being displayed, we still need to clean up the markup by formatting the field template.

Cleaning up the User Picture field

If we inspect the markup for the user picture field, we will notice an <article> element wrapped around each image. Currently, the <article> element is respecting the block display and causing the user image to display on a separate line. While we could easily adjust the CSS to resolve this, we want to respect the HTML provided in the mockup.

To bring our User Picture back in line with how it displays in our mockup, we will need to first modify the `user.html.twig` template.

Begin by navigating to the `core/modules/user/templates` folder and copying the `user.html.twig` template to our `themes/octo/templates` folder. Next, we will replace the current markup with the following:

New markup

```
{% if content %}
  {{- content -}}
{% endif %}
```

Make sure to save the template, clear Drupal's cache, and then refresh the page in the browser. You will not see a visual change just yet, but the surrounding `article` element is now removed.

Creating the Field User Picture template

We will need to modify an additional Twig template that outputs the image itself. We will be borrowing the markup and styling from an earlier template so that our user picture is framed similar to our Post image.

1. Begin by navigating to the `core/modules/system/templates` folder and copying the `field.html.twig` template to our `themes/octo/templates` folder.

2. Next, we will rename `field.html.twig` to `field--user-picture.html.twig`, based on the recommended file name suggestions.

3. Finally, we will replace the markup with the following:

   New markup

   ```
   {% for item in items %}
     <div class="img-thumbnail">
       <div class="user-picture">
         {{ item.content }}
       </div>
     </div>
   {% endfor %}
   ```

Make sure to save the template, clear Drupal's cache, and then refresh the page in the browser. Our comment threads are perfectly styled, with the user image for each thread aligned next to each other.

At this point, we only have one more item to adjust for our comment thread. Currently, the default date for each comment is displayed in a 24-hour format, often referred to as military time.

Date and time formats

There are multiple ways to address date and time formats within Drupal. In *Chapter 8, Theming Our Blog Listing Page*, we worked with Twig filters and field variables to format the date. However, the comment thread date is already formatted for us using the default medium date format. So where would we need to configure this to display a non-24-hour format?

If we navigate to `/admin/configuration/region/date-time`, we will get a glimpse of the date and time formats that Drupal configures for us:

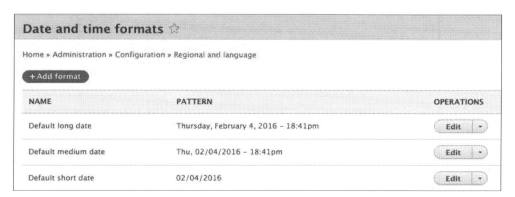

Each of the date and time formats that are shown can be used within Drupal by either managing a Content types field format or referencing the name with a Twig template or preprocessing function. As we can see, some of the formats can be edited, while others cannot. We can also add additional formats.

In the case of our comment thread created date, we can assume by reviewing the **PATTERN** of **Default medium date** that this is the format being used. Luckily for us, we can easily modify the pattern to change the time from 24-hour to 12-hour format by following these steps:

1. Click on the **Edit button** for the **Default medium date** format.

2. Replace **Format string** with the following pattern:

   ```
   D, m/d/Y - h:ia
   ```

3. Click on the **Save format** button.

We have successfully changed the default medium date format. One thing to note is that the date and time formats in Drupal take advantage of the Date object in PHP. We can get additional information regarding various formats by reviewing the parameters available in the manual at http://php.net/manual/en/function.date.php.

If we now navigate back to our Blog detail page for Post One, we will see that our comment threads now use the modified default medium date format:

Our Blog detail page is just about complete. While users can now read our Posts and comment on them, we are still missing the ability for users to share a post on their favorite social networks.

Implementing social sharing capabilities

Social networks such as Facebook, Twitter, and Pinterest provide another medium for content to be shared with family, friends, and coworkers. Most websites provide a mechanism for sharing content, and our Blog detail page is no different.

Based on our mockup, we allow users to share a post as well as see the number of likes, tweets, or pins. In fact, there are a number of different third-party libraries or APIs that make this functionality easy to implement. Services such as Share This, `http://www.sharethis.com/`, or even Add This , `https://www.addthis.com/`, provide either a library or contributed modules to implement this functionality within Drupal.

The Add This buttons

For our particular page, we will be using the Add This service. There are various button options and configurations that can be created, so to avoid any confusion with adding this service to our template, we will be using the standard buttons. The implementation of the Add This button requires each of us to have created a free account. However, for demonstration purposes, we will be using my account. Please remember to replace the `pubid` with yours once an account has been created.

The process of adding the Add This library to our Twig template requires us to configure the type of social sharing buttons we want to use, copy the JavaScript to our page, and then add specific markup that will enable the display of the buttons:

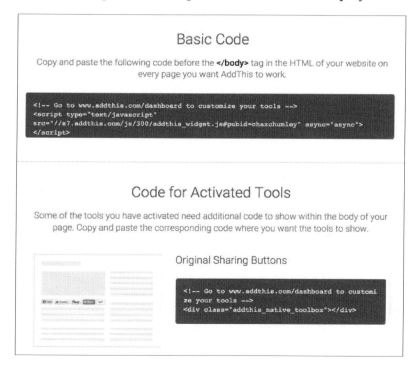

The basic code displayed above is a simple JavaScript block that needs to be placed within our webpage. We will be using our themes `octo.libraries.yml` file to configure this block and then using the {{ `attach_library` }} function to add it to our Blog detail page.

Creating a library entry

Begin by opening `octo.libraries.yml` located in our *themes/octo* folder. We will then add the following metadata to the bottom of our file:

```
add-this:
  version: VERSION
  js:
    //s7.addthis.com/js/300/addthis_widget.js#pubid=chazchumley: {
type: external, asynch: asynch }
```

Note that the JavaScript path is all on a single line. In the above metadata, we are pointing to an external script and are also adding a new parameter for calling the script asynchronously. Also, please remember to replace the `pubid` value with your Add This username.

Once we have added the metadata to our file, we can save `octo.libraries.yml` and then clear Drupal's cache.

Attaching the library to our Blog detail page

Now that Drupal has knowledge of our new library, we can attach it to our Blog detail page by following these steps:

1. Open `node--post--full.html.twig`.
2. Add the following Twig function directly below where we are referencing the owl-carousel:

   ```
   {{ attach_library('octo/add-this') }}
   ```

3. Save `node--post--full.html.twig`.

Make sure to clear Drupal's cache and then refresh the Blog detail page. We now need to add the markup required to display the sharing buttons on our page.

Displaying buttons

We will be adding some additional markup around the required div so that our "Share this post" section matches our mockup. With `node--post--full.html.twig` still open, we will add the following markup directly after the `{{ content.field_full_content }}` variable:

```
<div class="post-share">
  <h3><i class="fa fa-share"></i> Share this post</h3>
  <div class="addthis_native_toolbox"></div>
</div>
```

Make sure to clear Drupal's cache and then refresh the Blog detail page. If all the steps were completed successfully, we should see our new **Share this post** section displayed:

Congratulations, we have now completed the theming of our Blog detail page. Everything has been configured, styled, and modified to match our mockup.

Summary

While we revisited some common theming techniques, we also learned a few new ones. Slowly and methodically dissecting each section of our mockup, we walked through creating Twig templates, and worked with the new Comment field and a lot more to create a fully functional Blog detail page. We definitely covered a lot of material, so let's review everything we covered before moving on to the next chapter:

- We started by reviewing the Blog Detail mockup to identify key areas of our website that we would need to recreate.

- We familiarized ourselves with additional node templates and learned how to theme the default display of our Post content type.

- We dug a little deeper into the new Comment type and learned how to best manage the various Twig templates it provides. This included managing user profile pictures for each comment thread and configuring date and time formats for the comment created date.

- Finally, we implemented social sharing buttons using our themes `octo.libraries.yml` file, attaching the Add This library to our Blog detail page, and adding the required markup for our buttons to display properly.

In the next chapter, we will take a look at the new contact forms that are in the Drupal 8 core. We will add a default form to our page that users can interact with, and learn how to add a custom block to a Drupal-generated page. Even more excitingly, we will take a look at adding a Google Maps block to our page that provides a dynamic map with a map marker.

10

Theming Our Contact Page

Almost every website provides a mechanism for users to contact the individual, business, or association that owns the site, whether that be in the form of a simple e-mail link or something more advanced using a web form. Often, a contact page is part of the main menu hierarchy, as is evident in our mockup.

In this chapter, we will take a look at creating a contact page that uses the new contact forms that are part of Drupal 8 core. We will not be using any contributed modules, as core provides us with the configuration and templates needed to create most forms. We will also not be covering the extensive Form API, as it is beyond the scope of this book.

However, we will be learning the following theming techniques that will allow us to create a well-structured contact page:

- We will begin with reviewing the mockup of our contact page and identify how specific blocks or fields will need to be presented for display.

- Next, we will take a closer look at contact forms in Drupal and how to modify an existing form that we can use for our contact page.

- As Drupal creates the page that all contact forms utilize, we will make use of alternative regions within our theme to add additional content to our contact page.

- Finally, we will see how simple it is to add a Google map while working some more with libraries and Twig.

While we work through each section, we have the ability to refer back to the Chapter10 exercise files folder. Each folder contains start and end folders with files that we can use to compare our work when needed. This also includes database snapshots that will allow us to all start from the same point when working through various lessons.

Reviewing the contact page mockup

Like previous sections of our website, having a mockup to review makes planning how to develop a page much easier. Page structure, blocks, web forms, and other functionality we will need to consider can easily be discovered by looking at the contact page in the `Mockup` folder located in our exercise files. Begin by opening up the `contact.html` file within the browser.

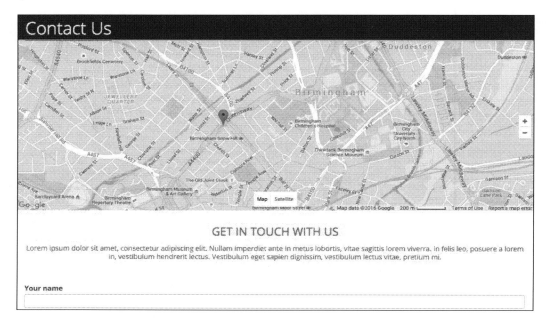

The contact page mockup has some fairly standard components that most websites seem to use today. Starting at the top of our layout and working our way down, we can identify three different sections that we will need to develop and theme for our Drupal site.

1. First, we have a Google map displaying the current address using a map marker. We will revisit building this section of the site after we have created our contact form.

2. Second, we have a simple block of information or callout telling users how they can get in touch with us.

3. The last section is the web form itself and is by far the most important component of the contact page.

Having identified these three different components, we will focus on the most important and most detailed piece of functionality first—the contact form.

Introducing contact forms

Contact forms in Drupal 8 have taken some of the characteristics of previously used contributed modules such as WebForm and placed the most common functionality into core. This new core feature allows us to create any type of form needed for users to be able to contact us. We can see the basic implementation of a contact form by navigating to /contact within our site.

By default, Drupal creates a contact form that contains fields for name, e-mail, subject, and message. As part of the database snapshot, we have a contact page already created for us. However, we can easily add additional fields and manage the display and format of fields just like we can with content types.

To get a better understanding of how contact forms work, we can navigate to the **Contact forms** admin by entering /admin/structure/contact within our browser.

We can see that two forms have already been configured:

- **Personal contact form** that each user of our site will receive.
- **Contact Us** (renamed from the default of **Website feedback**) that our global contact page will be using.

Editing a contact form

Contact forms can be managed similar to how we work with content types and blocks. Contact forms are also fieldable and can have additional fields added to them to capture a variety of information. We can get a closer look at how our form can be configured by clicking on the **Edit** button to the right of the **Contact Us** form.

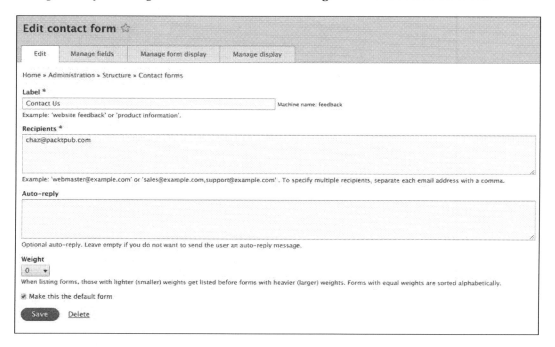

The Edit screen consists of several fields vital to a working contact form:

- A **Label** that identifies which form we are creating
- **Recipients**, which contains a required list of e-mail addresses that we would like the web form and its content to be sent to
- **Auto-reply**, which contains an optional message that we want to send users after they have submitted the form
- The **Weight** field, used to simply sort multiple forms on the contact form's admin page
- The **Make this the default form** checkbox, which designates which form to use as the default contact form

One thing to note is that the default **Website feedback** form has been renamed to **Contact Us** using the **Label** field. If for some reason the database snapshot has not been imported at this time, you will see the default form instead.

Whenever we create a new contact form, the machine name provided by the **Label** field is used to generate the predefined URL of `/contact/machine-name`. In the case of our Contact Us form, we were able to navigate to the form by entering `/contact` or `/contact/feedback`. Keep in mind that we cannot modify the machine name once we have entered a label and saved the form.

Managing form fields

Our Contact Us form is not using any additional fields. However, if we wanted to add any, the functionality is identical to how fields are added to content types or blocks using the Field UI.

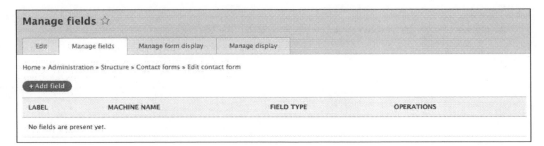

Managing form display

Any time we create a new contact form, there are five fields that are created by default that Drupal requires to handle functionality behind the scenes. Those five fields can be seen on the **Manage form display** screen.

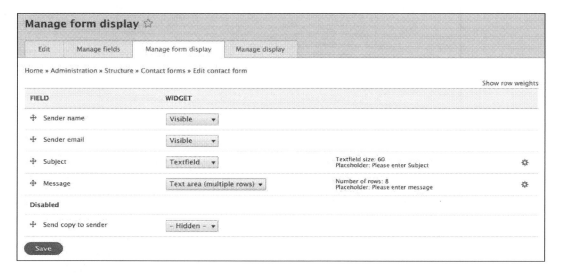

All contact forms consist of the following fields:

- **Sender name**—an input to collect the user's name
- **Sender email**—an input to collect the user's e-mail
- **Subject**—an input for the subject line of the form
- **Message**—a text area to collect the message or content of the form
- **Send copy to sender**—a checkbox to allow the user to receive a copy of the submitted form

For our contact form, we have chosen to disable the **Send copy to sender** control. This means that when a user submits the form, they will not receive a copy of their submission.

As we can see from the **Manage form display** screen, we have all the flexibility to enable, disable, and format our fields as needed.

Now that we have a better understanding of contact forms, let's navigate back to our default contact page located at /contact and discuss how we will begin to lay out the remaining components.

Contact page layout

So far, we have been working with mainly content types and blocks. Content created using any of our content types generates a Node and a Twig template with it. However, contact forms generate a page for us that is not quite like what we are used to working with. The only way for us to add additional content such as our Callout block or Google map is by using blocks. This requires us to rethink the layout of the Contact page a little.

We can begin by inspecting the markup to see what Twig templates Drupal is providing us.

```
<!-- BEGIN OUTPUT from 'core/modules/block/templates/block.html.twig' -->
▼<div id="block-octo-content">
  <!-- THEME DEBUG -->
  <!-- THEME HOOK: 'form' -->
  <!-- BEGIN OUTPUT from 'core/modules/system/templates/form.html.twig' -->
  ▼<form class="contact-message-feedback-form contact-message-form contact-form" data-drupal-selector="contact-message
    <!-- THEME DEBUG -->
    <!-- THEME HOOK: 'form_element' -->
    <!-- BEGIN OUTPUT from 'core/modules/system/templates/form-element.html.twig' -->
    ▶<div id="edit-name" class="js-form-item form-item js-form-type-item form-item-name js-form-item-name">...</div>
    <!-- END OUTPUT from 'core/modules/system/templates/form-element.html.twig' -->
```

It appears that the Contact Us form is output as a form element and is assigned to our Main content region. This means that we can add additional content both above and below the form using the Before Content and After Content regions. In fact, this is a perfect example of why creating regions in our design that can appear above or below the main content flow provides flexibility.

Adding a Callout block

We will take advantage of the Before Content region we created in our theme's configuration file to add our next component. The Callout block we identified in our mockup earlier allows us to add additional information that helps introduce our Contact form.

If we quickly review the `contact.html` page from the `Mockup` folder, we can identify that we will need to create a custom block that consists of a heading and a paragraph.

GET IN TOUCH WITH US

Lorem ipsum dolor sit amet, consectetur adipiscing elit. Nullam imperdiet ante in metus lobortis, vitae sagittis lorem viverra. In felis leo, posuere a lorem in, vestibulum hendrerit lectus. Vestibulum eget sapien dignissim, vestibulum lectus vitae, pretium mi.

This is a pretty simple block to create, so let's get started by navigating to /admin/structure/block, which will take us to the **Block layout** admin.

Next, we will follow these steps:

1. Click on the **Place block** button in the **Before Content** region.
2. Click on the **Add custom block** button.
3. Enter a **Block description** of Contact Callout.
4. Select **HTML No Editor** from the **Text format** dropdown.
5. Add the markup located in the Chatper10/start/content/ContactCallout.txt file to the **Body** field, as shown in the following image:

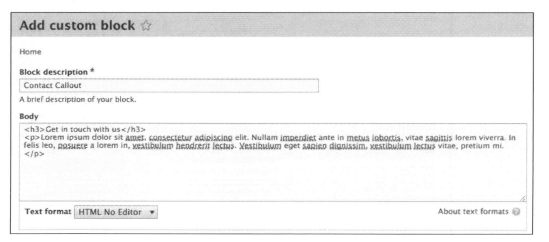

6. Click on the **Save** button to proceed to the **Configure block** screen.
7. Uncheck the **Display title** checkbox.
8. Select the **Pages** vertical tab within the **Visibility** section.
9. Enter a value of /contact in the **Pages** text area.
10. Choose **Show for the listed pages** under **Negate the condition**.
11. Choose **Before Content** from the **Region** field.
12. Click on the **Save block** button.

We now have our Contact Callout block created and assigned to our Before Content region. Let's make sure that our new block is displaying correctly by navigating back to our Contact page.

> ### GET IN TOUCH WITH US
>
> Lorem ipsum dolor sit amet, consectetur adipiscing elit. Nullam imperdiet ante in metus lobortis, vitae sagittis lorem viverra. In felis leo, posuere a lorem in, vestibulum hendrerit lectus. Vestibulum eget sapien dignissim, vestibulum lectus vitae, pretium mi.

Therefore, our content is displaying in the correct region but not quite visually what we were expecting. However, like any other block, we can remedy this by creating a Twig template and apply any additional markup or classes that may be needed.

Creating the Callout block template

Using the **FILE NAME SUGGESTIONS**, we can navigate to the `core/modules/block/templates` folder and copy the `block.html.twig` template to our `themes/octo/templates` folder. Next, we will need to rename the template to `block--contactcallout.html.twig` and then replace the markup with the following:

New markup

```
{% set classes = ['block';'contact-intro'] %}

<div{{ attributes.addClass(classes) }}>
  <div class="container">
    {{ title_prefix }}
    {% if label %}
    <h4{{ title_attributes }}>{{ label }}</h4>
    {% endif %}
    {{ title_suffix }}
    {% block content %}
    {{ content }}
    {% endblock %}
  </div>
</div>
```

Make sure to save the template, clear Drupal's cache, and refresh the Contact page in the browser. Our block should now look exactly like our mockup. Now we will move on to our next component, which involves integrating Google Maps.

Integrating Google Maps into our contact page

The Google Maps API provides developers with the flexibility to add interactive mapping functionality to any website. With our Contact page, we are implementing a map that provides a map marker pointing to a specific location based on the latitude and longitude that we will provide. As we implement this functionality, it is important to note that we will not be covering the in-depth details required to create a Google map or work with the developer API found at `https://developers.google.com/maps/tutorials/fundamentals/adding-a-google-map`.

Instead, we will take advantage of one of the many libraries that simplify the JavaScript knowledge required. For our next lesson, we have chosen to work with the `jQuery-gMap` plugin, which can be found at `https://github.com/marioestrada/jQuery-gMap`.

In order to implement our map, we will need to follow a series of steps that involve making sure that Drupal can locate the `jquery-gMap` library, create a library entry with any dependencies, create our custom block, and finally attach the library to our template.

Because the JavaScript to initialize Google Maps is quite long, we have broken the script into its own file. This allows us to keep specific functionality organized better for implementation. Let's get started by configuring the necessary files.

Configure Google Maps

In order to configure the Google Maps library, we will be adding two different library entries to our `octo.libraries.yml` file. The first will be pointing to our custom map script. The second will be pointing to the jquery-gmap library, which includes an external reference of the Google Maps API.

Before we get started, let's ensure that we have the proper files copied to our theme. Begin by navigating to the `Chapter10/start/themes/octo/vendor` folder and copy the `jquery-gmap` folder to our `themes/octo/vendor` folder. Next, copy the `map.js` file from the `Chapter10/start/themes/octo/js` folder to our `themes/octo/js` folder.

With the two files now accessible by Drupal, we can add the library entries:

1. Open `octo.libraries.yml`.

2. Add the following entry:

```
map:
  version: VERSION
  js:
    js/map: {}
  dependencies:
    - octo/jquery-gmap
```

Note the dependency to jquery-gmap; we will add that entry directly below the jquery-gmap entry.

3. Add the following entry:

```
jquery-gmap:
  version: 2.1.5
  js:
    vendor/jquery-gmap/jquery.gmap.min.js: {}
    //maps.google.com/maps/api/js?sensor=true: { type: external }
  dependencies:
    - core/jquery
```

Make sure to save `octo.libraries.yml` and clear Drupal's cache to ensure that our new library entries are added to the theme registry. To recap, we added two library entries that will allow us to enable Google Maps.

The first entry points to our custom JavaScript that initializes the map and then looks for any markup within our page that has an ID of #map, and renders a map. The first entry also has a dependency of jquery-gmap, which we have added.

The second entry points to our vendor library, which simplifies the creation of Google Maps, and because it obviously requires both jQuery and the Google Maps API, we add those to our entry.

With Google Maps now configured, we will need to create a new block and add the required markup that will render our map.

Creating our Google Maps block

We will take advantage of the Before Content region to add our Contact Map block. Being by navigating to `/admin/structure/block` and follow these steps.

1. Click on the **Place block** button in the **Before Content** region:

2. Click on the **Add custom block** button.

3. Enter a **Block description** of Contact Map.

4. Select **HTML No Editor** from the **Text format** dropdown.

5. Add the markup located in the `Chatper10/start/content/ContactMap.txt` file to the **Body** field, as shown in the following image:

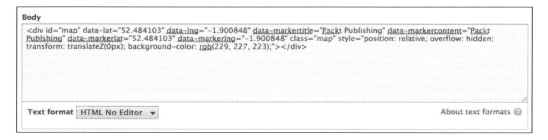

The markup we are adding introduces data attributes, which allow us to better describe the element being displayed while storing extra information. For example, we are adding data attributes for latitude and longitude that our custom script uses to render our map.

1. Click on the **Save** button to proceed to the **Configure block** screen.

2. Uncheck the **Display title** checkbox.

3. Select the **Pages** vertical tab within the **Visibility** section.

4. Enter a value of `/contact` in the **Pages** text area.

5. Choose **Show for the listed pages** under **Negate the condition**.

6. Choose **Before Content** from the **Region** field.

7. Click on the **Save block** button.

Once the block has been saved, make sure that the order of our Blocks with the Before Content region has the Contact Map displaying before our Contact Callout block.

Now that we have our Contact Map block created and assigned to the correct region, we will need to create a Twig template that will allow us to attach the library entry to it.

Creating the Callout Map template

If we navigate back to our Contact page, we will see the outline for our map represented by a gray box. Our markup is actually being output correctly, but we do not yet have a reference to the Google Maps script that renders the map. We can remedy this by using the **FILE NAME SUGGESTIONS** to create a Twig template for our block.

Navigate to the `core/modules/block/templates` folder and copy the `block.html.twig` template to our `themes/octo/templates` folder. Next, we will need to rename the template to `block--contactmap.html.twig` and then replace the markup with the following:

New markup

```
{{ attach_library('octo/map') }}

<div{{ attributes.addClass(classes) }}>
  {{ title_prefix }}
  {% if label %}
    <h4{{ title_attributes }}>{{ label }}</h4>
  {% endif %}
  {{ title_suffix }}
  {% block content %}
    {{ content }}
  {% endblock %}
</div>
```

Make sure to save the template, clear Drupal's cache, and refresh the Contact page in the browser then. Now we have our map rendering properly.

Summary

While our Contact Us page may have seemed at first to be a little more complex, it actually turned out to be quite simple as we were able to harness the power of Drupal 8's core functionality when it comes to both blocks and the new contact forms. In review, we covered the following:

- We began by reviewing the Contact Us page mockup to identify specific components and functionality that we would need to build.

- Next, we took a look at how Drupal implements contact forms for general website feedback and how to configure the fields and display of forms for use on our Contact Us page.

- Then, we used the Block layout admin to create two blocks for use on our Contact Us page—one to implement a callout and the second to render a Google map.

- Finally, we used libraries, scripts, and Twig to attach our jquery-gmap functionality to our Contact Map block.

In the next chapter, we will move on to Drupal's core search functionality as we tie back in our search block. We will also work with global search, use Twig to theme the results, and discuss how to best handle the search in Drupal 8.

11
Theming Our Search Results

Providing users the capability to search content within Drupal will help you ensure that the various content types are easily discoverable. Whenever a user cannot find content they are looking for, they will generally default to using some sort of global search. Earlier, we developed a Search form block that we placed within the main menu to globally search our site. In this chapter, we will circle around this block and focus on the Search results page that is displayed.

- We will begin with reviewing the mockup of our search page and identify how our search form input and any search results will need to be presented for display
- Next, we will take a closer look at search pages in core to learn how to configure what will be displayed in our results
- Finally, we will extend upon search by working with the Search API module to provide flexibility regarding which content types and fields can be added to search and how to use views to display our results

While we work through each section, we have the ability to refer back to the `Chapter11` exercise files folder. Each folder contains a `start` and `end` folder with files that we can use to compare our work when needed. This also includes database snapshots that will allow us to all to start from the same point when working through various lessons.

Reviewing the Search Results mockup

Like previous sections of our website, having a mockup already provided to us to review makes planning how to develop a page much easier. Page structure, blocks, web forms, and other functionality, which we will need to consider, can easily be discovered by looking at the Search results page in the `Mockup` folder located in our exercise files.

Begin by opening up the `search.html` file within the browser.

```
Search

DISPLAYING 1 - 1 OF 1


Post One

Euismod atras vulputate iltricies etri elit. Class aptent taciti sociosqu ad litora torquent per conubia nostra, per inceptos
himenaeos. Nulla nunc dui, tristique in semper vel, congue sed ligula. Nam dolor ligula, faucibus id sodales in, auctor fringilla
libero. Pellentesque pellentesque tempor tellus eget hendrerit. Morbi id aliquam ligula. Aliquam id dui sem. Proin rhoncus
consequat nisi, eu ornare mauris tincidunt vitae.
```

The search page mockup provides us with a look at how the search term `lorem` would look when Drupal has returned results. The nice thing is that Drupal already provides us with a Search results page regardless of whether there are any results, which we will see later when we test different search terms. Because we do not need to provide any additional content, we will have no additional blocks of content to worry about. In fact, the only item we will need to focus on to recreate the themed mockup is the following:

1. First, we will need to inspect the markup provided by the Search input including any form of controls displayed on our page and determine if we need to alter the HTML.

2. Second, we will want to take a look at what Twig variables the Search results page is displaying and determine whether we need to suppress anything from being output.

Having identified these two different components, we need to keep one thing in mind. Our mockup takes into account what our search results will look like once we have extended Drupal's default search using the Search API module, `https://www.drupal.org/project/search_api`, which you will learn about later in the lesson. For now, let's take a look at what a default search results page looks like, so we can determine what work we have in store for us.

Looking at default Search results

The easiest way for us to take a look at what Drupal will return is by navigating to the homepage of our site and clicking on the search icon in the main menu.

We can now enter the keyword or term of `lorem`, as shown in the following image:

Once we have entered a keyword, we can hit *Enter* on our keyboard, which will take us to the Search results page located at `/search/node?keys=lorem`. We now have our first glance at the markup that Drupal displays by default.

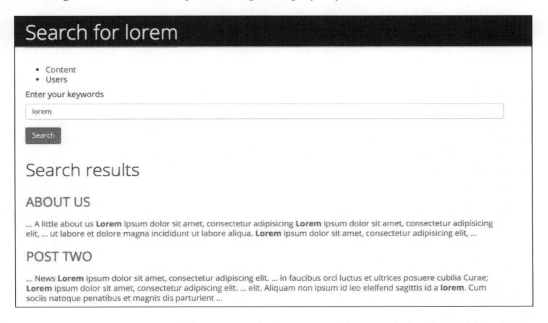

Comparing the results to our Mockup, we can visually see that each individual result is displaying as an ordered list. Within each result, there is also additional information such as comments, which we will need to suppress. Search provides us with a couple of Twig templates we can use to clean up our markup. But before we move on to theming, it would help to have a better understanding of the options we have within core search and how to configure it for our needs.

Introducing core search

The admin for search pages can be located by navigating to `/admin/config/search/pages`. Search pages are part of the core search and metadata that allow both users and content to be indexed and searched based on different factors. If we take a more detailed look, we will note that we can index content, configure minimum word length, and specify which search page to use for our results.

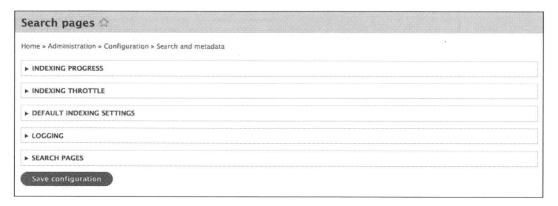

Indexing content

The most important aspect of search pages is the **INDEXING PROGRESS** status. Indexing is the process of crawling the site or database, which, in turn, stores a result set that allows content to be found when a user enters a keyword or term in the search form. Unless content has been indexed, we will not have any results to display.

In order to index our site, we need to complete two steps.

1. First, we must click on the **Re-index site** button, as shown in the following image:

   Clicking on the **Re-index site** button does not perform the actual indexing but merely triggers the indexing to occur.

2. Second, we must run a cron maintenance task, which can be located at /admin/config/system/cron by clicking on the **Run cron** button.

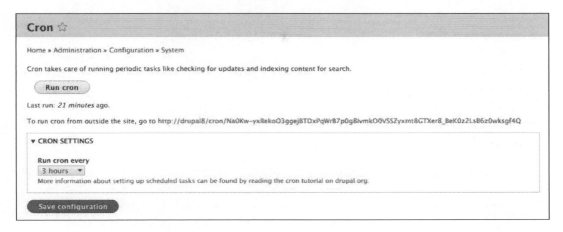

Cron allows specific tasks to run based on a set interval. The interval can be modified by changing **CRON SETTINGS**. By default, Drupal will run Cron every 3 hours. Cron is triggered when a user first visits the site after the 3-hour period has expired. Cron can also be triggered from a URL outside the site, which allows the manager of the Cron task to be run from the web server itself.

We will not be covering the configuration of Cron from systems administration level. Just know that we can manually run Cron when needed by visiting this page.

After completing the two steps required to index our site, if we navigate back to the search page's admin, we should now see that our **INDEXING PROGRESS** reports that **100% of the site has been indexed**.

Editing search pages

Another configuration within the search pages interface allows us to modify or configure additional settings for the label, URL, and content ranking.

In order to configure our **Content** search page, we will need to expand the **SEARCH PAGES** section and click on the **Edit** button, as shown in the following image:

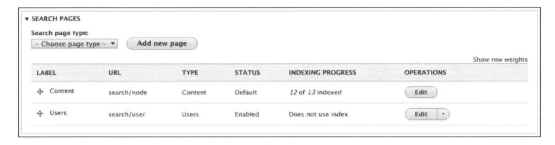

The most important configuration option is the **CONTENT RANKING** section, which allows us to influence certain factors that search uses, including but not limited to **Keyword relevance** and **Number of comments**. Content ranking, as shown in the following image, can be modified by changing the value next to each factor.

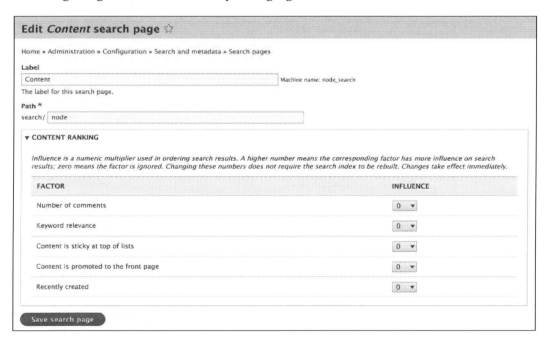

A higher **INFLUENCE** value determines the order of the search results, and modifying this value does not require reindexing the site. For demonstration purposes, we will not change the values on this page.

One important thing to note is that Drupal not only indexes content but also any users that have accounts within the website. Although this is great in order to create member directories, in our case, we only want users to be able to search on content. We can remedy this by disabling users' search pages.

Disabling search pages

From the **Search pages** admin, if we look under the **SEARCH PAGES** section, we will see **Users** currently enabled:

1. Click on the **Edit** button for Users.
2. Click on the **Delete** link.
3. Click on the **Delete** button for complete removal.

We can always create a new Users page at a later time by returning to the Search pages admin. One last step, make sure to reindex the site now that we have removed users and then it's time to move on to review the markup of our Search results page.

Working with Search Results templates

If we navigate back to our Search results page, we can inspect the markup to help locate which Twig templates Drupal uses to output the content. If we break the page into sections, we will be left with two different sections:

1. First is the search results list, which is currently being output as an ordered list. We can address this by modifying the `item-list-html.twig` template.
2. Second is the Search results itself, which contains the title and snippet with a highlighted keyword. We will address this by modifying the `search-result.html.twig` template.

Modifying the item list template

Using the **FILE NAME SUGGESTIONS**, we can navigate to the `core/modules/system/templates` folder and copy the `item-list.html.twig` template to our `themes/octo/templates` folder. Next, we will need to rename the template to `item-list--search-results.html.twig` and then add the following markup:

New markup

```
{% set classes = ['list-unstyled'] %}

{% if context.list_style %}
  {%- set attributes = attributes.addClass('item-list__' ~
```

```
      context.list_style) %}
  {% endif %}

  {% if items or empty %}

    {%- if title is not empty -%}
      <h3>{{ title }}</h3>
    {%- endif -%}

    {%- if items -%}
      <{{ list_type }}{{ attributes.addClass(classes) }}>
        {%- for item in items -%}
          <li{{ item.attributes }}>{{ item.value }}</li>
        {%- endfor -%}
      </{{ list_type }}>
    {%- else -%}
      {{- empty -}}
    {%- endif -%}

  {%- endif %}
```

Make sure to save the template, clear Drupal's cache, and then refresh the Search results page in the browser.

Our ordered list should now be displaying exactly like the Mockup. All we had to do to accomplish this was add a new CSS class to our template using Twig. We then added the new class to our markup using the Twig function `attributes.addClass()`.

Cleaning up each result

Now that our list is styled accordingly, we can focus on each individual search result. By default, each result returns the title, snippet, and additional information such as the number of comments if the result contains a Post. As each result is consistently styled, we will be removing the `{{ info }}` variable from the Twig template.

Using the **FILE NAME SUGGESTIONS**, we can navigate to the `core/modules/search/templates` folder and copy the `search-result.html.twig` template to our `themes/octo/templates` folder. Next, we will need to replace the markup by adding the following:

New markup

```
{{ title_prefix }}
<h3{{ title_attributes }}>
  <a href="{{ url }}">{{ title }}</a>
</h3>
{{ title_suffix }}
{% if snippet %}
  <p{{ content_attributes }}>{{ snippet }}</p>
{% endif %}
```

Make sure to save the template, clear Drupal's cache, and then refresh the Search results page in the browser. Each result is now consistent in the information it displays.

Search results

ABOUT US

... A little about us **Lorem** ipsum dolor sit amet, consectetur adipisicing **Lorem** ipsum dolor sit amet, consectetur adipisicing elit, ... ut labore et dolore magna incididunt ut labore aliqua. **Lorem** ipsum dolor sit amet, consectetur adipisicing elit, ...

POST TWO

... News **Lorem** ipsum dolor sit amet, consectetur adipiscing elit. ... in faucibus orci luctus et ultrices posuere cubilia Curae; **Lorem** ipsum dolor sit amet, consectetur adipiscing elit. ... elit. Aliquam non ipsum id leo eleifend sagittis id a **lorem**. Cum sociis natoque penatibus et magnis dis parturient ...

POST THREE

... Design **Lorem** ipsum dolor sit amet, consectetur adipiscing elit. ... in faucibus orci luctus et ultrices posuere cubilia Curae; **Lorem** ipsum dolor sit amet, consectetur adipiscing elit. ... elit. Aliquam non ipsum id leo eleifend sagittis id a **lorem**. Cum sociis natoque penatibus et magnis dis parturient ...

Search alternatives

Although working with the core search functionality in Drupal 8 can feel somewhat limited, it is not the only solution. There are alternatives to search that can be implemented to provide for more robust options. Two such alternatives are: Search API and Search API Solr Search. We will not be discussing Apache Solr as it is a little more complex to install and configure. However, the Search API will allow us to extend the default database search and is a perfect solution for our needs.

Search API

The Search API module at `https://www.drupal.org/project/search_api` provides a framework in order to extend core search. Multiple Search indexes can be created that then allow the use of Views to list search content. Each index can also can enhance the user interaction by creating a series of Facets that allow results to be filtered down to a granular level. Finally, each index based on the content type can be configured to let Drupal know exactly which fields should be included and the importance or weight of each field.

The advantage of using this great module is the flexibility it provides to display the search results. Instead of having to manage the display using a single Twig template as we did previously, we can use display modes for each content type. This, in turn, allows us to also have additional Twig templates for each result if needed.

Let's take a deeper look at enhancing our site's search functionality by installing and configuring the Search API module.

Installing the Search API

Begin by browsing the Search API project page located at `https://www.drupal.org/project/search_api` and extract the contents to our modules directory, as shown in the following image:

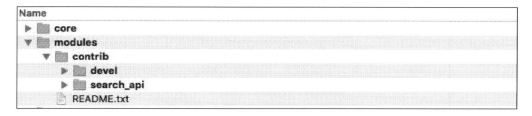

With the module in place, we can now navigate back to our Drupal instance and finish installing the Search API. Navigate to /admin/modules and locate the **Database Search** and **Search API** modules located in the **SEARCH** section.

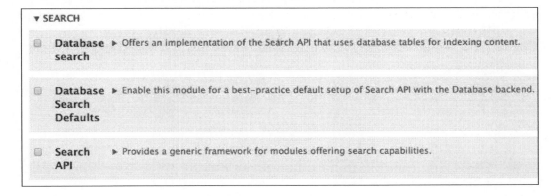

1. Select the checkbox for **Database Search**.
2. Select the checkbox for **Search API**.
3. Click on the **Install** button.

One important thing to note is that we will also want to uninstall the default Drupal Search module because we are replacing it with the Search API. We can do this by following these steps:

1. Select the **Uninstall** tab.
2. Select the checkbox for **Search**.
3. Click on the **Uninstall** button.
4. Click on the **Uninstall** button again from the **Confirm uninstall** page.

Now that we have replaced the default Drupal search with the Search API module, it is time to do some simple configuration.

Adding a server

The first step in configuring the Search API is to add a server definition for our index to use. In our case, we will be pointing to the default Drupal database.

To get started, we will need to navigate to `/admin/config/search/search-api`, which will bring us to the Search API admin page.

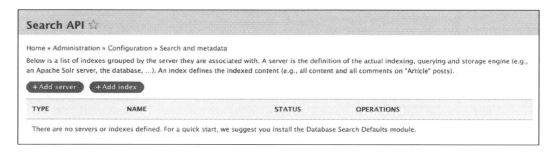

From here, we can follow these steps to add our server:

1. Click on the **Add server** button.
2. Enter a value of database in the **Server name** field.
3. Leave the remaining defaults, as shown in the following image:

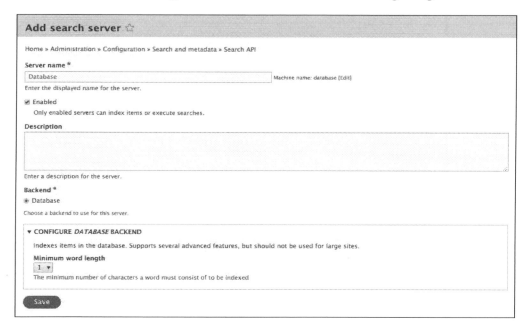

4. Click on the **Save** button.

We have now successfully added a search server that uses our Drupal database. We will point to this search server in our next step when we create an index.

Adding an index

Adding a search index allows us to be more explicit with the type of content we want Drupal to use when someone searches for a keyword or term. Having an index available allows us to use Views to create our Search results page and utilize our content's various display modes.

From the Search API admin page, we can follow these steps to add our index:

1. Click on the **Add index** button.
2. Enter a value of Content in the **Index name** field.
3. Choose **Content** from the **Data sources** field.
4. Choose **Database** from the **Server** checkbox.
5. Leave the remaining defaults, as shown in the following image:

6. Click on the **Save** button.

At this point, we have created an index but we have not defined which content types or fields our index will use. By default, all content types will be searched. While this may be okay in most cases, we only want our Post content to be searchable. Let's take a look at how to restrict which content types are indexed.

Configuring bundles

Content in Drupal is referred to as an entity, and the type of entity is called a bundle. We can configure which bundles are indexed by selecting them from our Edit page within the **CONFIGURE THE CONTENT DATASOURCE** section, as shown in the following image:

By default, all bundles will be indexed. However, we only want the post bundle to be searched, hence we make sure that we select the following:

1. Select **All except those selected** under **What should be indexed?**
2. Select **Headlines**, **Landing page**, and **Team** from **Bundles**.
3. Click on the **Save** button.

Now that we have configured our bundles, we will move on to choosing which fields will be searched on within our Post content type.

Adding fields to our index

The Search API module provides great flexibility when it comes to exactly what fields will be indexed. In the case of our Post content type, we only want to search on the **Title** and **Teaser** fields. We can start by selecting the **Fields** tab from our index and following these steps:

1. Click on the **Add fields** button.
2. Click on the **plus sign** next to **Content** to expand the field.

3. Click on the **Add** button next to **Title**.

4. Click on the **Add** button next to **Teaser**.

5. Click on the **Done** button.

We should now have our two fields added to the **CONTENT** section.

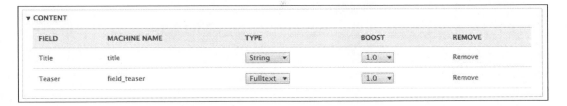

Although we are still within the **Fields** tab, we will want to take a quick look at some additional settings we have available to us.

- The first setting is the **TYPE** dropdown, which allows us to specify how a field will be treated when searched. In the case of our **Title** field, which is currently set to **String**, we will want to be able to do a **Fulltext** search on this field. We can select **Fulltext** from the dropdown to change the value. This will ensure that when a user enters a keyword, it searches all characters within the Title. If we left the default set to **String**, we would not get results returned properly.

- The second setting is the **BOOST** field, which allows us to give a field a higher level of importance when searched on. We will want our **Title** field to be more important than our **Teaser** field, so we can increase the **BOOST** value so that it has a higher number.

Make sure to click on the **Save changes** button to finish configuring our fields. Because we have made changes to both our bundles and fields, we will need to reindex our content. If we select the **View** tab, we can then click on the **Index now** button.

Now that our index is ready to use, we can create our Search results view.

Creating a Search Results View

We should be very comfortable working with Views, but this will be the first time we have used a search index as the source. To get started, we will need to navigate to /admin/structure/views and click on the **Add new view** button.

From the **Views** admin screen, we will add the following information:

- **VIEW BASIC INFORMATION**:
    1. **View name: Search**.
    2. Check the **Description** box.
    3. **Description: Search results**.

- **VIEW SETTINGS**: **Show**: **Index Content sorted by**: **Unsorted**.
- **PAGE SETTINGS**:
    1. Check: **Create a page**.
    2. **Page title: Search**.
    3. **Path: search**.

- **PAGE DISPLAY SETTINGS**:
    1. **Display format: Unformatted list of: Rendered entity**.
    2. **Items to display**: 10.
    3. Click on the **Save and edit** button.

From the **Search (Index Content)** admin, we will need to add some additional settings to our page. This includes selecting the display mode for our post to use, a filter criteria so that we can expose a form to replace our Global Search form, and a header to display the number of results.

Using the Search index view mode

We are familiar with using view modes to display content within a view. Our Search view will be using the Search index view mode, which we will need to add to our Post content type. Navigate to /admin/structure/types/manage/post/display and expand the **CUSTOM DISPLAY SETTINGS** field.

1. Select **Search index** from the **Use custom display settings for the following modes**.
2. Click on the **Save** button.

Next, we will want to enable only our **Teaser** field to display when the Search index view mode is used. We can accomplish this by selecting the **Search index** tab and adding our **Teaser** field, as shown in the following image:

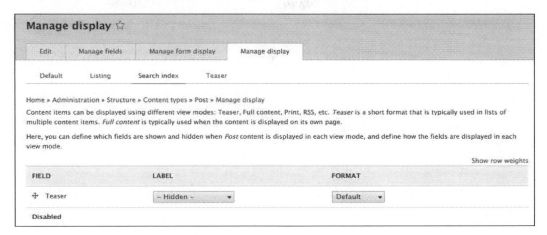

With the field now enabled, make sure to click on the **Save** button to complete our changes. We can now navigate back to our Search view and select our new view mode.

Begin by navigating to `/admin/structure/views/view/search` and follow these steps:

1. Select the **Settings** link next to **Rendered entity** within the **FORMAT** section.
2. Choose **Search index** from the **View mode for datasource Content, bundle Post** dropdown.
3. Click on the **Apply** button.
4. Click on the **Save** button to finalize our changes.

If we preview our results, we should see only the title and teaser fields being returned. Next, we need to add a Fulltext search filter that we can expose to our end users.

Adding filter criteria

Within the **FILTER CRITERIA** section, we can add various filters and expose them for use within our page. The form we will be adding will also be replacing our Global search form within the header:

1. Click on the **Add** button under **FILTER CRITERIA**.
2. Choose **Fulltext search**.
3. Click on the **Apply (all displays)** button.
4. Enter a value of 3 within the **Minimum keyword length** field.
5. Click on the **Apply (all displays)** button.
6. Click on the **Save** button to finalize our changes.

We now have a Fulltext search field added to our view. However, we still need to expose the form to end users. We can enable this by selecting the **Search: Fulltext search** link and following these steps:

1. Click on the **Expose this filter to visitors, to allow them to change it** checkbox.
2. Delete the **Label** value.
3. Replace the **Filter identifier** field value with the value term.
4. Click on the **Apply (all displays)** button.
5. Click on the **Save** button to finalize our changes.

Now that we have exposed our form, we will want to make it available within the Block layout page. We can do this by expanding the **ADVANCED** section of our view and following these steps:

- **EXPOSED FORM:**
  1. Select the link next to **Expose form in block**.
  2. Select **Yes**.
  3. Click on the **Apply** button.

- **OTHER:**
  1. Select the **Machine Name** link and change the value to search.
  2. Click on the **Apply** button.
  3. Select the **CSS class** link and change the value to search-index.
  4. Click on the **Apply (all displays)** button.
  5. Click on the **Save** button to finalize our changes.

With our exposed form now available to our Block layout, let's add it back to our Header region so that we can test our Search view.

Placing our exposed search form

If we navigate to /admin/structure/block, we will now be able to add our exposed form to the Header region. This new exposed form will replace the global search form.

1. Click on the **Place block** button next to the **Header** region.
2. Click on the **Place block** button next to **Exposed form: search-search**.
3. Uncheck **Display title**.
4. Add a value of search_form_block in the **Machine-readable name** field.
5. Click on the **Save block** button.

If we navigate to our home page, we can now test our exposed search form by clicking on the search icon. At first glance, we may not notice any difference from our original search form. However, we are missing the placeholder that once prompted our users to enter their search terms. Let's remedy this by adding some custom JavaScript to our theme that will add back this attribute.

Adding our placeholder attribute

So far we have only worked with Twig templates to add additional attributes to our markup. However, there may be times where simple JavaScript makes more sense to add to our project to add functionality. In the case of our Search form input, we would like to prompt our users what to enter, but the input is currently empty. Using some simple jQuery, we can target the element and add our placeholder attribute.

If we open up octo.js, located in our themes/octo/js folder, we can add the following snippet directly after the last function to accomplish this:

JavaScript

```
// Add Placeholder attribute
$(".search-block-form #edit-term").attr("placeholder", "Enter your
search terms");
```

Make sure to save the file, clear Drupal's cache and then refresh the homepage. If we now click on the search icon, we will see that we now have a placeholder prompting our users what to enter.

The JavaScript that we added uses jQuery to point to the element and then adds an attribute to the element with the specified value. This is an example of how easy it is to use custom script to add simple functionality.

Using our search form

Let's now add a search term to our input. We can enter the term Post and hit *Enter*, which will take us to the Search results page generated by our view.

Search

Post One

Euismod atras vulputate iltricies etri elit. Class aptent taciti sociosqu ad litora torquent per conubia nostra, per inceptos himenaeos. Nulla nunc dui, tristique in semper vel, congue sed ligula. Nam dolor ligula, faucibus id sodales in, auctor fringilla libero. Pellentesque pellentesque tempor tellus eget hendrerit. Morbi id aliquam ligula. Aliquam id dui sem. Proin rhoncus consequat nisl, eu ornare mauris tincidunt vitae.

Post Three

Euismod atras vulputate iltricies etri elit. Class aptent taciti sociosqu ad litora torquent per conubia nostra, per inceptos himenaeos. Nulla nunc dui, tristique in semper vel, congue sed ligula. Nam dolor ligula, faucibus id sodales in, auctor fringilla libero. Pellentesque pellentesque tempor tellus eget hendrerit. Morbi id aliquam ligula. Aliquam id dui sem. Proin rhoncus consequat nisl, eu ornare mauris tincidunt vitae.

The search results are returning all content that we included in our search index. The term we entered is used to look at both the Title and Teaser fields for a match to the value of Post. One thing we are missing that would enhance our page is the number of search results being displayed.

Displaying the number of search results

Because our search results page is created by our view, we have the option to add additional information to our page using the Views header. We are familiar with this capability as we used it in earlier views. This time around, we will use it to display the number of records being returned by our view.

Begin by navigating to `/admin/structure/views/view/search`, which will allow us to modify our Search view. We will be adding Result summary to our page by following these steps:

1. Click on the **Add** button next to the **HEADER** section.
2. Select the checkbox next to **Result summary** within the **Add header** modal.
3. Click on the **Apply (all displays)** button.
4. Within the **Display field**, we will wrap the content with an h3 heading, as shown here:

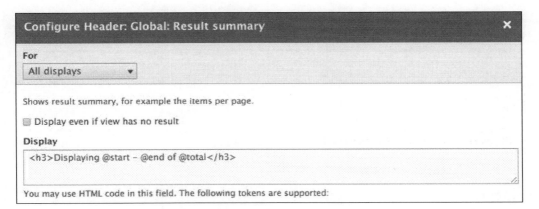

5. Click on the **Apply (all displays)** button.
6. Click on the **Save** button to finalize our Views configuration.

If we now navigate back to our Search results page by navigating to `/search`, we will see our newly added Result summary heading along with all results displayed.

Search

DISPLAYING 1 - 3 OF 3

Post One

Euismod atras vulputate iltricies etri elit. Class aptent taciti sociosqu ad litora torquent per conubia nostra, per inceptos himenaeos. Nulla nunc dui, tristique in semper vel, congue sed ligula. Nam dolor ligula, faucibus id sodales in, auctor fringilla libero. Pellentesque pellentesque tempor tellus eget hendrerit. Morbi id aliquam ligula. Aliquam id dui sem. Proin rhoncus consequat nisi, eu ornare mauris tincidunt vitae.

We can use the global search form to add different terms, and based on the term we enter, the Results summary will change to reflect the number of items in our results.

One last thing to test is what happens when we enter a term that has no results. Let's enter a term of Drupal and hit *Enter*. Our page returns no results, but we have not displayed that to the user. This can sometimes lead our user to believe that search is broken. It is always a best practice to alert the user that no results were found instead of just a blank page.

Adding a No Results message

If we navigate back to our Search view located at `/admin/structure/views/view/search`, we can easily add a message to our page when the search index doesn't return results.

We will be adding a Text area field to our page by following these steps:

1. Click on the **Add** button next to the **NO RESULTS BEHAVIOR** section.
2. Select the checkbox next to **Text area**.
3. Click on the **Apply (all displays)** button.

4. Within the **Content** field, we will add the following markup as shown here:

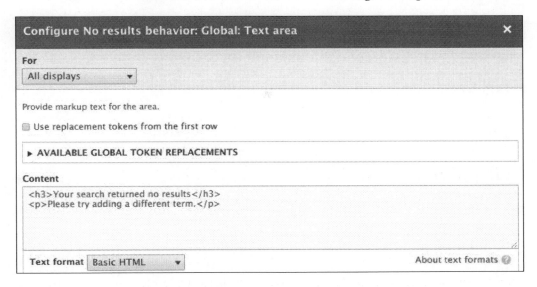

5. Click on the **Apply (all displays)** button.
6. Click on the **Save** button to finalize our Views configuration.

If we now navigate back to our Search results page and enter the term Drupal again, our page will now display the **No Results Behavior** section that we just added.

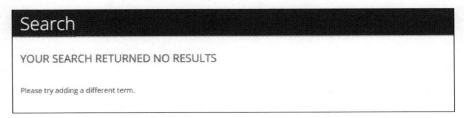

Summary

Congratulations! We have completed the theming of our Search results page. We began with the default core search and worked our way through replacing core search with the more robust Search API. The ability to extend Drupal using contributed modules is one of the primary reasons that makes it such a widely used platform to develop websites.

Let's review what we covered in this lesson:

- We started with our Search results page mockup and identified form elements and markup that would need to be modified in Drupal.

- Using core Drupal search, you learned the important aspects of configuration and how to control keyword factors. Once search was configured, we used Twig templates to override the Search results templates to match our mockup with minimal changes.

- Realizing that we needed to extend search to make it more flexible for our needs, we explored using the Search API module. Being able to create a search server, search index, and use Views to build our Search results page provided us with the ability to better customize the search experience.

At this point, we have themed every section of our website and successfully recreated our Mockup using Drupal 8 and Twig. So where do we go from here? Well, there are still a few tricks for us to learn in the final chapter. These are: theming a few Admin components, such as the local tasks menu and status messages, reusing Twig templates, and finally getting involved in the community.

12
Tips, Tricks, and Where to Go from Here

Now that we have followed the frontend developer's path of taking a design or mockup and converting it into a working Drupal 8 theme, we have to ask that burning question, what next? The answer to that question depends on the problems we need to solve.

For example, what about theming some more common, but often forgotten, admin sections, such as the local tasks menu or status messages block? How about extending Twig templates to reduce having to manage markup in multiple places? However, the most common question is what about contributed modules that can help us with our theming?

In this final chapter, we will take a look at answering these last-minute questions, as we cover the following:

- We will begin with cleaning up our theme by adding some additional Twig templates for both the local tasks menu and the status messages block.
- Next, we will take a look at extending Twig templates by using template inheritance to reduce the amount of markup we have to manage in our theme.
- Finally, we will take a look at the state of some common Drupal contributed modules, such as Display Suite.

While we work through each section, we have the ability to refer back to the Chapter12 exercise files folder. Each folder contains start and end folders with files that we can use to compare our work when needed. These also include database snapshots that will allow us all to start from the same point when working through various lessons.

Working with Local Tasks

One of the most common content blocks within Drupal 8 that is often forgotten about when creating a theme is Local Tasks, often referred to as Tabs. We can see an example of the Tabs block whenever a user needs to perform some sort of action, such as viewing and editing a Node, or even when logging in to Drupal. If we make sure that we are logged out of Drupal Admin and then navigate to /user/login, we will see the **Log in** and **Reset your password** links that make up the tabs on the user login page:

If we input our admin credentials and log in to our Drupal instance we will see that the local tasks menu changes to display **View, Shortcuts,** and **Edit** links. The local tasks menu will change, based on the type of page we are on and the permissions that each user has been assigned.

If we navigate to the About Us page located at /about, we will see that our local tasks menu now provides us with the ability to **View, Edit,** or **Delete** the current Node.

Now that we have a better understanding of how the Local Tasks menu or tab changes, lets dive into how we would go about theming it.

Theming local tasks

Local tasks, or the Tabs menu, is quite simple to theme. Drupal provides us with two Twig templates, `menu-local-tasks.html.twig` and `menu-local-task.html.twig`, which we can modify using techniques we are familiar with. For this exercise, we will simply add some classes to the template so that it styles our links as the pill buttons provided by the Twitter Bootstrap framework.

Begin by creating a copy of `menu-local-tasks.html.twig` located in the `core/modules/system/templates` folder and add it to our `themes/octo/templates` folder. Next, we will open the template and replace the markup with the following:

New markup

```
{% if primary %}
  <h2 class="visually-hidden">{{ 'Primary tabs'|t }}</h2>
  <ul class="nav nav-pills primary">{{ primary }}</ul>
{% endif %}
{% if secondary %}
  <h2 class="visually-hidden">{{ 'Secondary tabs'|t }}</h2>
  <ul class="nav nav-pills secondary">{{ secondary }}</ul>
{% endif %}
```

Make sure to save our changes, clear Drupal's cache and then refresh the browser. Our local tasks are now displayed inline and if we hover over each item, we will see the outline of the pill formatting. Next, we need to add the `active` class to each list item to help differentiate which action is currently being displayed.

Begin by creating a copy of `menu-local-task.html.twig`, located in the `core/modules/system/templates` folder, and add it to our `themes/octo/` templates folder. Next, we will open the template and replace the markup with the following:

New markup

```
<li{{ attributes.addClass(is_active ? 'active') }}>{{ link }}</li>
```

Make sure to save our changes, clear Drupal's cache, and then refresh the browser. The markup we added looks to see whether the list item is active and if it is, we add the `active` class to it. This then displays as a blue pill button within our webpage:

Great, we have now themed our first Admin component. The next item we will look at implementing is our Status messages block.

Working with Status messages

The Status messages block is what Drupal uses to inform users of specific actions they have completed, as well as to display any PHP warnings or errors. If we navigate to the Block layout admin, we can see that the Status messages block is currently assigned to the Highlighted region of our theme.

However, we are currently not outputting this region within our page template, which means that any messages Drupal is trying to display will not be seen. Let's remedy this by printing the region to our `page.html.twig` template.

Adding the Highlighted region

Begin by opening `page.html.twig`, located in our `themes/octo/templates` folder. We will want to modify our markup to add the `page.highlighted` region variable to our template. We can add it between our `title_bar` and `before_content` regions as shown here:

New markup

```
{{ page.title_bar }}
{{ page.highlighted }}
{{ page.before_content }}
```

Make sure to save our changes, clear Drupal's cache, and then refresh the browser. If we are on the **About Us** page, we simply need to click on the **Edit** button to modify the page content and then click on the **Save and keep published** button to trigger our status message.

It is easy to see how a user visiting our site could miss any status messages that we may want them to see, simply because we forgot to theme this component.

Theming our Status message block

It is important to ensure that any messages that we display to the end user are visible and invoke the proper message, based on whether the action was successful or whether the action returned an error. For this purpose, we can borrow from the Twitter Bootstrap Alert component.

If we inspect the page, we can see that Drupal is using the `status-messages.html.twig` template. Begin by creating a copy of `status-messages.html.twig`, located in the `core/modules/system/templates` folder, and add it to our `themes/octo/templates` folder. Next, we will open the template and replace the markup with the following:

New markup

```
<div class="container">
  {% for type, messages in message_list %}

    {% if type == 'error' %}
      {% set classes = ['alert', 'alert-danger', 'alert--' ~
      type] %}
    {% else %}
      {% set classes = ['alert', 'alert-success', 'alert--' ~
      type] %}
    {% endif %}

      <div {{ attributes.addClass(classes) }} role="alert">
        {% if messages|length > 1 %}
          <ul>
            {% for message in messages %}
              <li>{{ message }}</li>
            {% endfor %}
          </ul>
        {% else %}
          {{ messages|first }}
        {% endif %}
      </div>

    {# Remove type specific classes #}
    {{ attributes.removeClass(classes) }}

  {% endfor %}
</div>
```

Make sure to save our changes, clear Drupal's cache, and then refresh the browser. If we click on the **Edit** button and then click on the **Save and keep published** button, we will trigger our status message to display. However, this time it is displayed with the proper styling:

There are a couple of things to point out regarding our modification of the `status-messages.html.twig` template:

1. First, we added a block element to wrap our status message block with a class attribute of `container` to ensure we had proper margin and constraints on the content.

2. Next, we tested for the `type` of message Drupal was outputting and added the proper alert type to the `classes` variable. We then appended our classes variable to any existing classes on our alert element, using the `attributes.addClass()` function.

3. Finally, since we may have multiple messages of varying types being displayed, we removed the `classes` variable using the Twig function `attributes.removeClass()` through each iteration, so that we display the proper alerts.

We have now successfully themed both our tabs and status messages. This provides us with a cleaner user interface and allows for messages to be clearly displayed.

Reusing Twig templates

If we look at our `themes` templates folder, we can see that we have created quite a few Twig templates. While having an abundance of Twig templates is not necessarily a bad thing, it does become a little bit harder to manage our code.

One powerful feature of Twig templates is that they allow us to address this by extending or sharing markup between each template. This is great for global sections of markup. For example, the header and footer of our page never change, so why have the same markup in both `page` templates?

Using extends to share layouts

Twig `{% extends %}` allows us to share markup between templates by extending a template from another one. In our case, we could use this Twig function by extending the `page.html.twig` template from our `page--front.html.twig` template.

Begin by opening up the `page--front.html.twig` template in our favorite editor and add the following markup to the very top of our page:

New markup

```
{% extends 'themes/octo/templates/page.html.twig' %}
```

Now, if we were to save our template, clear Drupal's cache, and browse to our homepage, we would see Drupal complaining about how a template that extends another cannot have a body. The reason is that, while we are extending the `page.html.twig` template, we are not exposing any Twig blocks, which is a requirement for reusing sections of markup.

Working with Twig blocks

Twig blocks, not to be confused with Drupal Blocks, are just containers that we can place around a section of content which allow another template to be able to replace the content within it. So how does this work exactly?

First, a Twig block is referenced using the following syntax:

```
{% block content %}
some content or markup
{% endblock %}
```

In this example, some content or markup could be replaced from another template extending the parent template. It's not important what you call your `{% block %}`, just as long as you're consistent.

Continuing with extending the `page.html.twig` template, begin by adding the following Twig block around our `<main>` content section:

New markup

```
{% block content %}
<main>...</main>
{% endblock %}
```

Now we have a Twig block that can be referenced from within `page--front.html.twig` so that any content within the `<main>` content element can potentially be replaced.

Next, we will want to edit `page--front.html.twig` and first remove the `<header>` and `<footer>` blocks, as we will inherit those from the `page.html.twig` template:

New markup

```
{% extends 'themes/octo/templates/page.html.twig' %}
{% block content %}
{{ attach_library('octo/flexslider') }}
{{ attach_library('octo/scroll-to') }}

  <section class="intro" id="section1" data-speed="5" data-
  type="background" style="background-position: 50% 0px;">
    <div class="overlay">
      <div class="headline">
        {{ page.headline }}
      </div>
    </div>
    <a href="#" id="goto-section2" class="arrow-down">Get
     started</a>
  </section>

  <main role="main" class="main">
    <div class="layout-content">
      <section id="section2" class="section">
        <div class="container">
          {{ page.before_content }}
        </div>
      </section>
    </div>
  </main>

{% endblock %}
```

Now, if we save both templates, clear Drupal's cache, and refresh our homepage, we should see that our markup is being output correctly. So here's a quick explanation of what's happening here:

- First, our homepage is now inheriting all markup from `page.html.twig` including the header, footer, and Twig block. This is why we still see the header and footer of our website being displayed. However, we now only have to worry about managing that markup from a single template.

- Second, since we are including our own markup within the Twig block from our `page--front.html.twig` template, it is overriding the markup in `page.html.twig` and displaying the proper content for our homepage.

This is very powerful, as we can start to look at any content that is repeated across our templates and, with some proper planning, use `{% extends %}` and `{% block %}` to manage our markup.

This is just the surface of how Twig can be extended; for more information and more details of all the possibilities, take a look at the documentation at Sensio Labs: `http://twig.sensiolabs.org/`.

Where do we go from here?

We have covered a lot of information on how to use Drupal 8 and the new Twig template architecture to produce a great looking theme. So where do we go from here? One of the challenges of working with Drupal 8 in its infancy is the lack of contributed modules that have been ported over from Drupal 7. Just know that module maintainers are working hard to bring new and familiar ways to extend Drupal 8.

Some great modules worth taking a look at that have made great progress include:

- Panels: `https://www.drupal.org/project/panels`
- Page Manager: `https://www.drupal.org/project/page_manager`
- Display Suite: `https://www.drupal.org/project/ds`

Each module by itself is great, but together these modules will allow you to achieve a lot of different layouts quickly and easily, without the need to always create a Twig template.

As always, keep an eye on the Drupal 8 theming documentation located at `https://www.drupal.org/theme-guide/8` for detailed information on how to accomplish basic concepts.

Drupal also has a great community of people with various levels of knowledge and expertise, located at `https://www.drupal.org/`. While visiting Drupal.org, please become a member of the Drupal Association at `https://assoc.drupal.org/support-project-you-love` as well as creating a Drupal profile.

Finally, get involved and attend a local Drupal camp or DrupalCon itself for great sessions, training and fun. More information can be found at `https://www.drupal.org/drupalcon`.

Summary

Wow! Time to pat ourselves on the back; we shared a lot of information that has taken us from zero to hero with Drupal 8 theming with Twig. We learned basic site architecture, how to navigate all that is new with the exciting changes in the Drupal 8 Admin, Custom Blocks, Views, Twig templates and so much more. Before we know it, we will be challenging ourselves with the next great design and creating themes with ease.

So until next time, keep coding…

Index

A

About Us block
adding 266, 267
template, implementing 267, 268
About Us mockup
reviewing 196, 197
additional assets
adding 152, 153
Add This buttons
about 290, 291
displaying 292
library, attaching to Blog detail page 291
library entry, creating 291
reference link 290
admin interface
previewing 21-26
reviewing 20
admin menu
exploring 20
AMP stack
installing 2
Appearance interface
exploring 38, 39
assets
setting up 150, 151
attributes.addClass() function 206, 316

B

Bartik 39
basic page layout, design mockup
about 138, 139
interior regions, defining 139

basic theme, creating
about 87
core templates, copying 88
info file, creating 88
new folder, creating 88
screenshot, including 88
theme, installing 89
Welcome to Twig message, displaying 89
Before Content region
Features block, creating 187
implementing 186
refactoring 188
Services block, creating 186, 187
Block layout
exploring 56
block regions
demonstrating 58, 59
blocks
about 57
configuring 60, 61
content, managing with 56
Core 57
Custom 57
Forms 57
Lists (Views) 57
Menus 57
placing, into regions 59
System 57
block types
exploring 67
Blog detail mockup
areas 272
reviewing 272

Newsletter block 189
Social Icons block 190
custom themes
 about 76
 additional assets, adding 152, 153
 assets, setting up 150, 152
 configuration file, creating 147
 creating 146
 default files, handling 154
 installing 148
 regions, setting up 149, 150
 screenshot, adding 147
 theme folders, setting up 146, 147
 versus default themes 76

D

database
 backup 31, 32
 creating, for Drupal 10
 creating, phpMyAdmin used 11, 12
 export settings 32, 33
 restore 33
 snapshot, restoring 145
Default Comment type
 display, reviewing 277, 279
 fields, reviewing 277-279
default files
 handling 154
default Search results
 viewing 310, 311
default themes
 about 41, 76
 versus custom themes 76
dependencies 111
design mockup
 basic page layout 138, 139
 Blog landing page 140
 bog detail layout 141, 142
 Contact Us page 142-144
 homepage layout 134-136
 navigating through 134
 search results 144
Devel
 project page, URL 122
 URL 122

used, for printing variables 122, 123
variables, printing from function 124-126
display, Blog Listing mockup
 field label visibility 233
 fields, enabling 232
 fields, formatting 233
 managing 231
 modes 230
Display Suite
 reference link 341
Document Object Model (DOM) 176
document root
 about 8
 creating 8
Drupal
 core themes 39
 database, creating for 10
Drupal 8
 challenges 341
 configuration, managing in 77
 downloading 8
 folder structure, exploring 26
 installing 7
 reference link 101, 341
 security features, URL 145
 theming documentation, reference link 341
 URL 121
Drupal 8 installation, completing
 about 13
 database configuration 16, 17
 language, selecting 13
 notifications, updating 19
 profile, selecting 14
 regional settings 19
 requirements, verifying 14, 16
 site configuration 18
 site maintenance account information 19
Drupal API
 reference link 99
DrupalCon
 reference link 341
Drupal.org
 about 8
 reference link 238
 URL 8
Drupal Views
 and Twig templates 256, 257

E

elements
 inspecting, Google Chrome used 33, 34
exercise files
 downloading 31
 extracting 31
extends
 used, for sharing layouts 339

F

Field Comments template
 creating 282, 283
file properties
 reference link 74
filters
 reference link 95
FlexSlider
 about 182, 183
 enabling 183, 184
 reference link 182
folder structure, Drupal 8
 about 76
 core folder 26, 27
 custom themes 76
 default themes 76
 exploring 26
 modules folder 28, 29
 sites folder 29
 themes folder 30
Font Awesome
 about 163, 164
 reference link 163
footer
 custom blocks, creating 189, 190
 implementing 189
 main footer, refactoring 191
fundamentals, Twig
 about 91
 control structures 96, 97, 98
 filters 94, 95
 variables, commenting 91
 variables, dumping 93, 94
 variables, printing 92
 variables, setting 92

G

global footer
 adding 223, 224
Global Header
 adding 198, 199
Google Chrome
 used, for inspecting elements 33, 34
Google Maps
 block, creating 306, 307
 configuring 304, 305
 integrating, with contact page 304
 reference link 304

H

Header region
 Block templates, creating 168, 169
 custom JavaScript, adding 172, 173
 implementing 165, 166
 input element template, creating 173, 174
 logo, adding 166, 167
 menus, working with 174, 175
 menu template, creating 175
 printing 168
 search form block, implementing 170
 search form block, placing 170, 171
 search form block template, creating 171
 Site branding, enabling 167
 sticky header, creating 176, 177
 System Menu block template,
   creating 175, 176
Header Top region
 Font Awesome library, installing 163, 164
 implementing 162
 refactoring 164, 165
 Social Icons block, creating 162, 163
Headline Region
 Block, creating 177-180
 FlexSlider, enabling 183, 184
 FlexSlider library, configuring 182, 183
 Headline region, printing 181
 Headlines Block, adding 181
 Headline View, creating 177-180
 implementing 177
 library, attaching with Twig 183
 Parallax, implementing 184
 scroll effect, adding 185

Printed in Great Britain
by Amazon